DO, DIE, OR GET ALONG

DO, DIE, OR GET ALONG

A Tale of Two Appalachian Towns

PETER CROW   The University of Georgia Press *Athens & London*

© 2007 by the University of Georgia Press
Athens, Georgia 30602
All rights reserved
Set in New Caledonia by Bookcomp, Inc.
Printed and bound by Thomson-Shore
The paper in this book meets the guidelines for
permanence and durability of the Committee on
Production Guidelines for Book Longevity of the
Council on Library Resources.

Printed in the United States of America
11 10 09 08 07 C 5 4 3 2 1
11 10 09 08 07 P 5 4 3 2 1

Library of Congress Cataloging-in-Publication Data

Crow, Peter, 1942–
Do, die, or get along : a tale of two Appalachian
towns / Peter Crow.
   p. cm.
Includes bibliographical references and index.
ISBN-13: 978-0-8203-2863-8 (hardcover : alk. paper)
ISBN-10: 0-8203-2863-4 (hardcover : alk. paper)
ISBN-13: 978-0-8203-2871-3 (pbk. : alk. paper)
ISBN-10: 0-8203-2871-5 (pbk. : alk. paper)
1. Saint Paul (Va.)—Biography.   2. Dante (Va.)—
Biography.   3. Oral history.   4. Community life—
Virginia—Saint Paul.   5. Community life—
Virginia—Dante.   6. Saint Paul (Va.)—Social
conditions.   7. Dante (Va.)—Social conditions.
8. Coal mines and mining—Virginia—Saint Paul—
History.   9. Coal mines and mining—Virginia—
Dante—History.   10. Company towns—Virginia—
Case studies.   I. Title.
F234.S15C76 2007
975.5'743—dc22
2006014019

British Library Cataloging-in-Publication Data available
Cartography by David Wasserboehr.

To Beth, Amy, and Rob,
And to the people of St. Paul and Dante

In memory of Tom Fletcher, Nannie Phillips Gordon,
Roy J. Phillips, and James William Thomas

CONTENTS

PREFACE

The story you are about to read came to me in parts, at different times, told by a number of people. The more I heard, the more eager I was to tell it myself, to pass it on to students and others, to write it in my own words. But the more I worked at it, the more I found myself relying on the voices of the original tellers, until finally I had removed my own voice almost entirely. Why did I do this? I did it because their telling was more interesting than my telling. And I did it because I realized it was time for Appalachian scholars to stop talking about Appalachian people long enough for those people to speak for themselves.

Also, as a tool of research, learning, and growth, such an approach is much needed and overdue. For a number of years, postmodern thinkers suspicious of broad, abstract, so-called objective claims to truth have been drawn to authentic narrative at the local level. As early as 1973, anthropologist and ethnographer Clifford Geertz talked about "thick description" of "local knowledge" being the most productive way to interpret cultures.[1] In 1981, philosopher and ethicist Alasdair MacIntyre proposed that only by telling one's personal story (as contextualized by community) can an individual identify his or her own telos and thereby know what virtue or right action entails.[2] And more recently, a group of social psychologists and feminists, most prominently Mary Field Belenky, have demonstrated that encouraging people to tell their own stories empowers them, especially people frequently not taken seriously.[3]

Furthermore, reading a good story told by the principals of that story plays into the constructivist notion of learning originated by John Dewey, developed by Jerome Bruner and others, embraced by teachers everywhere, and roundly ignored by many state legislatures locked into standards of learning.[4] Reading such as story constitutes a journey of discovery, a quest for meaningful resonances, especially if there is not a monster at the end of the book called a test. And when the story involves community, as it does here, readers gain an appreciation for the kind of people with whom they want to share their journey. Such an experience encourages readers to strike out on their own, initiate their own conversations, and become involved in a life significantly of their own shaping.

As for my role in recording and editing these Appalachian voices, I realized early on that in order to capture intimacies of place, I had to limit the narrative to people associated with just one or two particular communities. I chose St. Paul and nearby Dante, Virginia, because fascinating links between their particular past and present seemed especially illuminative of issues confounding

Americans everywhere. I have made decisions about where to put what, how much of a given narrator's account to keep or cut, and so forth mainly on the basis of what would produce the most engaging overall story. That does not ensure objectivity on my part, but it does keep my eye on narrative rather than preconceptions about topics being discussed.

Though this work shares similarities with oral histories, the purpose and some of the methodology differ. Oral histories usually blanket the past of an area, showing that past to be interesting in its own right. *Do, Die, or Get Along* deals with the past mainly as a platform for the present and future. Here there are fewer narrators, but some of them become central figures in their own evolving story. Interestingly, an oral history about Dante becomes an important part of this story's plot because its construction awakened the town to possibilities for renewal previously unseen.

In instances where people's memories seemed uncertain or where they may have contradicted themselves, I have allowed them to reconsider and correct themselves. Where I am aware that people have simply erred on matters of fact, I have set the record straight in the notes. Where there are significant differences of opinion over important issues under consideration, I have tried to include voices from both sides where possible. If the most appropriate dissenting voice has little connection to either St. Paul or Dante, I have tried to track down that person for a comment in the notes.

Anyone involved in recording and transcribing speech has to decide to what degree, if any, to retain regional dialect in writing. I believe readers are more sophisticated than they once were about the relationship between language and intelligence, as well as about the importance of local language practice to personal identity and local culture, and the importance of local, regional culture to our national heritage and to global diversity. I have thus attempted to retain the grammar and diction I have recorded. But since there are no written words in speech, I have used standard spelling for the most part. Occasionally, common practice dictates otherwise. For example, nobody in the coalfields calls a hollow a "hollow." It's always "holler," so I've let the spelling reflect that usage. Also, I have sometimes tried to capture the informality of narrative by dropping *th* from *them* when the recording suggests the pronunciation "em." I have not, however, dropped the final *g* from *ing* words even though the speech often suggests such a spellin'. Practically nobody pronounces the final *g* on *ing* words very distinctly, and there are so many such words that dropping those *g*'s would impede the narrative.

I have eliminated false starts and sloppy phrases people have caught and repeated more coherently on their own, alterations that are common practice among oral historians. In addition, I have inserted names or places or even phrases where people have used pronouns or other references that would be unclear out of their original context, all in the interest of maximizing the narrative flow.

More people have been helpful in developing this book than I can possibly list. Foremost among the contributors are the twenty-six narrators who agreed to take part in the project and actually tell the story. Then there are my Ferrum College colleagues Dan Woods, Susan Mead, Carolyn Thomas, Vaughan Webb, George Loveland, and David Johnson, who have shared in the design and implementation of the Appalachian Cluster, a unique curriculum that has engaged us and our students in research ventures with a number of Appalachian communities. It was in such a context that several of the interviews included here took place. Friends, students, and colleagues not mentioned above who have read and commented on portions of the manuscript or provided other support include Rex Stephenson, Todd Fredericksen, Frederic Torimiro, Sam Payne, Tina Hanlon, Derek Ritenour, Cheryl Hundley, Sandy Doss, Scott Williams, Rich Sours, and John Bruton.

As director of three National Endowment for the Humanities summer institutes related to regional study and Appalachia, I have profited from the insights of such writers and scholars as Lee Smith, Denise Giardina, Robert Morgan, Patricia Johnson, Clyde Kessler, Stephen Fisher, Altina Waller, Crandall Shifflett, Anita Puckett, Charles Reagan Wilson, Dwight Billings, David Whisnant, Richard Couto, Mary Beth Pudup, Ben Judkins, Ralph Lutts, Casey Clabough, and Cece Conway, to name just a few.

In addition to the people of St. Paul and Dante, I want to thank the citizens and community leaders in Matewan and Caretta, West Virginia, and in Ivanhoe, Hurley, Grundy, and Alleghany County, Virginia, for hosting Appalachian Cluster and NEH Summer Institute research groups and for sharing those communities' heritage and plans. Franki Patton Rutherford, Marsha Timpson, and Kem Short of Big Creek People in Action (Caretta) and Mattie Christian of Hurley Community Development have been especially helpful. These visits have revealed how much of the St. Paul/Dante experience is unique and how much is common to the region. Others from southwestern Virginia who gave leads, widened context, found me a place to sleep, or helped check local spellings include William Wampler, Jean Kilgore, Ann and Allen Gregory, John "Woozy" Bryant, Larry McReynolds, Suzy and Bob Harrison, Betsy Fletcher, Vicki Dotten, Steve Lindeman, Mike Quillen, Gene Matthis, and David Fields.

I am indebted for grant support in background research for this project not only to the National Endowment for the Humanities but also to the American Council for Learned Societies and to the Virginia Foundation for the Humanities. I have also received substantial support from Ferrum College through a Cheatham Fellowship and through course load reduction as Williams Distinguished Professor of the Humanities, as well as through years of administrative support for interdisciplinary undergraduate teaching and community-based research.

The editorial staff at the University of Georgia Press has been extremely supportive and helpful throughout the publication process, especially Andrew Berzanskis, Courtney Denney, and Jane Curran. I would also like to thank the two anonymous reviewers of my manuscript for their recommendations to publish and for their useful suggestions.

My own enjoyment of this entire project owes much to timely encouragement, companionship, and practical help from my wife, Beth, who shares my interest in good stories and adds her own gift for photography. Including photographs was her idea. To my benefit, our grown children, Amy and Rob, supplied the "tough love" criticism I was used to dishing out to them, much of which accounts for the introduction going through nine major revisions. I didn't send them the last version.

INTRODUCTION

Much has been written about the difficulties of defining Appalachia. Is the region defined primarily by shared cultural values, by the Appalachian mountain range, or by a government agency (the Appalachian Regional Commission)? Should those studying the region focus on the south-central area dominated by extractive industries or extend their interest northward into Pennsylvania?[1] Is Appalachia really much more similar to other rural areas in the United States than its reputation suggests?[2] Or is what we think we know of Appalachia simply an elaborate invention?[3] Just what is Appalachia, and who are Appalachians?

Before the early 1960s, the American public held a frequently comic, but dark, stereotype of Appalachians as barefoot, ignorant, clannish, and violent, in need of civilizing intervention from the outside. This image of Appalachians, lodged in public curiosity, grew largely out of sensationalized journalistic coverage of feuding, especially the Hatfield and McCoy feud.[4] Traces of the stereotype still appear in jokes about West Virginia, on picture postcards and reruns of the *Andy Griffith Show* and the *Beverly Hillbillies*, and in a national TV network's recent attempt to introduce a hillbilly reality show. During the Kennedy and Johnson administrations, the curiosity began to turn to strident concern based on a new stereotype of Appalachians as tragic victims of outside intervention—sturdy, independent-minded, tradition-loving folk whose subsistence lifestyle had been destroyed by railroads, timbering, and coal mining.[5] Vestiges of that stereotype persist today among activists who believe the underlying issues remain valid even as they embrace a more complex understanding of causes and reject baggage associated with the term *victim*.[6]

Regardless of how it gets defined, perhaps in the very act of defining, Appalachia ends up apart from the rest of America. But is this a satisfactory portrayal? And if it isn't completely satisfactory, how might one begin to fill in the deficiencies? What is needed, it seems to me, is a different vantage point than stepping outside of something and trying to make out its shape. The twenty-six narrators of *Do, Die, or Get Along: A Tale of Two Appalachian Towns* step inside their experience and tell a story. From the inside, they assume that they are part of a place named St. Paul or Dante, which is part of a larger place they've heard called Appalachia, which is part of the United States of America. They think of these places not mainly as geographical or cultural entities with boundaries and definitions but as indeterminate extensions of themselves, part of who they are.

If we listen carefully to them speaking from this perspective, we begin to notice how their tale is an American tale with an Appalachian twist, not a separate tale to be played off against the American tale. Their story has American challenge—conquer the wild frontier. It has American opportunity—abundant wealth if you have what it takes to grasp it. It has American tragedy—grasping wealth entails turning people into stepping-stones. And it has American humor—human stepping-stones can bite you in the ass. It also has American ingenuity, racial tension, and other qualities associated with our national heritage, including exhibiting a melting pot of heritages. But most of all, it addresses the great American question—can we survive our own success?

Do, Die, or Get Along takes place deep in southwestern Virginia. St. Paul and Dante are coalfield towns six miles apart and about thirty miles west of Abingdon (and Interstate 81) in a region known as the Allegheny Plateau, which extends farther westward into Kentucky and West Virginia. It is an area of convoluted landscape and history whose Appalachian identity nobody disputes. Yet it is a part of Appalachia unfamiliar to people who know the region only from passing along one of the long north-south ridge or valley corridors such as the Appalachian Trail or the Skyline Drive/Blue Ridge Parkway or Interstate 81. Around St. Paul and Dante, there are no extended mountain ridges such as those that make up Shenandoah National Park and the Great Smoky Mountains. The Allegheny Plateau was formed some 200 million years ago from sediment from the much taller ancestors of those mountain ridges to the east (of which Shenandoah and the Smokies are a part). The tops of many disparate peaks are all that remains of what was once the plateau's surface, the rest having washed toward the Gulf of Mexico by the multitude of rivulets that flow together, often into "turkey foot" patterns, before becoming streams and then rivers. In fact, Dante (rhymes with *ant*) was originally called Turkey Foot. Exposed along the toes of the "turkey's foot" are seams of coal originating 350 million years ago when the land west of the long ridges was a tropical swamp teeming with flora matting into bogs (before sediment from the eroding mountains covered it up).[7] St. Paul lies on the Clinch River (which flows into the Mississippi by way of the Tennessee and Ohio rivers) just downstream from the mouth of Lick Creek, running out of Dante.

The twenty-six narrators come from a variety of social, ethnic, and economic backgrounds and political persuasions. And like everybody else, they are not always internally consistent. The same person who expresses despair in one breath (sometimes unconsciously in rose-tinted memories of the "good old days") can show resoluteness (and clear-eyed observation) in the next. A number of them have become resourceful community leaders, but none follows purist models of leadership. Not all of the narrators are long-time

Appalachians, though most are. Perhaps more than anything else, they reveal how fortitude and resourcefulness in certain individuals have helped their communities confront enormous challenges and move on. Their stories give twenty-first-century meaning to the idea of the good fight, not winning outright but stretching losing so far out of shape that sometimes it ends up looking and feeling and acting like winning.

As indicated earlier, the bituminous coalfields of southwestern Virginia, eastern Kentucky, and southeastern West Virginia are often considered the core of Appalachia. It is here that modernization issues play themselves out in boldest relief and set much of the context out of which communities such as St. Paul and Dante must look forward. The industrialization and thus the financial wealth of the United States were and still are largely powered by coal, yet the Appalachian counties that have produced much of that coal are among the poorest in the nation. Some companies may have taken better care of their workers than others, some may have profited less than others,[8] but none returned to the region anything remotely equivalent to what the trains took out.

Moreover, there are natural resources in the region arguably more valuable than coal. It is no secret that a wide diversity of wildlife characterizes the ecosystems of the Appalachian Mountains. As naturalist Scott Wiedensaul puts it, "At the southern end a naturalist finds longleaf pines, painted buntings and wild turkeys; at the northern end, woodland caribou, Arctic foxes and even (when the pack ice closes in on Newfoundland) a wandering polar bear or two. Few other continuous mountain chains in the world, and none in North America, encompass such biological diversity."[9] Not so well known is how much of nature's struggle against extinction takes place in Virginia coal country. According to comprehensive research by the Nature Conservancy and the Association for Biodiversity Information, there are more imperiled species (twenty-seven) in a section of southwestern Virginia centered on the Clinch and Powell rivers than in any other section of similar size in the continental United States.[10] Yet these species and their habitats have been and still are under unrelenting, deadly stresses. Deeply imbedded in the story of St. Paul and Dante is the clash between environmental and economic imperatives.

In the early days, Appalachian resoluteness frequently manifested itself in some form of "do or die," as St. Paul attorney Frank Kilgore puts it. If you didn't continually clear new slopes to replace cropland that was quickly worn out and washed out, you risked starvation. After the Civil War, the railroads had been largely destroyed between Lynchburg and southwestern Virginia. If a soldier didn't have it in him to walk two hundred plus miles, he might not get back home. If a couple of drunk miners got into an argument on the "Western Front" of St. Paul, fists were the method of choice for settling the matter. Before unions and mechanization, a miner got paid only for the coal he hand-loaded, not for setting safety timbers or for traveling sometimes miles to the coalface. If the company inspector found too much shale in a load of coal, he dumped it out, and the miner got nothing. Before mid-1900s federal safety regulations, a miner's safety was almost exclusively in his own hands and those of his buddies. A less-than-vigilant miner was not only a walking dead man; he was a liability to his entire crew. Living that life produced the hardscrabble brand of resoluteness captured in so many memorable characters of Appalachian novelists such as Harriette Arnow, Lee Smith, Robert Morgan, Denise Giardina, and Charles Frazier.

Almost unnoticed outside the region is how the "do or die" attitude has changed, changed to finding ways to "get along," again Frank Kilgore's words. "Getting along" doesn't mean "knuckling under." In the first half of the twentieth century, it meant workers from diverse ethnic backgrounds suppressing their differences sufficiently to organize labor unions. It meant companies and labor unions being forced by federal law to coexist—an admittedly uneasy form of "getting along," the jagged edges of which manifested themselves as late as the Pittston strike of 1989–90. At the same time, however, a deeper change of attitude was taking place. The coal companies didn't own every town in the coalfields. At junctions on major rail lines, there grew up incorporated towns, such as St. Paul, where citizens had space to dream of a life for their children beyond coal. So education became important, and not just education tied to the economic interests of the coal companies. With education came greater likelihood of using courts to settle problems, town council debates to steer a community's future, understanding of how state and national decisions are made and how to work the system. Over time, women took leadership roles, often with less confrontational leadership styles than men. And environmentalism began shaping "getting along" in an ecological image to which many mountain people seem particularly receptive.

Unfortunately for people living in localities once owned and operated by coal companies, "doing" and "getting along" frequently have not prevented their towns from "dying." But persistence and resourcefulness have enabled at least some former company towns to "die" at least partially on their own terms, perhaps not even to end up "dead." To inanimate objects such as towns, "dying" might mean losing significant economic viability but hanging on in some reconfigured manner for an indefinite period, perhaps re-emerging with a vitality driven by something other than market economics. Such a town is Dante.

In some places, *Do, Die, or Get Along* supports recent scholarship about Appalachia, undercutting popular misconceptions about subsistence farming, offering nonfeud-related reasons for indigenous violence, illustrating the profound effects of social stratification in community life. In others, however, the narrative challenges stereotypes that have emerged from academic writing itself, stereotypes, for example, about myopic missionaries, idealistic but uninvested Volunteers in Service to America (VISTA) workers, and self-serving local elites.

The twenty-six narrators who tell the stories of these two towns not only come from different backgrounds, but each also represents an important source of information not readily available elsewhere. And each displays a different style of narration. Retired St. Paul postmaster LeRoy Hilton speaks from the perspective of a man who by profession, personality, and longevity has known a lot of people and witnessed a lot of the town's past. In detailing the early years of St. Paul, he shows particular interest in the "Western Front," a row of buildings (mostly gone now) along the railroad tracks that at the height of the coal boom housed saloons, brothels, and a prohibition-era phenomenon known as "blind tigers." Hilton speaks with the weathered ease of a fisherman for whom the pleasure of describing unbelievable exploits is exceeded only by the joy of demonstrating their veracity.

Terry and Dean Vencil often tell their parts of the story in tandem. Dean is a retired coal miner in whose possession are a variety of coal-mining memorabilia along with the hair-raising tales that frame them. These tales, however, like those of many miners, are buried so deeply in his psyche that one has to dig them out like coal. His wife is a big help in this endeavor. Terry herself teaches science at St. Paul High School, where her students pass down from year to year a wetlands project that has won nationwide recognition.

Terry's boss, principal Tom Fletcher, son of St. Paul's most re-elected mayor, speaks of coaching high school football during integration, leaving the area for coaching duties at major NCAA universities, and finally being drawn back home to end his career at St. Paul High School in an Appalachian county (Wise) with a long record, surprising to many, of academic excellence. Of all the narrators, he seems most aware of his public role as community spokesperson.

Bruce Robinette and Charles McConnell unravel a tangled web of bureaucratic intrigue and backroom politicking that led ultimately to relocating the Clinch River in St. Paul at the very time the Environmental Protection Agency was figuring out just how much clout it had under the Clean Water Act of 1972. Lou Ann Wallace describes how the town's relationship to environmentalism had shifted by the mid-1990s, when she initiated a town-supported effort, called St. Paul Tomorrow, to combine economic planning and environmental sustainability. Support for this project came from the Nature Conservancy's Bill Kittrell, who discusses that organization's discovery that the Clinch is the most biologically diverse river in the continental United States.

In Dante, Roy Phillips, Lucille Whitaker, and Nannie Phillips Gordon reflect on the old days—mining and town life during the Depression, omnipresence of the company, unionization. Younger citizens such as Catherine Pratt, Pete Castle, and Shirley Glass speak of the decline of mining, the slow pullout of the company, communal despair, and finally the resolution to "live on." Oxygen tank at his side, Matthew Kincaid speaks of continuing hazards of mining even as he describes enormous rewards he experienced in the profession. His wife Emogene takes a painful look at hardships African Americans experienced in a segregated community but also takes pride in how her family dealt with discrimination and in how most of the town accepted racial mixing, once mandated.

Two St. Paul High School students, Chelsea Salyer and Jason Boone, add youthful perspectives often missing in Appalachian considerations. Other voices add color and detail to a story in which a number of the tellers become important figures themselves. As the story progresses, Frank Kilgore and Kathy Shearer emerge as centering voices.

Frank Kilgore is likely the most notorious living person associated with St. Paul. In the 1970s while a student at what was then Clinch Valley College (now the University of Virginia at Wise), Kilgore started a controversial group called Virginia Citizens for Better Reclamation, an organization instrumental in bringing to passage the federal Surface Mining Control and Reclamation Act of 1977 (SMCRA). During the Pittston strike of 1989–90, Kilgore's law firm was the one retained by the United Mine Workers of America to defend the miners. Recently, Kilgore has been heavily involved in the Appalachian School of Law in Grundy and other regional economic development initiatives, often in league with former adversaries in the mining industry.

In 1993 as the representative of a regional social service agency, Kathy Shearer began helping the people of Dante understand a hard choice. They needed either to put in a septic system and stop pumping raw sewage into Lick Creek or to risk having the state effectively shut down the entire town. Her involvement in that project led to a growing fascination with the people and history of Dante. At the same time, telling their stories to Kathy helped the townspeople understand the importance of their own community and its history. That understanding led to a book entitled *Memories from Dante: The*

Life of a Coal Town, the possibilities of a future for the town with so many memories, and Kathy's starting her own publishing company.[11]

Kilgore and Shearer make an interesting study in contrasts. One practices law in St. Paul and has a long family history in the region. The other is a New Jersey–bred outsider and former VISTA worker assigned by her job to Dante. One likes to generate ideas and then pull people together to carry them out, calls himself "aggressive," and says he doesn't mind "ruffling a few feathers." The other is a thoroughgoing grassroots organizer, one who engages herself in energy, inspiration, and admiration exchange with her clients. Yet, despite starkly differing politics and motivational styles, Kilgore and Shearer have recently conspired to create a book based on Frank's extensive postcard collection.[12] While there may be characteristics of a "local elite" in Kilgore and of a "hopeless idealist" in Shearer, it would be a mistake to dismiss either on the basis of those stereotypes. They are two of the most committed, productive community leaders I have met.

Do, Die, or Get Along begins at some remove in the past. Easily a third of the narrators, without notes or forewarning, can recite much of their ancestry back to the Civil War, some beyond that. And several have read accounts of early Europeans settling in the area, of their conflicts with Indians and among themselves. But distance can be deceiving, especially distance in time. As ontologists such as Martin Heidegger remind us, much of who people are involves interplay between what they have read, heard, and lived directly and how they project themselves into the future. The narrative proceeds much in the fashion of a roomful of people, each of whom has a different angle on significant experience common to them all, each of whom has a different orientation to what lies ahead for their shared community. One narrator picks up the story from another as chronology and knowledge dictate, some narrating extensively, some only briefly, some presenting prevailing notions, some representing countercurrents.

Of course, also present in the room is the host holding a recorder. What is my role in all this? As anyone knows who has read Lee Smith's *Oral History,* a collector of authentic Appalachian stories may not always get what the collector expects. If not accepted, the interviewer can become the lightning rod for interviewees' frustrations and malaise, and hence perhaps the unwelcome subject (rather than collector) of storytelling. *Oral History* makes clear that storytelling is an insider's game. Bootlegger Almarine Cantrell's estranged great-granddaughter Jennifer, tape recorder in hand, learns this the hard way when she tries to dredge up her family's past to fulfill a college assignment. Richmond highbrow Richard Burlage, who came to Black Rock first as a teacher and later as a photographer, had been similarly rejected. Fortunately for me, about half of the people I interviewed are used to a public presence in their lives, and they were eager to tell their stories. They introduced me to the others, whom I got to know over a seven-year period of visiting the area, often with students and colleagues. I learned from experience (and also from Parrot Blankinship, the one outsider in *Oral History* accepted by the mountain folk) that a love of listening to and telling stories goes a long way toward making you Appalachian, even if you have no other claim.

No doubt, other people living in the area would tell the story differently, or could tell a different story altogether. But of these things I am confident: There is an important and, until now, largely untold tale of Appalachia. That tale has all the standard elements of a good story—conflict, romance, despair, hope, death, six-barrel lust, an uncertain ending, and even baseball. The tale also involves persistence, adaptability, and eclectic redefinition of the American Dream. And these twenty-six narrators tell it well.

THE PEOPLE WHO TELL THIS STORY

Jason Boone was a St. Paul High School senior at the time he was interviewed, a member of Team Estonoa, and an all-conference, all-regional football player. Currently, Jason is a student at Virginia Highlands Community College in Abingdon, Virginia.

Carl E. "Pete" Castle, lifelong resident of Dante, is a retired postal carrier from Dante who may be found playing his guitar and singing at most any community function.

Tom Fletcher returned to St. Paul to become assistant principal and then principal of St. Paul High School after nearly thirty years away from the area coaching NCAA Division I football. Tom's father, Holland Fletcher, was mayor of St. Paul for almost three decades beginning just before World War II. Tom Fletcher died July 10, 2006.

Shirley Glass is a lifetime resident of Dante and treasurer of Dante Lives On. When I first met her, she was wearing a red elf hat and raising money for the community from an eager crowd awaiting the annual visit of the Santa train.

Frank Gordon, son of Nannie Phillips Gordon, was one of the first Dante residents in the mid-1990s to understand the importance of putting in a town sewer. His influence "up the hollers" was instrumental in helping Kathy Shearer convince a skeptical community.

Nannie Phillips Gordon was battling cancer as she recalled moments of humor and joy amid the mostly painful memories of her family's poverty and her father's struggles with alcoholism during the Depression and afterward in Dante. Nannie died April 6, 2005.

LeRoy Hilton has excelled during his eighty-three years in golfing, arrowhead collecting, woodcarving, and fishing, to name but a few of his many interests. A retired postmaster of St. Paul, he is widely acknowledged to be the unofficial town historian. He becomes most animated when telling fishing stories and describing the wild side of St. Paul when there was once a row of saloons and brothels called the "Western Front."

Frank Kilgore is an attorney in St. Paul with a maverick reputation and a long family history in the area. Along with Kathy Shearer, he emerges as one of this story's centering narrators, explaining with LeRoy Hilton important elements of the area's past and speaking of his own central involvement in strip mine legislation, the Pittston strike, and regional redevelopment efforts.

Emogene Kincaid talks about coal town life for an African American woman who endured the pains of segregation and discrimination but later watched her children play sports at integrated schools. Currently, she is a member of the board of directors of Dante Lives On.

Matthew Kincaid describes life in Sawmill Holler (designated by the coal company for black miners and their families), courtship with his eventual wife, Emogene, hardships and rewards of coal mining, and coping with black lung disease (including difficulties of getting benefits).

Bill Kittrell established the Nature Conservancy's field office in Abingdon, Virginia, when that international organization discovered in the early 1990s that the Clinch River Valley was home to more endangered species than anywhere else of similar size in the continental United States. He outlines a strategy for working with communities located on the Clinch, such as St. Paul, to develop both viable and environmentally sound economies. Currently, Bill directs conservation programs at the Nature Conservancy's Charlottesville, Virginia, office.

Charles McConnell, director of the Wise County Redevelopment and Housing Authority, found himself during the 1970s in the middle of a complicated project to minimize flooding in St. Paul, permit the expansion of U.S. 58 to four lanes as it skirts the town, and pay for relocating people living in substandard housing in the floodplain. What stood in the way was first the challenge of relocating a portion of the Clinch River, then a national economic downturn, and finally the newly established Environmental Protection Agency.

Debbie Penland, St. Paul High School librarian, discusses family tensions over the Pittston strike of 1989–90. Her father and a brother were striking members of the United Mine Workers of America while her husband was a salaried employee of the coal company involved in the strike.

Roy Phillips discusses coal mining during the Depression, expresses gratitude to the company for keeping him working, and reflects on God's presence in Dante during bad times and good. Roy died December 30, 2005.

Catherine Pratt, the first chairperson of Dante Lives On, describes growing up in Dante, watching the town go through an extended period of decline, and later learning how to be a community activist and run a grassroots organization.

Bruce Robinette was one of the first regional planners in southwestern Virginia. He outlines difficulties in getting local communities to buy into the idea of planning and then cites the Clinch River relocation project as an example of the challenges, bureaucratic shenanigans, and rewards of planning.

Chelsea Salyer was a St. Paul High School senior at the time she was interviewed and a member of Team Estonoa (the Estonoa Wetlands project), the PACE (Partnership for Academic Competition Excellence) team, and the basketball team. Chelsea is currently a student at Duke University.

Bob Salyers, retired from Norfolk and Western Railway, lives at the edge of the Clinch River near the section where the relocation occurred. Though his property was enhanced by the changes, he speaks of respected neighbors, now deceased, who were bitterly opposed to being forced off their family land.

Dink Shackleford, whose father and uncles were coal mine owners, is executive director of the Virginia Mining Association. Dink takes pride in awards Virginia operators have recently received for exemplary mining and reclamation practices. He expresses enormous frustration, however, with people who he believes see little contradiction between opposing current coal-mining practices (such as mountaintop removal) and living a lifestyle heavily dependent on electricity and other kinds of energy.

Katharine "Kathy" Shearer was a social service agent in the 1990s assigned to convince the people of Dante that they needed to put in a sewer system rather than straight-pipe sewage into Lick Creek, which flows within a few miles into the Clinch River. Along with Frank Kilgore, Kathy becomes a centering voice for this narrative as she describes how her involvement with the people of Dante grew into an oral history project, a book about the town, and finally a grassroots effort to keep the town alive. No longer employed by People Incorporated of Southwest Virginia, Kathy now owns and operates her own publishing company, the Clinch Mountain Press.

Jackie Stump, as district president and international board member of the United Mine Workers of America (UMWA), was one of the union's primary negotiators and spokespersons during the Pittston strike of 1989–90. During the strike, he was imprisoned by a federal judge for fourteen days for refusing to instruct miners to desist from acts of civil disobedience. Jackie served in the Virginia House of Delegates from 1990–2006, when he resigned for health reasons.

James Thomas at the time of our interview was a resident of Dante's Sawmill Holler and deacon of First Mount Calvary Baptist Church, from which position he was instrumental in organizing an interracial gospel sing and fundraiser for Dante Lives On. James died May 25, 2005.

Dean Vencil is a former medical technician and retired coal mine examiner. A proud member of the United Mine Workers of America, he currently assists his wife Terry in advising and nurturing St. Paul High School students involved in Team Estonoa, the Estonoa Wetlands project.

Terry Vencil has received local, state, and national acclaim through her leadership of a St. Paul High School wetlands preservation and learning project called the Estonoa Wetlands project. She and her husband Dean met when they were both working as medical technicians in a small office in Dante.

Lou Ann Wallace lives in "Minneapolis," Virginia, a town just across the river from St. Paul that was supposed to exist but doesn't. Lou operates a graphics design company in St. Paul and heads a community development organization called St. Paul Tomorrow. Working with the Nature Conservancy, St. Paul Tomorrow is attempting to revitalize the town through sustainable, environmentally friendly economic development.

Lucille Whitaker was one Dante citizen Kathy Shearer found eager not only to put in a sewer but to pursue an oral history project and later a book venture. Lucille tells fascinating anecdotes about life in Dante from the 1930s on. She currently lives with her daughter in Richmond, Virginia.

DO, DIE, OR GET ALONG

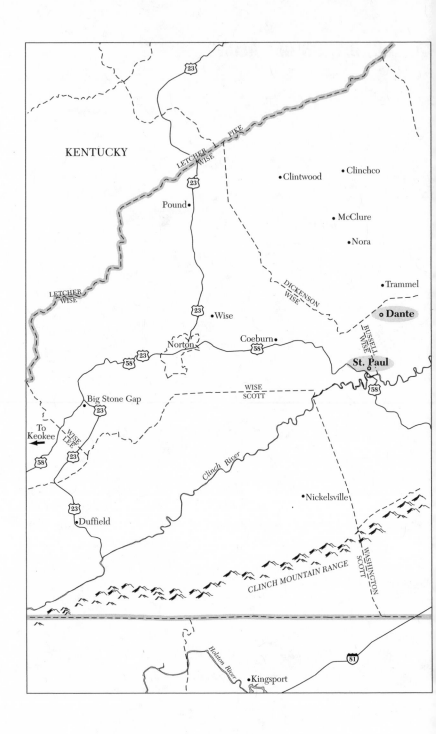

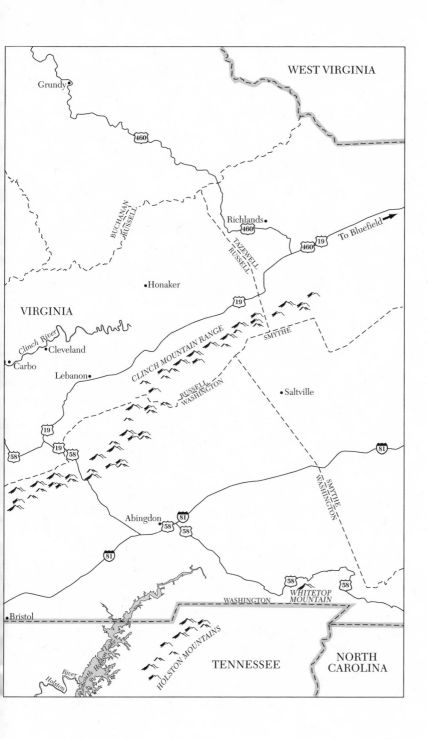

The Indians didn't kill him. . . . It was
white thieves.

ONE

Frontier Times

Frank Kilgore: Coal was formed about 320 million years ago in this area when this was a flat, inland sea that was filled with swamps that would be inundated every few million years by water and silt and sand. That silt and sand would cover the matted, rotted plant life that was pressured first into peat moss, then lignite, and later under more pressure and heat, it became more and more pure, and it's now bituminous coal.

The further east you go, the coal seams there have been upended and pressured more from geologic forces pushing from the east. There's a streak of anthracite coal in Virginia that runs parallel with the Blue Ridge system. Anthracite coal is one of the harder, more purer forms of coal and it's been under more intense pressure. And it's more pure. Its hallmark is that it is almost smoke-free, it has high BTUs. That means British Thermal Units. So it heats well and has very little ash because it's been purified over years, and the impurities—the iron and the sulfur—have been burned out, squeezed out for lack of a better term. Because it's been there longer and it's been exposed to more severe geologic forces. Pennsylvania still mines some anthracite coal. But bituminous coal is by far the most plentiful coal throughout the world.

The Appalachians have been the major source of coal for the United States for a century.

LeRoy Hilton: When you come into town I think you will see the sign that says, "chartered in 1912." But really St. Paul started about 250 years ago in the early 1700s. And the reason for the settlement here—we'll get to that later. But let's just go back 250 years. In 1769 the first settlement was just across the river in Castlewood, Virginia. That was the first settlement. So in 1769 they come to Castlewood to settle, when all the Indian wars were going on.

Frank Kilgore: A lot of people view the central Appalachians as 99 percent Caucasian and western European influence. And that's true to a certain extent. But there's a lot bigger story than that, especially when you count the Melungeon influence. Brent Kennedy over at the University of Virginia at Wise studied it, found out he is of Melungeon descent, and has written several books on them.[1] According to his theory, the Melungeons had traces of Turkish blood and Portuguese blood, some African American blood, Native American blood, but the bloodline DNA goes back to the Middle East, where, after a battle or some invasion between the warring factions there, captured prisoners were pressed into servitude. These were traded around.

They ended up with some of the Spaniard barons, who then either brought them to the New World, or some of them escaped to Portugal and the Portuguese brought them to the New World around the 1500s. They settled on the coast of the South, most likely South and North Carolina, intermarrying with the Indians. They had a lot of native intelligence. Instead of fighting with whoever was the perceived enemy, they would trade with them, make friends with them, intermarry with them. And so when the white Europeans would want the Native Americans' land, they would just kill the Native Americans and drive them out. Whenever they wanted the Melungeons' land, the Melungeons would say "okay," and they'd just back up further into the mountains and settle high, dry ridges. And that's where they remain today.

It was just sort of an unspoken truth around here for years that these dark, curly-haired, dark-skinned, olive-skinned children that came to school—every one of them has the same story: "My grandmother was full-blooded Cherokee." That's what every one of them said. And that was their political position as to their characteristics. And it dawned on me even in high school: where are these Cherokees? I've never seen one. If it was their grandma, it looks like she would still be around. But what it was, they were of Mediterranean descent, maybe some Negro blood, and Indian blood. And they chose to say "Cherokee" because in the Appalachian Mountains Native Americans are honored much more than they are out west. So that seemed to be to them a more dignified position. And some of our area's best leaders are people of Melungeon blood.

As to my own roots in this region, there were two to five brothers that were all my ancestors at the Battle of King's Mountain during the Revolutionary War.[2] I don't know which one was my grandfather six or seven times removed, whether it was Charles or Robert or James or Hiram. There was a fifth one. I can't remember his name, I never can remember his name. So we'll call him Bubba. Anyway, there was one of them, he and his son built what is known as Kilgore Forthouse that still stands in Scott County. Anyway, their children scattered out. There's a fairly significant Kilgore influence in Texas in a town called Kilgore, Texas. A fairly sizable contingent of that family went on to Oregon. As you know, one of our Scott County Kilgores is attorney general of Virginia and touted to be the next governor, so we'll have to wait and see how that turns out.[3] But mostly my forefathers have been engaged in the last two or three generations in coal mining and some farming.

Dink Shackleford: We were the first American melting pot, I think. We have the Melungeon heritage, where you had three thousand Mediterranean people coming in and interbreeding, intermarrying with the Cherokee Indians. And this was the primary middle ground between the Shawnee and the Cherokee, and this is where a lot of those people settled. And this was the Wild West. These Indians weren't like the Plains Indians; these were some tough Indians around this area. I mean, they would eat you.

And Chief Benge, the red-headed Indian chief, was killed here in Norton just down the road a little bit. He single-handedly held up westward migration in this area until he was killed in an ambush. He chose the wrong side in the Revolutionary War and fought for the British. His father was John Benge, an Indian trapper and trader. And he came through the mountains—he was raised on the backside of the mountain over here in Scott County. That's why people thought he really had to be psychologically disturbed because he'd come back and really raided and killed a lot of the people he grew up with. He was Cherokee and Scotch, Scotch-Irish. Dr. Lawrence Fleenor has wrote several books that include him—one was *Benge!* and the other, the first one, was *Bear Grass* [*The Bear Grass*, a history of upper east Tennessee and far southwest Virginia].

He killed some folks one time and set down, and he and his cousin Pumpkin Head got together—and they had another one called Double Head—and they said he might have been that because he was schizophrenic. But they set down and killed some pioneers and ate their brains, in the old Iroquois tradition that you could acquire their power if you really got with it there evidently. So he had a few bad cannibalistic traits there, but he did some funny things too. He went into a camp one time, and the men jumped up and all ran, and the women all sat there stunned. And he got tickled that all the men ran from him, so he built the women a fire and tucked them in and let them live and went on his way. And can you imagine being a husband and have to come back and see those women after that?

He came through on one of his raids and they shot him down. A little girl saw a moccasin print on the river over there, and they found out he was there. And they formed a militia and tried to head him off at the pass. They had tried several times, but he had got by them. And they slipped and got him that time. And once he was killed, that opened up westward expansion through the Cumberland Gap. People were just afraid to come over this way. He was killed in 1794. Benge was a real interesting character, and they still have his hatchet down at the Museum of the Cherokee in Cherokee, North Carolina.

LeRoy Hilton: It was called the French land. All this used to be Augusta County. And then it was split off into Russell County. And then from Russell County, you had Lee, Scott, Wise, and Dickenson. And so the first settlement in Wise County was like in 1791, and Mr. Kilgore owns that farm now. It's called Sugar Hill. And there was a Frenchman by the name of Francois Pierre de Tubeuf during the French Revolution. And he had a 55,000-acre grant of land in this area here. And he was given safe passage by the King of France to come to Virginia. So when he came to Virginia, he got a loan of six hundred pounds sterling from the state legislature of Virginia, and he came to Castlewood and built a road from Castlewood, which had the courthouse over there, into what is now Mr. Kilgore's land. And when they surveyed it, it ended up being 150,000 acres. And his land went all the way down into Lee County and all the way to Kentucky.

And he was murdered in 1793, and after he was murdered then his family was still here. And so because they couldn't pay the taxes, then they sold the land off. And many of the old deeds and titles now refer to it as the French land, which is here in St. Paul. If you look out from the church, this little old high hill here is called Sugar Hill, and that was the first settlement in Wise County in 1791.

I used to have a friend who owned it. As a matter of fact I think I sold it to Frank Kilgore. This friend of mine owned it, and he passed away. He and I were good fishing buddies. He lived on the river, his family. They owned the old French quarter up there. And his wife asked me, said, "LeRoy, you know all the people down around there." Said, "I need to sell the old farm." And so I contacted Frank Kilgore and got Frank to go talk to the lady, and consequently he bought the farm from the Glover family who owned it.

The old sills and the foundation had big white poplar logs that were like three feet wide, from virgin timber. It was one of the most beautiful structures you ever saw in your life, the big old logs. And it also had the portholes, you know, when the Indian attacks would come. Had the portholes in this old building, and it was an old big log building. The old nails were square-cut iron nails that put this structure together. And it was just an absolute beauty, is what it was.

During the bicentennial, some local people asked my opinion on what they should name a new local wine. I said, "The oldest settlement in Wise County is Sainte Marie on the Clinch." And I said, "It is a red wine you are producing for the bicentennial days. Very appropriate it would be to advertise both the oldest settlement and the wine as St. Maria's Rosé." So they adopted this, and they made a label and put it on the bottle, the picture of the old bridge and the first hotel. And my name ended up on the bottle, as naming the wine. And my wife says, "I don't know if this is good or bad." Says, "Several years down the road when all the winos drink their wine and throw their bottles under the bridges, the first thing you'll see is LeRoy Hilton's name on the bottle."

We had a meeting of the historical society to make a national treasure out of this thing, being the first settlement in Wise County, and we were getting ready to make this thing a park, the National Register. And the very day it came out in the paper, that very night it burned to the ground.

Frank Kilgore: It was a beautiful place. I was in it twice before it burned down, and Mr. Hilton has been in it many times more than I have. It was where the Frenchman lived. John English built the house before the Frenchman came, but his whole family was wiped out by Indians. So he moved back to Moore's Ford, and this Frenchman came along looking for a place to live. He had a fifty-thousand–acre land grant, but no building. So John English was happy to sell him that, and he just assumed the Frenchman would be killed by Indians. And the Indians didn't kill him; they never once attacked he or his family.

It was white thieves making their way through Russell County to the Ohio Valley to trap. They came by, he fed them, he was going to put them up for the night. And they killed him and robbed him. And one of his servants got killed trying to swim the Clinch River to go get help. There is a paper done by Rhonda Roberts, who's now the head of the Wise County Historical Society. She did this years ago as a college paper. It tells the whole story about the Frenchman's settlement ["St. Marie on the Clinch (The French Lands)," unpublished manuscript].

I've put in about eight miles of trail. The last three miles we put along the river, the state helped us put it in. It's the only publicly accessible trail on the Clinch River in Virginia.

LeRoy Hilton: The one Civil War thing that was really mentioned in St. Paul was a General Burbridge. He come down through Saltville into what is now St. Paul at Wheeler's Ford. And he was fording the river at a time when it was really high. Lick Creek, coming out of Dante, enters the Clinch River at that point. It was said, according to the history books, Summers' history, and the story of Wilburn Waters [Lewis P. Summers, *Annals of Southwest Virginia (1769–1800)*, and Charles B. Coale, *The Life and Adventures of Wilburn Waters: The Famous Hunter and Trapper of White Top Mountain Embracing Early History of Southwestern Virginia Sufferings of the Pioneers, Etc., Etc.*, 1878], which are old history books—very authentic happenings of this country—his troops were swept and his cannon and horses and whatnot, were all swept downstream from there. And there's been many, many artifacts—old cannon balls—actually been found, and parts of old wagons, and they even found a bucket of old pennies at one time apparently was lost when the Union troops were coming through with General Burbridge, coming through that Wheeler's Ford section.

Frank Kilgore: On my grandfather's side, Grandfather Kilgore, and also my grandmother's side, there was a good blend of Holbrook family. James Holbrook was my great-great-grandfather, who was in the Confederacy. And I have researched his war records at the state archives in Richmond. He couldn't read or write. He was a small man; he was young. He lied about his age to get into the Confederacy. People in the coalfield section of Virginia, 99 percent of them did not own any slaves, but they joined either the Confederacy or the Union depending upon their loyalties one way or the other, or depending upon who was on the other side. If the family they had squabbled with or feuded with for some reason took the Union side, the opposing clan would take the Confederacy side. So it didn't have as much to do with North-South sentiments as it did local, political issues. There is an interesting book out about that phenomenon—it's roughly called *The Civil War in Buchanan and Dickenson Counties: A Bushwhacker's Paradise* [Jeffrey C. Weaver, *The Civil War in Buchanan and Wise Counties: Bushwhacker's Paradise*, 1994].

To get back to my great-great-grandfather, James Holbrook, he helped his family build a little cabin up on Honey Branch before the Civil War broke out. Part of it is still standing; we were the last family to live in it. I do remember as a little boy you could see through the cracks in the chinking of the logs—when it was cold, very cold. I found his Confederate military records, and it said he was not educated. He was seventeen years old when he enlisted. And it gave his height and so on—I have a picture of him. And there is this communiqué from the captain that had mustered these men together in Russell County to fight for the Confederacy. And this one communiqué from him to the colonel, I think it was a colonel in Abingdon, stated, "Men will not cross the Clinch River until they receive their $50 sign-up bonus." And then about three weeks later you see another memo from him to the colonel, I think it was a colonel, and it said, "Men have now crossed the Clinch River; thank you for sending

1. Frank Kilgore's great-great-grandfather, James Holbrook, about 1861. Courtesy of Frank Kilgore.

the $50 sign-up bonus." So my great-great-grandfather may have done it for the money. I don't know.

But he fought in skirmishes and minor battles and did end up in Pickett's service in Richmond and was captured at the Battle of Five Forks along with thirty thousand other Confederates who were barefoot. Most of them didn't even have firearms. So my great-great-grandfather Holbrook was captured along with a lot of his comrades, sent to Hart's Island off the coast of New York City as a prisoner of war for just a few weeks. The war ended, and he was shipped back down to Richmond, got a train to Lynchburg. The tracks were out from Lynchburg west, so he walked barefoot from Lynchburg back home. And for those four years he was in the war, he never wrote home because he couldn't read or write.

So his parents gave him up for dead, and they were outside—this is the family legend. He walks up Honey Branch; it's just a cow path, wagon trail. He walks up, and he's only twenty-two or twenty-three years old, maybe even younger, probably twenty or twenty-one because he joined early. And he was haggard, had a beard, kind of bent over, and he was gaunt, starving, barefoot. And he told them he was their son. And they didn't believe him, so they questioned him pretty tightly about things that happened around the house before he left. They were finally convinced he was their son.

And I can just imagine that. He's gone four years, you don't hear a word, he comes back. Leaves as a fresh face, sixteen, seventeen years old. Comes back haggard, battle-worn, battle-weary, bearded, dirty, skinny, shoeless. And just imagine how his parents must have felt when that happened. Anyway, he married my great-great-grandmother. And my grandfather Frank Kilgore, who worked forty-some years in the mines for Clinchfield, told me stories of playing checkers with his grandfather Holbrook. And Grandfather Holbrook would jump up and knock the checkerboard over, stick his cane out the window and say, "Let 'em sneak up on us, why don't you?" And of course my grandfather was only seven, eight, nine years old, didn't understand that Great-great-grandfather Holbrook was suffering from post-traumatic stress, from four years of fighting and being shot at.

For generations, my family has lived here in Honey Branch or up on Sandy Ridge, St. Paul being the trade center of this little community, this little region. But of course Dante was at one time too. We just always gravitated towards St. Paul. Dante is due north of St. Paul, and in between Dante and St. Paul is Honey Branch.

LeRoy Hilton: In the wintertime the river would be high, and Abingdon was the only place you could get materials because that was the railhead that come down and brought all the materials. Regularly, there would be wagons from Kentucky and all the places west of here come through here to Wheeler's Ford, and they would get on the ferry and ferry across the river. My grandfather come out of Dickenson County, and every month or every two months he would get an order from all the neighbors and they would go to Abingdon. In this picture here, you can see the old trail going up the river to Wheeler's Ford. Wheeler's Ford would be the last place you can see if you look at the top of the picture. See the bend in the river? That's Wheeler's Ford [upstream from present-day St. Paul, from approximately where the photo was taken]. And if you can see the old roadbed going along the edge of the river, they would go up and ferry the wagons across to the other side. And Mr. Wheeler was drowned. He got on the ferry and broke loose, and a week later they found him six miles down the stream. And he was drowned. Mr. Wheeler come from Liverpool, England, originally.

Frank Kilgore: I think there were a lot of great primitive artisans in the last one hundred years who built what they needed, either to farm with or use as household furniture. So I've developed an interest in Appalachian primitive furniture and tools. I think we are rapidly losing it. And I try, if I find one, especially if it is from this region, I try to buy it, preserve it. It's not so much

2. Wheeler's Ford, at the bend in the Clinch River beyond the iron bridge, upstream from St. Paul, 1902. The long white building to the left of the bridge was the Riverside Hotel. The house at the extreme left of the photo (with two windows showing, one above the other) is the oldest building in St. Paul, now housing the Railroad Museum mentioned by Lou Ann Wallace in chapter 17. The bridge in the photo had been partially washed out by a flood. Courtesy of LeRoy Hilton.

who made it, because most of the time you can't find out who actually made it. But if I find a piece I know was built in Russell County or Wise County or Lee County or Buchanan County, if I can trace that back and verify it, then to me that's valuable. If they built a pie safe, they built just what they needed. They didn't usually build them for sale. In general, when you were doing subsistence farming, you did everything, from the farming to building your own furniture. And you had so many children, as they grew up, if you had that skill, you were busy making them furniture for their house.[4]

The coalfields, as opposed to just east of here in the karst topography or the limestone country, had much steeper slopes and thinner soils, didn't have much clay to hold the soils in. Consequently, when you had black loam soil that was made up of rotting leaves and trees over millions of years of a decaying process, you had a thin layer of very rich soil on top of rocky area, cliff-like environment. And so when people settled in what is now the coalfields section of Virginia, West Virginia, and eastern Kentucky, they would farm, and erosion over a two- or three-year period would completely deplete the topsoil. So then they would have to go around the mountain to another location, cut and burn the trees (the ones they didn't make lumber out of), dig out the stumps by hand and by horse, have the horse attached to it and chop out around the smaller roots and then keep pulling it till they got it out. Moving three or four large stumps could be an all-day job, or maybe even one stump in a day.

So it was very hard work, and then you grow corn on it, which within itself depletes the nutrients in the soil. Combined with erosion, they would run out of land to keep clearing. They called it "new ground." They'd have to go around the hill and cut off and plow up new ground. And they would raise big families in order to help on the farm, but then the bigger the families the more they would have to raise. And the more they would raise in corn and potatoes and some wheat—wasn't a lot of wheat—some oats, they would have to get horses. And then they would have to raise more corn to feed the horses through the winter. So it became a sort of vicious cycle that depended on those very thin layers of topsoil. As that was depleted, this area looked completely different. At the turn of the century, you see old photos and the whole surrounding area of a town or community would be completely de-nuded. No matter how steep the slope would be, there would be pastureland or cornfields. And that couldn't go on very long because of erosion.

The first encroachment upon the great forests was by the subsistence farmers. And then as the worldwide demand for timber picked up in the late 1800s, early 1900s, that's when the timber industry really discovered the central Appalachians.

LeRoy Hilton: Everywhere you looked there was a sawmill. One of my other great-grandfathers come to Dickenson County, and that was his profession. I had many uncles work for the Ritter Lumber Company.

Frank Kilgore: The Yellow Poplar Lumber Company built towns, they built bridges to get their lumber out. So in the turn of the century up through the twenties, almost every acre of southwest Virginia was cut over. And so I guess that pretty much knocked out all our old-growth forests. Down in the creeks they would drag logs through the creek or mill logs close to the creek. But because they used horse logging, the hillsides would grow up fairly fast and not lose as much topsoil as subsistence farming would cause because they weren't plowing the ground up on steep slopes. So the land actually recovered a little better, I think, from those old cutting, logging methods than it did from subsistence farming.

When you combined the two, then you are talking about trillions of tons of sediment, topsoil and sediment, coming out of the central Appalachians down into the Gulf of Mexico. And then you add to that in the 1960s, '70s, and '80s, strip mining simply exacerbated the erosion problem, sedimentation problem. So the lands in the central Appalachians, in the coalfields, has been overfarmed on steep slopes, it's been overlogged, and then strip-mined. So just about anything you could throw at the steep landscape has been done here.

Kathy Shearer: Dante is actually located in the northwest corner of Russell County, almost in Dickenson County, in the coalfields. And originally when settlers came here from North Carolina, back in the early to middle 1800s, they named it Turkey Foot because Lick Creek branches into three distinct toes. And we have the left fork, the middle fork, and the right fork, which are also called Sawmill, Straight Holler, and Bear Wallow Holler. And those are the three toes of the turkey's foot. There's also a little hollow, Hospital Holler, which is kind of the small toe of the foot, a little spur off of the downtown area. There used to be the company hospital up there, and it has been torn down, most of it. There's one little part left.

But before coal was developed there, as far as we know, Turkey Foot was just a tiny little rural community. We don't know if there was a store there. There was no post office. The Phillips family settled there. That's the first name, the earliest name, we found in the record. Laborn Phillips came up from North Carolina with his wife, and they had their children there. One story has it that he was married to a Cherokee woman. Her name was Maria. And that they had had to leave where they were because white men weren't supposed to marry Cherokees, but now that happened a whole lot. So I don't know about that.

They lived in a log house. Clarence Phillips, a descendent of Laborn, says it was located about where the Clinchfield office building sits today. So it would be right in the middle of town, right where those branches divide. And that would make sense, because they would build their house right where they had plenty of water all around for drinking and washing. And also there would be a good place for a garden, probably raising a corn crop and whatever. From that point out the hollers are very narrow and the hills are very steep. They settled on what was the only flat land around.

They had a bunch of children. There were eight children, all born in Russell County. We're not sure they were all born right at this location, Turkey Foot, but I presume they probably were. The first one, Mary Ann Phillips, was born in 1829, and the last one, Patsy, was born about 1847. Laborn

Phillips was born about 1794. They moved in sometime probably prior to 1829. They're buried up there on Roanoke Hill. Nobody knows where the graves are; they are unmarked because people didn't have big stones then. The representative to the Virginia General Assembly from that area, Bud Phillips, is a sixth-generation resident of the area. He actually lives up on Sandy Ridge above Dante. And his son makes the seventh generation.

But I imagine they were just looking for land. Maybe North Carolina was getting crowded. And now we've got Phillips everywhere.[5]

Kathy Shearer and Nannie Phillips Gordon: We were talking about remembering your roots. The Phillips family just spreads out. You go back seven or eight generations. Laborn was the first.

Was my daddy's grandpa.

And there's another Laborn behind . . .

Maybe great-grandpa, but anyway I've heard Daddy talk about Uncle Laborn Phillips many a, many a time.

In 1890, the first railroad train come
into St. Paul.

TWO

Incorporated Town—Early Years

LeRoy Hilton: I had a great-grandfather in Dickenson County sold the Virginia Mining Company, which is Pittston, 127 acres of coal land in Dickenson County for $127, a dollar an acre, and this produced something like $40 million or whatnot of coal. His name was Rainwater Ramsey, my great-grandfather. And also in the deed the company could use all the timber, trees they needed to build their trestles and roadbeds and whatnot for free; they could use the timber for free—$127 for 127 acres.[1]

Rainwater Ramsey. He was a Civil War veteran. My grandmother used to tell me they were just real jealous—her aunts and uncles—said they would— a hundred and some dollars was a lot of money—said they would go down and buy them a brand new suit, and said you would see them out digging a groundhog out from under a stump with a brand new suit on. Said they was just real jealous that they had so much money—a hundred and some dollars—had so much money that they could just go out and buy a new suit and dig groundhogs in it. They was just real jealous, you know, because of all the money they had—$127. And that was in this million-dollar McClure area in Dickenson County. Hard to tell how many millions of tons of coal they took out of that section over in there.

Bruce Robinette: Wise County in 1961, when I moved to St. Paul out of college, had five separate railroads. They had the L&N [Louisville and Nashville], the N&W [Norfolk and Western], and the Southern, and the Interstate, and the Clinchfield, and over at Pound they had the C&O [Chesapeake and Ohio]. So they had six railroads. But the Interstate was local. So we had five interstate railroads and one intrastate railroad, operating in Wise County.

Cook County in Chicago, which was the rail hub of the nation, only had twelve railroads. So we had five, we had almost half.

And it was all coal related, every bit of it was coal. And now, we've got, let's see, two—the one at Pound, the C&O—that's part of CSX [consolidation of C&O and Seaboard railroads]. Southern bought the Interstate in 1960, and then what, ten or twelve years ago, the N&W and Southern merged to make Norfolk Southern. And now the Clinchfield was bought by CSX, so it went from six railroads to two.

LeRoy Hilton: St. Paul was originally a half mile up the river at Wheeler's Ford. And that was where the CC&O [Carolina, Clinchfield and Ohio] was supposed to join the N&W. It is now called Boody. That's where the settlement was. And this is the only road to Dante. In olden times, you'll notice here along the river, there's a trail [see figure 2]. This is the only road through St. Paul, come from Kentucky to Wheeler's Ford, which is a ford across the river to Abingdon. That was the only way to get to Abingdon, coming out of Kentucky, was through St. Paul and up this road here.

And then they came on down here. In 1889, John Dingus, who lived in Nickelsville, he come to St. Paul and built the first hotel, and that was because the N&W railroad was coming to St. Paul at that time. And he also brought his nephew John Hillman, brought him to St. Paul with him. And they operated the first hotel, and they had a small coal mine and a little farm that they raised some cattle and a lot of vegetables and whatnot. And John Hillman operated this hotel for his uncle.

And at that time the name of St. Paul was Estonoa. And the reason it couldn't be St. Paul—the idea was twin cities, like St. Paul and Minneapolis— and when they started to name the town St. Paul, they found out there was another St. Paul in Carroll County. So John Hillman and John Dingus and a bunch of the local men needed this because of the twin-city concept—the shipping point on the railroad was St. Paul but the town was Estonoa—so they went to Hillsville in Carroll County and paid this man a hundred dollars to release the name of St. Paul so they could bring it here to this community. So after three years of being Estonoa, Virginia, it ended up being St. Paul.

The CC&O and the N&W railroad were supposed to come to St. Paul at the same time, about 1890. So the N&W come, but at the time they were developing this, all the people that owned the CC&O railroad that had the money going to come and help develop this area, they were killed in an accident—the financiers. And their families didn't want to put any money into it. So it was 1910—nearly twenty years later—before the railroad finally come here from Kentucky to join the N&W.

So they were copying the Twin Cities, St. Paul on this side of the river and Minneapolis on the other side of the river, on the south side. And the CC&O railroad would come through St. Paul and go south, through Minneapolis. And the N&W come from Bluefield and Roanoke and go through into Norton. One would go north-south; the other would go east-west. So St. Paul is the north-south, east-west crossing point of the railroad.

And they sold many, many lots of land in Minneapolis. They even laid the pipes—the sewer lines and the water lines—and they had a pump station upriver. Streets were graded. It was ready to be developed. Platted as "Minneapolis." All this was done. And Jay Gould and the Vanderbilts and all, they made the trip down from New York. And they come to St. Paul and they stayed in the old hotel and signed the registry. And I think they saw the hilly country or such a limited amount of flat land that you could really do some developing on. I think they were really discouraged.

Once they saw what they were into, and the development was very limited in this mountain country, I think they sort of pulled out and lost interest. So the Minneapolis part never did develop. I understand that many fortunes were lost, where they paid thousands of dollars for the lots across river, and it's mostly hilly, bluffy country. It's called South St. Paul now.

The biggest landowners in this area was Senator M. M. Long and Ed Mason, other than the men who come and developed and plotted and platted this particular three hundred and some acres in St. Paul. The St. Paul Land Company, which was Senator M. M. Long, here way back before 1920. And nearly all the property on Gray Hill, which is the latest development in St. Paul, was the St. Paul Land Company. He owned everything not immediately downtown. He owned a lot of lots in St. Paul. And he was the biggest landowner. Senator Long was an attorney when he come to St. Paul. Of course, he was representing people in land management and so forth and so on. Some of the local history says that a lot of his lawyer fees came from him representing people, and they paid him in land. That's how he acquired some of his many pieces of land that he had here.

Ed Mason, who lived just across the Clinch River, which is just inside of St. Paul, owned a vast amount of acreage along the river on the other side in Russell County where Minneapolis was supposed to be.

Lou Ann Wallace: About ten years ago, my husband and I purchased a plot of land that was next door to a subdivision that we lived in. We found out that it was formerly incorporated as a town known as Minneapolis. The land was surveyed, it was subdivided, the streets were named, the water line was being lain. In fact, in 1971 when the subdivision was built, and the dozers came in to doze out the roads and everything like that and the power lines, they unearthed the old pipes that was laid in the ground. So I presently have a map of that on my wall, which is absolutely wonderful. And I love to share it with anyone who wants to come and visit. Our house was built on what they say is the site of the grand hotel. Up the side of the hill from St. Paul, up on top of the hill, which I'm about two hundred feet on a river cliff or a river bluff. And so there was a trolley road built, and all this was done by hand, pick and shovel. And we have found also hand tools from the people that came and worked on this project. It was done in the late 1800s, and according to the incorporation of our map was done in 1890.

LeRoy Hilton: So in 1890, the first railroad train come into St. Paul. And it brought all the people that were going to work in the coal mines, so they come to St. Paul. So this was the last of the frontier, St. Paul. Norfolk and Western ended here in St. Paul. And they had a turntable here because it was a couple or three years later before they went on through the rest of Wise County. The turntable was here in St. Paul. So the trains come down from Bluefield and from Norfolk—it was all the way across the state—and it would come into St. Paul, and they would turn the train around and send it back. So people come here for the reason of the coalfields.[2]

George L. Carter . . . saw Dante and that little seven-mile line as an important part of his plan.

THREE

Company Town—Early Years

Kathy Shearer: I think people knew there was coal and used coal all along. I would imagine the Phillips knew to dig it out of banks. I doubt that they actually blasted into the hillsides. But people were burning coal; the Indians apparently burned coal. So it was something people knew to use as well as wood to keep warm and to cook with. Eventually, after the Civil War I think, maybe because of the Civil War, engineers were roaming around, realized there were some riches there, and said, "We will remember to come back." They were surveying in the late 1800s. I don't know whether this was done by the state of Virginia or the federal government or what, but they marked the immense timber and coal reserves.

And there was all this land that was basically there for the taking. People had gotten patents on it early on and were probably the first speculators. They would get patents on like sixty thousand acres or six hundred thousand acres. Veterans of the war in 1777, 1778, the War of Independence, they were able to get land from the federal government because of their military service. They got huge tracts of land. So back in the 1880s, people then were saying, "Well, what can we do with this land? We would like to go down and buy it and use the timber, market the timber, market the coal." People started coming in, and we've got a deed here in 1887. Henry Phillips, who was one of Laborn Phillips's sons, sold the mineral rights to their land for fifty cents an acre. They sold it to trustees for the Virginia and Tennessee Coal and Iron Company.

So little companies were starting to spring up. Entrepreneurs were coming in and saying, "Okay, enough of this farming. We're going to make some serious money here." The farmers, for their part, were probably pretty excited to get fifty cents an acre. We talk about that today and say, "How could they have done that? How could great granddaddy have done that?" But, you think, they were living on a barter system. Real money was new to them, exciting to them. And if they had had a couple of hard years, that would have been wonderful to have that money. For the mineral rights, you gave somebody permission to come in and dig—prospect basically on your land and take it out. In the early days there was no protection for the homeowner, the landowner. There was nothing in there about repairing the surface of the land. You couldn't ever imagine that all the coal could be removed, or mined out. Usually there was a little provision saying the property owner can take whatever coal he needs for his own home use.

Eventually the whole parcel of Turkey Foot property was sold to the Taze-well Coal and Iron Company. Now actually the Phillips lived there, and there's some dispute about that, as to where they actually ever owned it or not. Because the huge tract of land was owned originally by an Englishman who had patented the land, and then he started selling off chunks of it. Richard Smith. He owned hundreds of thousands of acres, including all of what is now Dante and St. Paul. He owned everything. We don't think he ever even came to this country. He just saw an opportunity after the Revolutionary War and took it. So he sold off chunks of it. Nowhere in the deed books is there mention of the Phillips ever owning the place where they lived. So probably they were squatting, but they were squatting at a time when everybody was doing it. There was so much wild land that people never came and checked on their land.[1]

So in 1889, the heirs of Henry and Nathaniel Dickenson, who now owned the part that was Turkey Foot, sold that Turkey Foot land to Tazewell Coal and Iron. They were, as far as we can tell, the first local owners of this land. Everybody else had been from out of the area. There had been a couple of brothers from Pennsylvania who had owned a lot of the land. Now when they sold the land in 1889, the heirs of Henry and Nathaniel Dickenson, they sold 4,205 acres for $40,050, $9.52 an acre. The original deed we are talking about is fifty cents an acre for the coal deal. This Dickenson sale is an outright sale. But even so, that's a huge jump in value. So you can tell, people are getting a little smarter about this. It's more competitive.

So Tazewell Coal and Iron owned it for a few years, and they tried to develop it. But they didn't have the transportation figured out. There was no railroad in or out. So any coal that was taken out had to be trucked, or hauled by horse or mule or whatever. They started working on a railroad after the land was sold again. The coal lands were sold to Stilson Hutchins. He had been the owner, editor of the *Washington Post*. So he was another outsider. He was very entrepreneurial, and he knew that people were developing the resources all over the country. And he wanted to own a coal mine. So he bought it for $18 an acre in 1901, so again the price is going up. So it's gone from $9.52 an acre to $18 an acre, almost double, from 1889 to 1901, twelve years. Stilson Hutchins is the man who understands you've got to have a railroad to get that coal moving.

He has a vice-president of his company—the company is called Dawson Coal and Coke—his vice-president is William Joseph Dante. And together they organized this railroad company, which they called the Lick Creek and Lake Erie Railroad, because it is their intention that it's going to run from Lick Creek all the way up to Lake Erie. These guys had great dreams; they thought big. And it's going to carry this coal out of the mountains all the way to the Great Lakes. At that time, the Great Lakes must have been a major shipping destination. A lot of goods must have gone from the Great Lakes over to Europe, or other places in the United States. So he got a little short line installed down to St. Paul, which was just about seven miles long. It was just a little north of St. Paul. It's called Boody today; it was called Fink then. And they got that little railroad built. They leased the train that ran on it. They were tying into the Norfolk and Western there. That was their southern terminus. They never pushed any further though; they ran out of money or energy or what. But they got that much done, and if they hadn't done that, we might still be in the backwater today.

At this point, George L. Carter enters the picture. He was busy in the coalfields already, and he saw that this could be part of his empire, or the Clinchfield Coal Corporation. And he got involved. He didn't actually buy the company at this point; he got himself on the board of directors. And so he was then able to kind of manage their business, what they did. He was a Virginian, had a remarkable career. He was one of nine children who grew up on a farm in Carroll County [in southwestern Virginia, three counties east of Russell County and Dante]. His father was a disabled Civil War veteran. George's first job was working for something like fifty cents a week as a clerk in a store. He worked his way up until he became a bookkeeper of an iron company. In 1877, he was working at the Wythe Lead Mine Company in Austinville, first as a buyer, then as the bookkeeper and manager. So this fellow is working his way up. He was born in 1857, so at this point he is only twenty years old.

The company is just about to go out of business because the owners can't make the improvements necessary to expand. And he realizes that somebody is going to buy this and make a pile of money. He gets options to buy adjacent land. Now he couldn't have had any money of his own. And he goes up north, and he finds buyers for the lead mine company in New Jersey. The

New Jersey Zinc Company is going to come down and buy it. He works that deal out through them. Then he exercises his options on all the surrounding land, thereby making a pile of money. He was really good about working with other people's money, because as a young man he wouldn't have had the resources. But he was smart enough, and he must have been a real good talker because many times in his career he would go somewhere else to the men who had the money. He talked them into it: "Let's take a chance on investing in this." Invest in me, basically, because I know what I'm doing. And he would convince them. And even when the business went bust, he would come out on top.

He was involved in one venture, Virginia Iron, Coal, and Coke. They were just getting going, and they had all this property, all these resources and everything, which he had purchased by borrowing money from a New York banking company. In 1901, his company owned ten coal and coke companies, 150,000 acres of coal land, 60,000 acres of iron ore, as well as 136 miles of the Virginia and Southwestern Railroad. At that point, higher-quality Mesabi iron ore was discovered in Minnesota. And so everything that he was working toward abruptly ended because now there was no market for his product. They defaulted, and you would think this guy would have been totally broke. However, he sued as a creditor. He went right to the head of the list when they went bankrupt because he had so much of his own money involved. And the judge, rather than recusing himself because he was a good friend of Carter's, just said, "fine," and awarded him this judgment. The judgment was against his own company. The company went bankrupt, but he got in line as one of the main creditors. So he collected $500,000 as an individual suing his own company. And because the judge was a friend and a former attorney for the company, he was able to work this out. So George L. Carter had friends in just all the right places.[2]

So he saw Dante and that little seven-mile line as an important part of his plan to further develop the coalfields. He kind of turned his interest away from iron ore and got totally absorbed in coal. And he proceeded to combine several small coal companies. The idea was, as he was developing the Carolina, Clinchfield and Ohio Railway, then he would purchase all these little coal companies. And he would have something for his railroad to haul. His idea, just like Stilson Hutchins's, was that his railroad would go all the way to Ohio. He thought it would end up in Cincinnati. It would start from a port in South Carolina. He was purchasing a lot of trackage. He bought up a whole lot of different old railroad companies that had made little short lines, or some of them were quite a bit longer. But his idea was to have docks down in South Carolina and come all the way, I think at Charleston or Sumter, and come all the way up through the coalfields and on up north to Cincinnati and to the Great Lakes eventually.

So that was his plan. But there were several panics back then in the early 1900s, several times when the investors got very nervous. They had major construction on the railroad company beginning in 1905, but by 1908 the money started drying up, and he had to reduce his plans. So at this point he decided it would simply go as far north as Elkhorn City, Kentucky, where it would connect to other lines. And that's what it did. It got that far. It took quite a while to do all this because he had to go through a lot of mountains, tunnel through. He had a really good engineer. There's twenty-two tunnels and eight bridges on the entire line. And we're talking about just this western section. He didn't actually ever get all the way to South Carolina. He again used other lines. The southern terminus is in North Carolina, I think. The longest tunnel on the line, just north of Dante, is two miles long. And when they finished it, digging from both ends, they were only off by half an inch. That's incredible. 1914. Think about the technology. They didn't have computers. They didn't have GIS [geographic information systems]. They were just digging.

To build this two-mile-long tunnel, which is just north of Dante and comes out at Trammel, they used a lot of immigrant labor. The immigrants would come here, largely unknown. No one knew them. They came here as single men. And their idea was to work long enough and send money home and bring their wives and children over here. And so nobody knew them. They didn't speak English. And when they died during an accident or work injury or whatever, no one knew who to contact back home. And often they would just take their bodies out of the tunnel and apparently bury them along the side of the railroad track in shallow graves, and also in the area which is now the Dante ball field. Clarence Phillips says, "My grandfather told me you'd be surprised at people that's bones is up here in this baseball field." So that's a really grim thought, but I've since read that this was true all over this country, that as the Chinese and the Irish came and worked on the railroads, they were just single men far from home. The engineers on these projects would just say, "Dig another hole, put 'em in, and let's get another worker on this section."

Stilson Hutchins had started building up the town and in 1903 renamed Turkey Foot *Dante* in honor of his associate William Joseph Dante. In the earliest pictures, I think you can see the hotel was already built. The railroad station, not the one that's there now but an original one, a framed station. There was a little company store. The steam heat plant may have already been built then, and there was some basic housing. [The year] 1906 was when

3. Clinchfield Inn, Company Store B, depot, company houses in downtown Dante, 7 April 1907. Courtesy of the Dante History Project, Collection of Clinchfield Coal Company.

the Clinchfield Coal Corporation was organized. And the pictures we have from about that time period show those buildings already in place. And they couldn't all have been built just within a few months. So they must have already been there. But when George L. Carter took over, the Clinchfield company constructed many, many more houses for workers as they envisioned this big coal boom coming. So they really built the town.

And then he left. One of George L. Carter's hallmarks is he would get excited and start a venture, and then he would get bored with it. He would leave it and go on. He left southwestern Virginia in 1911. And he went to West Virginia, where he built Coalwood, which was a model coal town.[3] He built it with really nice houses and conveniences. He must have had the idea by then that a more comfortable worker makes a better worker, more productive. He had a habit also of getting up and leaving places if people got too contentious with him. He really liked being in charge. He didn't like competition. He didn't like people crossing him.

The records show that he and his wife made donations to the Mountain Mission School in Grundy, and there's some indication that he supported some individual children so that they could get their education. He really had a sense that education was important. It's interesting because he was such an industrialist, such a man interested in his own good fortunes. And very secretive about that. We have no records remaining because he left directions to his son that all his papers be burned at his death, and apparently they were. But he did see the value of education.[4]

FOUR

Immigrant Labor

Kathy Shearer: The story is, a lot of immigrants were brought to Dante starting around the early 1900s, say around 1906 or so when Clinchfield got started
up, until World War I. They came to build the railroad and build the coal
town. And many of them died, and no one knew where their families were,
how to get in touch with them. And, as I said, many of them are buried in
the ball field on either side of the tracks. It's kind of like a huge graveyard.
Italians, Hungarians, Poles—they were flooding in from Europe. The war
was heating up over there. They were coming here for, they thought, a safe
place to work, where they were promised a decent place to live and work.
And many of them just died.

The coal company and coal towns like Dante had a problem. They had to
bring in all these "foreigners" and people from out of the state because they
found the local folks would work in the cold weather, and then when it was
time to plant a crop, they would leave. And they would go back to the farm,
and they would take care of their farming duties. And they'd just take off. So
they couldn't get a regular, year-round workforce until they brought all these
other people in who didn't have land for them to go back to. And it was a
lot easier if you had foreigners who didn't own anything. And it was a whole
lot easier to control people who didn't own anything. Because you had total
control over them. If a miner died in that household, they were in a company
house with no miner in it, they could be put out on the street. And they were.
You had to have a miner in the home.

Frank Kilgore: I would say that there was probably two main reasons immigrants were recruited. One would be immigrants who had certain trades
or skills that indigenous people didn't have. That would be bridge building

and building tunnels, excavating tunnels, rock work and maybe a lot of masonry work. And so those folks were brought in because of those skills they had. And then when the coal demand got so high, particularly before, during, and immediately after World War I, the coal companies actually ran out of a labor pool of indigenous people who would or could mine coal. So they recruited foreigners and black sharecroppers just simply because there was a labor shortage. And about that same time, the unionization of the mines was picking up steam in southwest Virginia, and the coal companies responded by laying off, firing, a lot of the native miners and bringing in more immigrants and black sharecroppers to cross the picket line.[1] So I think we probably have two versions of immigrants coming here: one was labor shortage in skilled labor made it necessary, and, secondly, to help replace native coal miners who were trying to unionize and were being fired.

My grandfather told me about when the immigrants were brought in, how hostile the locals were toward the immigrants because they were brought in as strike breakers, how he was blackballed for two years for signing a union card, and these immigrants took over all their jobs. But apparently the coal operators discovered that experience did mean something, started hiring back some of the native Appalachians to work in the mines. And then the immigrants, they learned what the true score was in the coalfields and the coal camps. They were much more slave-like than the natives, because the natives owned land and could at least farm a little. But the immigrants lived strictly at the mercy of the coal companies and the coal camp housing, had to buy from the coal camp store.

He told me about that, and then they forged friendships with these immigrants, especially the second generation of immigrants. And they became some of the strongest supporters of the union. So the plan was a temporary fix for the coal operators to bust the union, but as it turned out they imported immigrants who became among the strongest union loyalists. And so those different ethnic groups, even though some of them couldn't even speak English, eventually joined with the native Appalachians to form the union. And there were southern African Americans brought up for the same purpose, and they became very strong union supporters.

I think a lot of coal operators would go recruit these workers down south or at Ellis Island and lie to them. Basically, my grandfather's recollection was they would tell the black workers, who were tenant farmers down south, that the coal was laying in piles here, and all you had to do was shovel it in the coal cars, and that was it. He said that he had actually witnessed several occasions where these black plantation workers would be brought up here, and when they started taking them into the mines, they would become claustrophobic and bolt and run, and try to find their way back home. That's how he found out what they were told because they would say, "This is not what I signed up for."

And some of them came and went into the mines and became some of the best coal miners. And so their offspring are still in the coalfields, not as many as there used to be. But like Bluefield (West Virginia), Pocahontas, Dante— large black contingencies of coal miners. And we still have a lot of the ethnic surnames around here—not as much as we used to—more apt to move out of here once the coal was gone and go back to a culture or society where more of their own folks lived. But a lot of them elected to stay, or couldn't leave for economic reasons, and became a part of the fabric of the communities.

So it's quite an interesting history to have all that. The second largest melting pot in the nation, I've been told, was the coalfields of Appalachia, the first being New York City. There were thirty-two nationalities represented in Wise County alone in the 1920s and '30s. There is a little town called Pocahontas, that's on the West Virginia border near Bluefield. You go up there, and they have a Hungarian Catholic Church in the middle of their town. They have a big mountainside graveyard where you find Hungarians, Poles, Italians.

When you see these rock walls around St. Paul and Lebanon, and these hand-hewn rock basements in Wise and all these other places, those were Italian rock masons. Entire families of rock masons would come over from Italy and Sicily, and they would do rock work for the coal companies and the town, and you still see that everywhere around here.

Terry Vencil: My mother's father came over from Wales when he was sixteen. He was a coal miner at that time, and he came by himself onboard ship. My grandfather said there was not enough work over there, and he came to this part of the country because underground he felt like he was home. You've got to remember that the United States and Wales originally were side by side, and they split. So the coal seams here look exactly like they look in Wales. And he came into Ohio and down the Ohio Valley into Kentucky, coal mining. And finally found his way into Virginia and bought and owned a coal mines here in Virginia. He settled in St. Paul because of it being a bedroom community. He was a rough Welsh miner, and he found this pretty southern belle, my grandmother, who majored in college in poetry and needlepoint.

All their lives, it was just a love affair between this rough coal miner and this little southern belle. He bought our house in 1932, and he placed his family in that house and then he would go into the coal mines and work. Then he would come back out. We've been in this house since '32, our family has been. And it's been handed down from grandparents to children to children. And I hope it can go on. I grew up in St. Paul, my mother grew up in St. Paul. She graduated from St. Paul Elementary School and High School, and I did too.

The schools grew up with a high, high expectation for their children because the parents had very high expectations of the schools. My mom once told me that she feared, feared getting in trouble at school. Not because of the principal, because of her daddy. You went to school to learn; you didn't go to school to cause trouble. And I think we still, we address our kids that same way. We expect good things out of our kids.

*There was more fighting going on in
St. Paul on the Western Front than there
was on the front in Europe.*

FIVE

Wild Times in St. Paul

LeRoy Hilton: The reason for the settlement in St. Paul was because of the
two railroads coming here. And also for bringing all the workers who would go
from here north into Dante and Dickenson County and all the other counties
to develop the coalfields. And it was 1910 before they finally brought the
railroad down from CC&O. It was finally then (because they had lost their
financing) before they finally brought the two railroads together. So when
they come from Dante, they come to here, and here they crossed over, and
they used the same tracks to go to Spartanburg, South Carolina. The Norfolk
and Western come through and went into Norton and connected to the other
coalfields out of Lee County and the area down there.

So they come to St. Paul, and this was the last frontier. So they come here,
and all the immigrant workers and whatnot that come into this territory, they
would stop at St. Paul, and this was a wild and woolly town. It was really.
They had a government distillery here, and they made liquor in the holler
over here. And they had a government taster who would come periodically
and taste the liquor. The biggest thing was the bordellos and the saloons and
the gambling and such related things. We had seventeen saloons in St. Paul.
All this was legal.

Now here's a picture in 1910 of St. Paul [see figure 4]. You'll notice this is
the Western Front section right here, along the river. There are no buildings,
no houses. Now here's 1930, and here is the Western Front [see figure 5]. All
these buildings were built somewhere between 1910 and 1930. In a twenty-
year period all of this developed, you see when there was nothing.

Speaking of the wild days of the Western Front in St. Paul, St. Paul lies
exactly on the banks of the Clinch River. Once you cross the Clinch River,
you are in Russell County. And apparently, they had a deal between the law

4. St. Paul, 1910, with arrow indicating future location of the Western Front. Courtesy of LeRoy Hilton.

enforcement people. When Wise County was dry, Russell County would be wet. And people would come to St. Paul and get in a boat and go to Russell County to get their liquor. And so the next couple of years, they would vote Russell County dry and Wise County wet, and the same thing would happen there. Well, I remember as a boy seeing all these men go in a little bus station they had down here. I guess it's all right to say it was the Maurice, later the Maurice Cab Company.

They had a place there they called a "blind tiger." I don't know if you've ever heard of a "blind tiger" or not, but liquor was very common—a lot of bootlegging. And you could see people carrying it in on their backs, bringing their fruit jars in, bringing them to these little holes-in-the-wall. And they had one they called a "blind tiger." We'd see these men coming in and coming out, and after a while, we would see them tipsy, walking up and down the street on the Western Front. Well, come to find out, they had a little hole inside the building, and you would open up a little door, and you'd put two dollars in the door and close it. Well, after a while, they would open the little door, and there would be a pint of liquor in here.

So the reason for doing the "blind tiger" was that the proprietor never

5. St. Paul, 1930, with arrow indicating buildings of the Western Front. Courtesy of LeRoy Hilton.

did see his customer, or the customer never did see the proprietor. So when they'd catch them on the street drunk and ask them, where did you get this liquor and who did you get it from, they couldn't tell them. And they were perfectly honest when they said, "I don't know where or who I got it from." It was a "blind tiger," and it operated in St. Paul on the Western Front. And when I was hunting in the woods, ever once in a while I would run into an old still where they had had their old barrels and tubs and whatnot.

I had an aunt who went to Radford College; she lived in Clinchco. And she had to come to St. Paul in order to catch the train to go to Radford. And she said she was only a young girl and she come to St. Paul. And, of course, the railroad station is just opposite the Western Front. Said she had never seen a drunk man before. And so when she come to St. Paul and she got off this train, the train pulled out and left her standing there. Said here these drunks come staggering by, a bunch of men. She said, "I've never been so scared in my life. A bunch of drunks there, and I'm a young girl in a strange place."

But there was all kind of killings. Several people were found dead. The train would run over them where they would get drunk and lay on the railroad tracks. Coss Holley, that was one in particular I remember. Then they had others. Kelley McGorick, which is a friend of ours, he was a young boy, and he would hop the trains. And he got his legs cut off. I mean there's all kind of accidents up and down the railroad. But as far as actually shootings, you'd hear of all the fights. It was a common thing on Saturday nights. You could really go over—back in the early '20s just after World War I. All quiet on the Western Front—that was the thing that they said in Europe as the war went on. Said there was more fighting going on in St. Paul on the Western Front than there was on the front in Europe. But it was nothing to go down there and see people—you know, fist fights and whatnot. There was several people who were shot, but right off I don't remember their names. We're talking about seventy years ago.

A Mr. Bolton told me this story about a killing in the middle of Fourth Avenue, just opposite the bank. He had a store at the time, Bolton Grocery Store. It was about 1921. And there was a jeweler here in St. Paul who apparently had a girlfriend, the same as the local sheriff. And there was a controversy over this girlfriend, and Mr. Bolton told me that he was there and saw the sheriff kill this Mr. Addington. Both were courting the same woman. Apparently the sheriff had the gun, and Mr. Addington did not. So he ended up dead in the middle of the street on Fourth Avenue in St. Paul. And I understand that Mr. Addington was related to Maybelle Carter.[1] Fred Bolton was the man that told me the story. Later on, they had the oil company, Bolton Oil Company in St. Paul.

But in the Western Front, you had one grocery store, and you had a café and a poolroom and another café and a beer joint and a bar and a bus station and a little boarding house. And then above all these buildings, that's where your "overnight guests" were spending whatnot, you know. Once they legalized liquor and did away with all the old saloons, then there was really no need for all these illegal hole-in-the-walls and liquor and bordellos. And the only merchant was Tom Dean and Company. He moved uptown. The highway come through, and they relocated the highway further over, away. So it was really a matter of there was no other need. The old hotel was replaced by a newer, modern one uptown. And all the grocery stores, the bakery, and the bank—all these things were established uptown. Plus the housing development was here. And there was no housing at all on the Western Front, except the boarding houses and whatnot. So it was just a way of the world. There was no need for them anymore. It phased out like the Old West.

Jason Boone: As far as the drug use, more out in town, and I see quite a bit of it. If I ever decided to use any drugs, I could be someplace and in forty-five seconds to a minute get anything I basically wanted. But as far as the school, there's not much drug use at all that I know of. But as far as the community, yeah, there's quite a bit. But never been pressured into using any kind of drugs or any illegal substances. Nobody really influences me, one way or the other.

LeRoy Hilton: I hear scuttlebutt, and it's strictly scuttlebutt. But I hear people talking. I talk to my friends. But I don't think there's any real underground Western Front operating today. There are some drugs being sold, but these are people that come in with a car or a van and get in a parking lot or near a service station or a shopping center. And they set up there. There's no establishment. There's no buildings in town that I know of. And I can just about call everybody by name and what they do and what time they get up in the morning, what time they go to bed. I know of no hole-in-the-wall buildings in St. Paul that are doing anything like this. But I have heard of one or two people supposedly has been selling OxyContin. But they drift in, like I say, in a pickup truck or a van, and they set there on a parking lot. The people that are looking for it, they're going to find it.

I could find it probably if I looked hard enough. But I'd go to a parking lot somewhere looking for a strange van or out-of-town vehicle. I about know everybody in St. Paul, and I know what kind of car they drive. If I'm looking for something, and I go down and see a strange van setting more than thirty minutes or an hour in a parking lot down here at one of the shopping centers, I know that there is something not the way it is supposed to be. But alcohol—probably beer and wine—nearly anybody can go anywhere in the grocery store and buy this. If you're sixteen and you want a bottle of wine, I'm sure there's an eighteen- or twenty-year-old can go get it for you. And they know who they are. I'm honest when I say, in my vision in my mind, going through every building in St. Paul, I know of no places where a bunch of rough crowd hangs out or where you would be going and expect to find something like this.

Jason Boone: Anytime I wanted to, I know a few people at school and I know ten or fifteen people out of school that I could go and get drugs from anytime. I mean, that's not my thing, but there's people all over town. The older folk probably don't know them. Anybody that's, like, my age up to probably around thirty or forty definitely knows of them. They're local. Everybody's local here. They get busted pretty frequently, probably once a year, or maybe once every couple of years. And they will "narc out" quite a few people, and it gets to be a big mess around town.

Chelsea Salyer: I don't know where the main, like, original source is, but as far as, like, what I've known and I've seen, it's local people that the people are getting it from. I don't know where they're getting it from, but all I have ever seen is local people. I've heard people talk about, they supposedly went to, like, North Carolina. It was, like, a big drug convention, kind of. And, like, they were supposed to make, like, thousands of dollars. I don't know if that's how they always do it. But I know that one time they supposedly went down there and did that.

I always knew that pills were kind of big here, but apparently they've talked to people from the outside, and we're known for pills. I didn't really realize that. St. Paul. Somebody called it St. Pill. Apparently, that's what we're known for, the pills. But I personally don't really think it's much worse than any other area.[2] And I personally don't feel pressures. I don't know if it's just the way I've been raised with self-confidence. I don't know. I don't feel pressure from anybody.

> If you lived above the tracks on the north
> side, then I never saw a drunk.

SIX

Civility in St. Paul

LeRoy Hilton: The town sort of separated in two sections. Once you crossed the railroad tracks, you were in a different world. The drunks, and the restaurants, and the bordellos, and the saloons—most of them operated across the tracks, but once you come over here in town—you've always heard of these people who live on the wrong side of the tracks—well, if you lived above the tracks on the north side, then I never saw a drunk, unless I was over across the tracks on the Western Front. Two different worlds. The solid citizen types— of course, all the men, even the solid citizen men, they would go across and do their drinking and their gambling or whatnot on the other side of the tracks. But I would say mostly your women and your well-thought-of people never ventured across the tracks anyway. So it was really two different worlds, is what it was.

I've lived in St. Paul almost eighty-one years; I'm eighty years old. And I guess the reason they call me the local historian is because I outlived nearly everyone else who moved here. My family came to St. Paul in 1924. When we first come to St. Paul, the Boltons were in charge of the store, the post office, the hotel—they were also operators of the Blue Sulphur Hotel, which was built in 1910—Charlie Bolton. And there's a story of a salesman who come to town—it was the horse and buggy days—but he did something that wasn't right, so the police took him down to the J.P. And the J.P. happened to be Mr. Bolton.

Well, the salesman said, "There's something wrong here. Yesterday when I come in here, I registered at the hotel. Mr. Bolton was running the hotel, and he registered me. I went over to the post office to mail a letter, and there was Chub Bolton, his son. He was the postmaster. Now I get a fine, and I come to the justice of the peace. It's Mr. Charlie Bolton, his daddy." He said,

"Now you talk about a one-horse town. This is a Bolton one-horse town." Fred, Chub's brother, he told me all of this.

I come out of the army in 1945. And at that time the postmaster was a neighbor of mine. One day he said, "LeRoy, I need some help at the post office. Would you come work for me?" And I said, "I'm just freshly out of the service. I don't know." He said, "Pretty good pay. It's eighty-nine cents an hour." And that's the rate I started at in 1946. I started at eighty-nine cents an hour. And then I said, "I won't stay here long because I've got to find another job." So he said, "I'm sick, and I have to go to Hot Springs. They've told me to go down and take a couple of months off. Would you mind working while I'm gone?" So as an accommodation to him, I worked. And then he come back and said, "Christmas is coming on and we don't have any help." And nobody wanted this eighty-nine-cent job, so I worked during Christmas as an accommodation.

And this is the time of the spoils system. You got a public job ever what if Democrats or Republicans, that's how you got your job. But since it was such a low-paying job and the Democrats were in at that time—Roosevelt had just gone out, and Harry Truman—so I had this job. And they asked me if I would like to make an application for the postmaster. I said, "I don't know." And they said, "We'll appoint you. You don't have to take an examination or nothing." The Democrats said, "We'll appoint you as postmaster." Well, they appointed me.

Then Eisenhower was elected. And about the time the election was over, I had six or seven well-known Republicans come in and told me I wouldn't be working very long. And I go back to Mr. Bolton, and this is the honest-to-goodness truth. When I moved to St. Paul in 1924, we moved right across the street from the Boltons and have become well acquainted with them as neighbors. And Fred and I used to do some arrowhead hunting and whatnot, and he was the chairman of the Republican Party. And I was always a Democrat, my family.

Well, he said, "LeRoy, don't you worry about your job." He said, "I've known you and your family too long. We had a meeting last night and I told 'em, 'Leave that Hilton boy alone.'" So by the grace of Fred Bolton and the Good Lord, I ended up getting the postmaster's job and stayed there thirty-seven years until I retired.[1]

But industry, we've never had a great industry here except World War I, we had what they called the extract plant. It was Swift and Co. in 1914 established an extract plant, and because of their great holdings in the cattle business and whatnot, they made material for WWI. And they made a tanning acid in this plant that was located here in St. Paul. They had great wooden vats up on concrete stands, and they had what they called a hog and a pig. That was two machines that ground the chestnut wood, which made the tanning acid. The hog would grind the tree, and the pig would grind the bark, and they would put these into these large vats and had a big steam boiler where they would put hot water into these vats and made a tanning solution. And so they did the harnesses and the boots and the shoes and everything for the war industry. It closed in 1920 after the end of the war. Really this was one of the biggest industries from many years back was the extract plant. Other than that, the coal industry, which has supported this area all these many years.

During the Depression, all these at-one-time-affluent people would come, they would come on the trains. About every fifteen minutes somebody would knock on your door looking for work or something to eat. And these people that come through, you know they called them bums, but they were not. They were really nice people. They were just down and had no place to go. They were searching and hunting a place to just find work, a way to support their families. A lot of them stayed here and, of course, got work in the coalfields.

But when I first had anything to do with coal, I was like fourteen or fifteen years old, and my father had a truck and we would haul coal for $2 a ton. Now this was back in the mid-thirties. And just before the big boom finished, it was like $80 a ton.

And there was a lake where the Episcopal Church sets, Lake Estonoa. There was another one across where the Methodist Church is. There was a series of ponds—we called them lakes. These houses were only built in the '30s when they started making the road to Dante. Every bit of it, plumb to the sidewalk where the houses are, was all water. It was like a four-, five-, six-acre lake, and it went all the way to the school building and all the way to the sidewalk here on Buchanan Street. They only filled that in and built houses during the Depression when they was building the road to Dante in 1932 or '33 or whatever. And here, there was a cave. This was built on a cave and a lake. My neighbor, John Hillman, who was one of the founders of St. Paul and had the first hotel in 1890, he would come, and his ducks would go back into the cave right here where this church sets now.

So what they did, they blasted this thing and broke the crevice in the rock, of course, and drained the lake and filled it in and built the church here, the Methodist Church. When I was young, like six or seven or eight years old, we had boardwalks. And the one here just behind this building on the next street, it was like four or five feet off of the ground because of the swampy area that was always through here. And the cows run loose in town. The streets were only paved here during the Depression—called it WPA, Works Progress Administration. They laid the groundwork for every road in St. Paul because there was big erosion ditches four or five feet deep, and the cattle run up and down the streets. Ten cents an hour was their wages, you know. And they graded all these streets. And they'd bring rock in, and with sledgehammers the workers you would see them break up the rocks and beating them into the ground. That's the roadbeds for all the streets in St. Paul.

Back in the late '20s and early '30s, it took all day to go to Bristol. I mean the road wound across the river, went every little curve. Everywhere the cows walked, that's the way it went. And we'd leave like seven o'clock in the morning. Maybe once every six or seven months we got to go to Bristol. Bristol had everything. It had movie theaters and stores. All the women had to go do their shopping. The big city. Oh, it was a big deal. You'd have so many people in the car, it would be stuffed. But you would leave at like seven o'clock in the morning. It was a two or three-hour trip just to Bristol, which was only forty-five miles away. You would talk forever about it. Went to Bristol. You would pack eight or ten people in a car to go to Bristol to see *Gone with the Wind*, you know. It was really a big deal.

Tom Fletcher: For all these many years, St. Paul has been pretty much one square mile. The population has gone up and down, but it's stayed around a thousand people. So we have a square mile of a thousand people.

And this was the movie theater right here. It's called "The Gaiety." I think you can still read it. That was the first movie theater. That was the Ben Franklin store for years; it's a restaurant now. And Giovanni's and a barber shop. The second theater was built right here across from the Lyric. The Phillips building. The reason I know of this is, this is where I lived. This is where I grew up. My grandfather built that home, and it was a post office across the street. My grandfather, he was building homes, he owned a lumber business. He was going to build it for my dad and mom, and they tried to talk him out of it. They said, "In ten years, that's going to be the business district." He said, "Ten years from now, I won't care." So this theater was built, flourished. It went seven days a week. Mr. Coleman built that one. Then Mr. Turner built this one, across the street, the Lyric, and it was a step up in luxury and whatever. But they all three actually operated at the same time—late '40s, early '50s.

My dad was elected mayor, I believe, in 1941. Interesting enough, he had run for mayor since he had been twenty-one. I believe this was the third time he had run. And he was elected. Then war broke out, and he went into the navy. He came back in '47 and was elected and remained mayor, I believe, until sometime in the '70s, all except for one term. He was involved with the lumber business my grandfather had started, actually had a hardware when

6. The closed-down and boarded-up Lyric Theater and Lyric Shop in 2005, though St. Paul Tomorrow still hopes to convince the town council to purchase the building as part of its revitalization plan. Photo by Beth Crow.

7. The old post office and pharmacy, in 2005 a novelty shop and restaurant. Photo by Beth Crow.

World War II started. It was a branch of the lumber business, and then when he came back, they had sold the hardware while he was in service. The only thing it left was the lumber business itself.

Terry Vencil: This is the house my grandfather bought in '32. Then my mom and dad bought it for something like eighty-nine hundred in '53. And then once my dad died in 1980, Dean and I built an apartment on the back for Mom, and we have been living here since Dad died in 1980. Mom stayed with us, we stayed with her, through her cancer, and we were lucky enough to keep her here right up to her death. So this house is very special.

The Lyric Theater was open when I was in school. The other one had closed out. You could go to the theater on Sunday afternoon and get in for fifteen cents. Mom would give me twenty-five cents for a Coke and a box of popcorn. And Dad always gave me an extra little bit of money because he had to have a box of popcorn brought home. And then right beside the Lyric Theater was the Lyric Shop [see figure 6]. The Lyric Shop was hamburgers, french fries, that type thing. Ma Whitenack ran the Lyric Shop, and Fats Whitenack, her husband, ran the theater. They were characters, and they raised half the kids in town. Mom let us have a charging account there because she knew Ma wouldn't feed us anything that we shouldn't have. And I've been cut off plenty of times: "One Coke is enough, Terry."

And there was the drugstore. Doc Hall—he wasn't really a doctor, he was a pharmacist, but we all called him Doc Hall—was the proprietor. And he owned the house that LeRoy lives in now. You go in there, and the floors were wooden floors. They were oiled, so you walk in, and you have this definite smell. They had the old Cocola tables, with the little wire things. And they made the best strawberry Cokes, fountain Cokes in the world. You could go up three steps inside the pharmacy and get inside the old post office. So you had internal connections between the pharmacy and the post office. And again, it had the oil floors. When I was growing up, we had our own post office boxes, and I used to love to go get the mail [see figure 7].

And everybody grew up, every time the church doors opened, we were expected to be there—Wednesday night choir practice, Sunday morning, Sunday night, GAs [Girls' Auxiliary], RAs [Royal Ambassadors], whatever it happened to be. Our social life revolved around churches. And we passed that down from generation to generation. We have eleven churches within a half-mile radius of St. Paul. We have a population of a thousand people. That's a large number of churches for a small amount of people. Are we very religious? Well, we're in the Bible Belt. The church makes a big impact on our lives.

SEVEN

Great Depression and Dante

Frank Kilgore: My grandfather, Frank Kilgore, was born in the late 1800s. He had lived through the Depression, he had lived through union organization, he had lived through subsistence farming. He could read and write a little bit. He never drove a car in his entire life. He walked everywhere he went. He walked seven miles over to Dante, seven miles one way to work and seven miles back, would work ten-, twelve-, sixteen-hour shifts in the mines hand-loading coal when carbide lamps were used and the dust was so thick you couldn't even see. And the oxygen was so diminished back in those deep mines that sometimes their carbide flame would go out and they would have to back up into the main way to light it because there wasn't enough oxygen to burn it.

He hand-drilled coal, he hand-loaded coal, he hand-pushed coal. Sometimes they would shut the mines down or during a strike they would be blackballed or laid off and have to go somewhere else and live in a boarding house and mine coal and bring money back to his family. He did that for forty-three years. And he talked about the union to me. He lived in a two-room house where he raised his seven kids. He and my grandma lived a mile off the road up Honey Branch. I would carry groceries to them, I would go up and chop wood for them, carry water for them, coal. And sit and listen to him talk about growing up on a farm and then becoming a coal miner. And how rough things were.

Kathy Shearer: People walked from Chaney Creek several miles to get to work each day. Hazel Mountain. Anywhere along Sandy Ridge. From West Dante certainly. And some of them probably came up over the mountain from Trammel. Honey Branch. Frank Kilgore's grandfather worked in these mines.

And people just didn't have cars, mostly till after World War II. Not many cars here. Many people would live in company houses close to the entrance of the mine so they could get right in there. But still when they got to the mine, they would have to walk a way into the mountain to get to their work place. And before the union came in, they didn't get paid for that time. They had to be at the working face, or they were loading coal and they got paid by the ton.

Pocahontas started earlier than Dante, but Dante was about the second coal center, and Clinchfield had its headquarters here. So it was the big place, certainly in Russell County, and one of the largest coal communities in southwestern Virginia. We know in 1930 there were thirty-eight hundred people living here. Now during the Depression, things really went downhill.

Clinchfield was big enough to survive the Depression. It kept everybody in their company house. You could get at least one or two days a week, sometimes one day every other week, but it was enough of a check or payment coming in every week to pay your house rent. And so, by and large, people did not lose their houses during the Depression. But I don't think Dante recovered after the Depression to the extent it had been in the beginning of the '20s and '30s. So I would say the peak was in the late '20s.

And then there was another spurt during the war, and then after the war people tell me they came back from World War II and everything had been mechanized. And if you could run machinery, you could still have a job. But if you couldn't make that transition, you were out of luck. And they laid off lots of people. And the mines here in Dante, the active mines in Dante, closed down entirely by 1959 except for some private trucking that went on after that. But the major push in coal was over in Dante in 1959.

Nannie Phillips Gordon: I came here when I was three weeks old. That was in 1925. And as far as I know, I've been in this area the balance of my life. And now I'm getting on up in years, and I forget a lot of things, but some things I still remember a lot. I can remember how my dad worked in the coal mines and how my mother used to take in laundry. There was a Hungarian, Dominic, I can't think of his last name. My mother did his shirts. He wore white shirts all the time. My mother washed and ironed them every week. And I have an older sister, and I only had the one brother, and he got killed in '52. A man just walked up and shot him. I have a sister that lives in Kingsport, one in St. Paul, one in 'Lizabethton, and I have two sisters that's dead. My brother's dead. And, of course, both of my parents are dead.

My dad was born here. I can show you the place, but the house is tore down. My dad worked in the coal mines as a water boy when he was seven years old, up old No. 2 at Straight Holler here. And then after my dad met my mother and married, he brought my mother here. My mother was born in Coeburn. My dad and his dad, they lived right down here. When my dad was just a small boy, he carried water to the miners in an old bucket. I've got an old bucket in there like the one he carried. Not hisn, but I've got one.

Daddy at one time was a moonshiner, before he ever got on for Clinchfield. That was before he started picketing for the union. But he made moonshine. That's how he raised us children, and we were small at that time. But we lived over in Russell County, over on Honey Branch. I was just small, but we moved from over here in Bear Waller to Honey Branch and stayed over there a long time. And then Daddy moved back to Dante. We lived on a farm down here above Dante, down at Grandpa's old place. My mother always canned. I had an aunt and uncle that lived in Castlewood, over behind the cemetery. Mommy and Daddy would go over there in the summertime and pick blackberries. And Mommy would bring them home and can them, make jam or jelly, whatever. A lot of it I've forgotten. I was raised right here in the Dante area, and I'm not no spring chicken, you know.

I've got a picture of my daddy—he butchered hogs. I've got big pictures of him where he killed hogs. We always killed our own hogs. And when we lived over on Honey Branch, he killed us a beef every year. Take a long butcher knife and go out to the smokehouse, cut off big steaks this big, that thick, bring them in, and fix them. Oooh, you talk about good eating, that was good eating. You don't get that anymore. Then when he moved to Dante, he got to raising hogs. And he killed two hogs weighed a thousand and some pounds. I mean, they was like cattle.

My mother kept us in church, and we went to the Assembly of God Church. The Assembly of God Church up in Bear Waller now is not the same. It was way down here at the Bear Waller curve. That's the haunted house. It was just always called that. Anybody ask Mommy where she went to church, she said, "the haunted house." That's what Mommy always said.

Our Christmas was very small. We always had plenty to eat. That was one thing my daddy and my mother always looked out for: we had plenty of food. We didn't have a tree until about three years before my daddy died. He started putting up a Christmas tree. When he started decorating, he decorated everything—outside, inside, everywhere. And after my daddy died in '82—I was married and had a family—after Daddy died, Mommy gave all the stuff away. Daddy decorated everything, everything. When people come by my daddy's house, some of them would call, "All right, Ora [rhymes with Tory], turn your lights on; we're coming up."

I can remember the first time I learned there was not a Santa Claus. My

8. Ora Phillips's hog-butchering operation in Bear Wallow, 1946. Ora stands third from the right, Nannie Phillips Gordon fourth from the right. Nannie's husband Bill and two of their children are at far left. Courtesy of the Dante History Project, Collection of Jim Wood.

mother had bought all our stuff at the company store right here at Dante. And she hid it—back then they didn't call it a couch, they called it a davenport— mommy hid all our stuff under that. And we didn't know it. Mommy had gone somewhere, I can't remember where. Anyway, we found our toys. I had a little doll this long, and my sisters did too. And my brother had only one little bitty car. Wasn't like a car, it was more like a wagon. And under that couch, that was where was hidden for our Christmas. We didn't get a lot of clothes, a lot of toys, and stuff like that because they was expensive at that time. But now, you go buy stuff like that, it's nothing. You'd think nothing about it.

What we did, we pulled them out and looked at them. We knew from then on there was no Santa Claus. They was not wrapped; they was in boxes. So we put them back under the davenport. And Mommy didn't know until Christmas time when she went in to get the stuff and put them out. Because we had to go to bed, and Santa Claus come after we was in bed, which was Mommy and Daddy, you know. And we'd get up the next morning and find them, but see we'd already see our Christmas stuff. And one of my sisters, that lives in Elizabethton right today, she—we always called her "big mouth"—she looked at Mommy and said, "We knowed what we got for Christmas." Mommy said, "*What?*" She said, "We'd already seen everything we had." Mommy wore us out. I'll never forget.

I can remember that my daddy was a sick man at that time. And he was in the hospital right here at Dante. Dr. L. C. McNeer was the man over the hospital. And they operated on my daddy, and we thought he was going to die. And he kind of put us in a hard place, because if you didn't work, you didn't draw no scrip, uh uh. There was nothing. That's when my mother started taking in ironing for people, to feed us children. It bothers me talking about all this. My daddy and mommy, they had a hard life. They had a big family. Mommy made our slips out of feed sacks, if you know what I'm talking about. Back then you bought feed in regular sacks. And Mommy would take them and make us underwear and slips out of them. That's what we had. It wasn't burlap, it was like a pillow case.

And at that time, my daddy drinked a lot. And I'll never forget the day he quit drinking, never in my life. He came down the road, he'd been up somewhere on Hazel Mountain. "I killed my beef." And Mommy said, "Now young'uns, let's get ready because your daddy'll be home drunk." Naturally we was scared. We was afraid Daddy was going to come home drunk. Well, Daddy come home, and we had so many steps he had to come down. He dropped a glass jar on the steps, and we thought it was full of booze, but it wasn't. And from that day till the day my daddy died, he never drank another drop. But he done that to convince Mommy that he could go places and do things and not be drinking.

When you think about it, those was hard times, but they was good times too. Nobody had more than anybody else. And I can remember when the bank was right here next door. I can remember the day when that bank went broke. My daddy worked at No. 3 mines. Charlie Bartee, my daddy's boss, said to him, "Now Ora, I need you to go to the bank for me this evening. The banks is going broke. I need you to take out everything I've got and bring it to me tomorrow." My daddy came right here, and took his money out, and kept it in his pocket, until the next morning he took it to him at work. Old No. 3 mines. I can remember that, and that's been many, many years ago. When the bank went bust, I was more or less you would say, a child. 'Cause it went bust, I'm gonna say, in '32 or '33.

Roy Phillips: I'm Roy Phillips, Roy J. Phillips. We moved to Dante when I was fourteen years old. And I've seen a lot of changes, I tell you. My father died when I was sixteen and a half. It was '32 when he died, and I went to work in August of '32. And they passed a law you had to be eighteen, but I had two sisters and my mother. And I was in a company house. Mr. Long, he always tried to take care of boys growing up from around here, give them work. And he kept me someway and cut off the others.

Talk about work, I started work at twenty-five cents an hour. Glad to get it.

Before I stopped work, some of them were getting a hundred dollars a day. I said, "What about twenty-five cents an hour?" They wouldn't believe me.

But I was glad to get it. We didn't have anything at all. Nobody had anything then at all hardly. I was glad to work. They paid scrip, and I managed a lot of time to buy some scrip, trade a little some way. We didn't have very much, but I was careful. Some of them used it wrong. They would get it, and it was very hard times here then.

And I was glad I did because I had a mother and two sisters. Course now, your power bill wasn't nothing. We didn't have nothing at that time but a radio and lights. I've seen a lot of changes, a lot of things. And so I was glad to get it, and I tried to always give them a good day's work. And I never was cut off but one time. I was at No. 2 in '56, I was working up there about a month. Before they closed down, they sent me over to Carbo to work. Plenty of work over there till I got ready to retire. So they was always nice to me. That one time was the only time. I was off two months; they called me back.

I've seen a lot of changes. We see a lot of people, crippled back then, because they didn't practice safety back then, you know. All they had in mind was to get coal. This black lung I've seen back then. Many years ago, I visit this fellow—he dumped coal at No. 2 tipple. He got sick, and I visited him. And they said coal dust won't hurt you, and you couldn't get nothing out of it either. You wouldn't get no pay, you know.

Anyhow, I've seen so many changes in the mine, like I worked outside most of the time. I would pick slate out; some pieces had scree [rock debris]. They would tell you what size they wanted. Some of that large, boy, you had a hard time on your legs. Because that box, you had to keep moving. That slate coming down on you, sometimes you would get one leg about covered up, and you would have a hard time pulling it out. And you would have to move, you know, to get it out of there. Keep me skinned up a lot.

Sometimes you worked one, sometimes two days a week, but most of the time you worked two or three. [The years] 1936, '37—Clincho over here, they worked six days a week. They had what you call "lake orders" [apparently coal orders from the Great Lakes, orders instrumental in keeping Clinchfield in business during the hardest times of the Depression]. And we'd go over there because, man working that many, you could go over there any day about, and they would give you a place to go in the mine and load coal. I even went over and worked in the mine car shop those two years.

But we had a lot of people back then loading coal with shovels, had much more people. But machinery began to come in, gradually would cut down labor. I know, I was a blacksmith a good while. After a while in several years, it come where torch and welders, you know. My job was obsolete really. But they would still keep me, and I would work in repair work. And if you needed any tools sharpened, that's all the blacksmith and I would do. So I've seen so many changes, but each time we get new machinery, it cut people off. And so it just went on down to where the miner is just about obsolete himself, isn't he, praise the lord.

Anyway, I worked forty-six and a half years. One time they opened a new mine over at Duty. One month I had to visit the hospital, an old hospital. They had thirty men that were hurt, some of them real bad. One a back broke, others arms—it was just awful. When they first started, they just didn't practice safety much, but in later years we would have schools and things, teach us things, so it was much better in later years.

The union helped us a lot too. We had a safety committee, and that helped very much. The union was organized in 1945. They tried before but didn't get it. That's when they got the contract. It was very hard to get the union here because Mr. Long actually treated his men pretty good, you know. It's pretty hard to get organized, and I wouldn't sign. And I know I about got whipped a time or two for not. But I was a stubborn old boy. Some of them would try to make me, and I wouldn't be made to do nothing at that time, bless the lord. But after all this machinery come in, kept cutting off men, you know. Well, I understand the company because it costs a lot to keep a man on the payroll. And I could understand their view too.

I thank the lord I'm here this morning. I finally went to sleep, woke up, and felt better this morning. I thank him for that, praise the lord. We've got a God that understands and takes care of us so many times. But you know mining has changed so much even before I went to work. One feller I worked with told me he went to work when he was ten years old. But see that was a way back, and all he done was stay where the coal would come out, and he would have to keep them switches there and kind of sweep around that little station he had there, and answer a telephone once in a while.

But we see so many changes in everything anymore, you know. But back then, it's almost unbelievable to tell what happened, that took place, but it did. And so we are glad that the lord has blessed us to work that many years, and not get hurt too bad. But I did get hurt some.

Lucille Whitaker: I run around with a bunch of girls, and there wasn't nothing we wouldn't do. You name it, and we done it. Our schoolhouse had a fire stair to go down. And we was in the study hall, and a bunch of us was setting around in the chair. And we didn't want to stay in that study hall. Mr. Butt, he was our principal, and the teacher went out. So there was five of us, and we sneaked down that fire escape. And they had a funeral at the Catholic

Church, a gentleman that got killed in the mines. Well, we was coming down through the schoolyard, and I looked up and there was Mr. Butt looking out the window at us. I said, "Girls, we're in trouble." They said, "What we gonna do?" And I said, "Well, we're going down here to this Catholic Church." We went into that Catholic Church. To keep Mr. Butt getting a hold of us, we went up front. We went up front, and we just acted like we was the family there. So Mr. Butt came into the church, and I looked around and seen where he was setting. And I told the girls, "He's gonna get us this time, really lay it onto us." So when we come out of the church, Mr. Butt slipped out, and he just went around the corner where the door was at. When we came out of the church, he said, "Come on. You ladies come with me." So he really worked on us. We had to stay in after school for two hours, and did he give us work to do. And I didn't try that no more.

Later, I worked at the company store, and I got $75 a month. It was in '35, '36, somewhere along there. Anyway, the company changed me around and put me in what we call the beer garden. We sold beer; we had sandwiches and stuff to serve and everything. This gentleman came in and he was drunk, and I waited on him. And I knewed him; I knewed this gentleman very well. He had ordered up a bottle of beer and wanted a bowl of soup. Well, I served him, and I forgot to take him a spoon. He kept hollering at me, and I was waiting on some more customers. And I turned around and looked at him, and there was a little bar shovel setting there. I just reached over and got that bar shovel, and I took it over and said, "Here. You can use this until I have time to give you a spoon."

If something come in the area like a carnival, a group of us would get together. We didn't go by ourselves; the girls were in groups. We would meet boys, and they would walk us home. And then a skating rink came in. Now, I went to school with Harry, but I didn't have nothing to do with him. And there's a skating rink come up here at the ballpark. And my sister Marie wanted to learn how to skate. Harry skated, and I wouldn't learn. I wouldn't learn how to skate. So he helped Marie, told her how to skate and everything. And I had a date with a guy. I don't know; we separated some way or another.

Harry walked up to me, and he said, "Can I walk you home?" And I said, "Well, no." And he said, "Aw, come on, I'll walk you home." And I said, "Okay." So he walked me home, and we went together, started going together and everything. And he went in the service, Harry did. We went together five years. When he come home in '46, he said, "Let's get married." I said, "I don't know if I want to marry you or not." But we did, we got married in '46.

I never was in no cars with no boys. Our mother was real strict on us. We walked to the movies, but we walked in groups. I never was in a car with

Harry up till we got married. That was the only time I was in a car with him. I was working at the shirt factory in St. Paul, and me and Harry talked about getting married. And I never did mention it to my mother that I was planning on marrying Harry because she was real strict. So I got up and I got dressed and I packed my suitcase, and Momma said, "Aren't you going to go to work today?" And I said, "No, me and Harry's going to get married." She said, "You're going to do what?" I said, "Yeah, we're going to go up Lebanon and get our license and everything. We're going to Mr. Monday's house, and we're going to get married today."

She said, "You better think about this, young lady." I said, "Why?" She said, "If you get married and it doesn't work out, you can't come back home." I said, "Okay, if it doesn't work out, I won't come back home."

Nannie Phillips Gordon: The first permanent I ever got was done at the old Dante hotel. They had a beauty shop there, and the police stayed there. Caney Boyd [company policeman], he stayed there. And they had rooms. Mr. Matthews and Mr. Long and Mr. Thacker, all of them, if they had to go on a business [do business], or if somebody had to come in to be with them, they all met at the hotel. And then they had upstairs—Daddy always called it the "golden room." They was rooms and rooms and rooms. One of my daddy's sisters worked right here at the Dante hotel. She was Beulah Phillips, and she married Abraham Rife. She lives in Bristol now, and that was my daddy's sister.

You're not going to believe this. My husband tended to me when I was a baby. My husband was twice as old as me when we married. I was eighteen, and he was thirty-six. I had very few boyfriends. My daddy was a very strict man. He knew my husband from years and years back. I never dated but one other guy. Daddy never allowed us to date any boys and go with them in a car without we took our other sisters, our brother, whatever.

One other time I remember. My husband had a pickup truck, and he just loaded it full of children in the back. And me and one of my sisters would ride in the front with him. And we went on Honey Branch just riding around in the truck. And coming up Honey Branch, Bill stopped, my husband stopped, and one of my sisters—Mildred—she got out of the back of the truck and started to get back in, and he pulled out and kind of throwed her. And scared her to death. And he got out and told her, said, "Mildred," or "Muchie"—we called her "Muchie"—"Muchie, I'll wear you out if you do that again." And when he took us home and told Daddy that, Daddy never let us go anymore. That was the end of it. I could go with Bill to the movies when we had the old theater.

They would play on the same field, but at separate times.

EIGHT

Race Relations in Dante

Matthew Kincaid: I was born right here in Dante in Sawmill Hollow, down the street there. My mother and my father moved here from Tennessee. My father moved here to mine coal. He shore did. And that's when I was born. I had two older brothers. One of them, Earl, passed away just two years ago. At Christmas when we were kids, me and my brothers, we'd get our little toys and go to the next-door neighbors and get with them. And we just had a good time. Didn't have too much, but what we had we enjoyed it. I remember when we used to get our little cowboy outfits and everything. Especially during wartime, you didn't get no capbusters or nothing. Everything was wood. And right down here, where the church is down here, up on the side of the hill there, it's flat. That's where we used to go and play cowboys. And we would go from this end all the way over to the church. We'd get a tree limb, and we'd make a horse out of it.

When we got a little older, we stayed on the ball park, playing baseball. We had about ten or twelve games a day. We'd lose a few, and we'd win a few. Just guys from the neighborhood. What it was was upper end, and right along in here was middle, and then lower end. They would have baseball where the lower end would play the upper end. Then whoever would win on that, they would play the middle. And I tell you what, if your momma wanted you, there wasn't no telephone. If she wanted you, she would just get out there and holler. And the next-door neighbor, it would just go up the line like a telephone. You would get the message. Those were the good old days.

When you would come into this community, you wouldn't be hungry. They'd set up with you all night before they'd let you go to bed hungry. And especially when they would have something with people from out of town, you wouldn't have to worry about something to eat. That was the least worry.

There was a woman we called the "fish mammy," Mrs. Morefield. She used to sell fish and have big fish fries. And she was blind too. She'd walk up the side of the fence, but she knew where she was at all times. She just walked up and down the fence, knowed every house. She had a song that she would hum up and down the road through there.

And I would go to the movie theater many a time, especially every Thursday. That was the Western night. Back when I was growing up, you didn't have to go out of Dante to buy nothing, to do nothing. We had our own hospital, our own doctor's office, post office, barber shop—you name it, we had it—service station. We had all of that. You didn't have to go out of Dante. And the stuff you got from the commissary and everything, it was good stuff. It was a little high, but it was good. I furnished my house down there. And my brother and my daddy furnished their houses out of the store down there. And if I'm not mistaken, we've still got some furniture down at my mother's house when she died, it's a bedroom suite. It was cherry, and heavy as a ton of lead.

Right down here at this little white church, that's where I went to school. But they built another school right up here, Arty Lee. My wife graduated from up here. She lived up about two miles from here. We got together when she started riding with me to work. She was working in St. Paul for a lady down there, doing housework. And she would ride down with me. She rode with me a year, and we didn't even speak. Now, ain't that something? We just didn't have nothing to say to each other. I finally said something. That was in 1958. We got married in 1959, standing right there in her parents' house. Her dad was strict and real particular. Oh, he was. Probably if he had been living, I wouldn't be married to her.

Emogene Kincaid: My mother and father lived in Straight Holler, and that's where the majority of all my sisters and brothers live. There was eleven of us. Black families lived at the upper end of Straight Holler, and our white neighbors lived right down below us. And we all played together. Uh huh. They would come to our house; we would go to theirs. We played dollhouse and then mostly go to different ones' houses. We played dollhouse, and we would play ball, too. And then we had a theater downtown. And we'd go to the theater on a Thursday and Saturday. And really that was about all there was to do. We just had a lot of fun because we had more people, more kids to intertwine with. And we was going to school, and that was about it.

When we would go to the movies, now we have set with our white friends. Yes we did. And then sometimes they would go off on a section by theirselves, and we would be over here in what we call the black section. And that's the way they viewed it. And we would sit on our side. It was sort of like that's the way it was. But it was a hurtful thing. And at times you'd get mad. I guess it was something we was just born and raised up with. But that's the way it was. And sometime we would mingle together. We would get in the movies and say, "We're going to do what we want to do." We'd sit down and watch the movies, and when the movies were over with, we'd leave and come back home and socialize after the thing was over. Sometimes after a movie we would even walk back to Straight Holler together. We'd walk down to the movie together and walk back to Straight Holler home together.

When I graduated from high school, they hadn't integrated then. I never did go to school with white kids, but my kids did. Sometimes me and the white girls got in fights, as kids do. That was just us being young. But as far as the racial part, we were called names. And sometimes we'd get in a fight over that. But we'd go right back playing. When all this changed [with integration], it really didn't make a . . . well, it made a difference to us, but with our friends and stuff, we already knew them, and they knew us, and we were raised up together. So I guess we didn't think about it much because we were young.

It continues, not as much, but it still continues today. It's a hateful word, and you hate to hear it, but it's not much of it. *Nigger*. The word *nigger*. I've heard that so many times. I remember when it was integrated, and they had a drugstore down here. I'll never forget the day when they did. I dressed up every one of my children and went down to the drugstore. White people set there and eat, but we couldn't. But I dressed up all my children and went down to the drugstore and set down and ate. Didn't have any trouble at all because, like I said, everybody knew everybody.

Kathy Shearer: But now baseball was a big deal here in Dante. It was the biggest sport. Football was nothing; it was baseball. Mr. Long was the vice-president of the company in charge of the Dante operation; Mr. Adams was over, also with Clinchfield, at the Clinchco operation. So these were rival mine superintendents, with rival baseball teams. And they would both recruit ringers. They would bring college boys in for the summer, and they had to have a job in the mines to play on the mining teams, so they would give them a job painting houses. But every afternoon was practice. So you would paint a little in the morning, and then you would go to practice.

And this caused some irritation with the local fellows because they thought they were pretty good too, and they had to work in the mines. And from what I understand talking to Lefty Noe, now deceased, he was actually offered a place with the Cincinnati Reds. But at that time, baseball didn't pay anything. And his wife was pregnant, and she said, "No, you don't. You're not leaving me and going on the road for just no money at all." Several of the players could have gone on into the professional leagues; they were that good. Being miners, it kept you in shape. Hand-loading gave you muscles, but professional baseball didn't pay anything. It wasn't any kind of life, so these boys just stayed here and played miners' ball.

I do want to say this. The company supported the white ball team. They gave them uniforms; they arranged all the games and everything. The black team was separate. They had to come up with their own support. They traveled far and wide to get games. And they would play on the same field, but at separate times. And black teams would come in and play the black team here. And they were excellent too. And they would have exhibition games. Sometimes professional teams would come through and play the local teams. That was a big deal for everybody. So it was a big thing. This was the main entertainment—the movies and the baseball.

I will ask people I have known now for ten years about racial problems, and they will tell me there were and are none. I know that surely there are problems. The pecking order in housing had to do with how close you were to the mouth of the mine. And the black community up in Straight Holler was right at the entrance to the old No. 2 mines. You got all the dust, all the noise, constantly. If they were running three shifts, you got everything. The worst housing was right there. And Sawmill is actually also in the floodplain. So you had everything.

It was not a problem in that they all accepted it. They are all of that age where they knew their place, they knew not to be forward around any white women, not to make any comment that might be taken wrong. There were no problems because everybody got along. You talk to white people, and they will say, "Our people in Sawmill were good people. There were never any problems." Which means they never tried anything. Everybody knew how to treat everybody else. To this day, they call them "colored people," they call it "nigger holler." They do, you know. It has to do with the age, and the perception, and knowing you've got to get along here.

Tom Fletcher: I was the football coach at Castlewood High School when we integrated. And I always thought that was, in my lifetime, that was one of the most interesting experiences I'll ever be a part of. This was in the football season of 1965. Arty Lee High School in Dante—the students were brought from there. And I'm not so sure they were enthusiastic about coming. And there wasn't a lot of enthusiasm about them coming, by the people receiving them or them going. There was a lot of anxiety in the air, and how that was going to fit, and how it was going to work out. And all at once they were going to be there. There wasn't any gradual thing to do—it was court ordered. I think you have all seen the movie recently *Remember the Titans*. Matter of fact, we went undefeated that year. We did.

What happened though is that we had about ten black guys try out for the football team. There was a lot more around, but only about ten came forward to try out because they didn't know how they would be treated, they didn't know how it was going to happen. I didn't know how things were going to happen. But we had at that time almost three and a half weeks before school started. And we had a camp at the school site, meaning we had the kids come that morning, and we kept them all day. They ate their breakfast meal. We fed them their lunch, and we fed them their dinner. And we kept them all day long. And we had activities going, skull sessions and doing this and breakdown meetings, trying to do this. But a lot of it was trying to get everybody to come together, and we really came out of that a lot stronger. I talk to kids who were on that football team—Dennis Hensdill, Billy Keith, Billy Gillen Water, Raymond Holloway, Terry Booker. But I remember, one of the black kids was Frank Kincaid [son of Matthew Kincaid's brother Earl]. He made all-state and was quite a guy, and he has two sisters that are school teachers now in our area. And I went to his father's funeral a couple of years ago, and Frank lives in New Jersey now. And he just wanted to talk about those days and how they felt, an uneasiness, but how smoothly in the end it went. And that was my point in this, how it really assisted the integration process. They were the leaders. Everybody just followed their lead. We weren't totally error free or problem free, but we really had a good experience during that. And I think they had been coached by their parents to understand that there was going to be some difficulty, but to stay the course.

Emogene Kincaid: When I was coming up, like I said, I never did go to school with whites, but my kids did. We didn't know Castlewood High School existed until our kids started going over there. Then they started playing sports, and Castlewood become a big name. Laying all jokes aside, Castlewood was not recognized until the black kids started going over there. I had a boy, Ken, he played baseball and won a scholarship to college in baseball. And he played basketball. Then I also had a son named Kelly—he was good in baseball, basketball, track. Him and Ken, anything that Kelly and Ken, sport-wise, they would take a part of it. And then also my daughter Lisa; she graduated from high school in Castlewood. She played basketball, and she also run track.

I never will forget one night we went to Castlewood, and they was playing a tournament. My son Ken was reaching for his thousand points. He was nervous that night, and he couldn't make it, and it looked like every basket he tried he couldn't make it. And then when he did make his thousand points, they stopped the game. Then he throwed the ball up to me, and then they resumed playing the ball, playing the game.

> John L. Lewis come in here, . . . and he
> changed a lot of things around.

NINE

Unionization

Kathy Shearer: Women worked hard.

Nannie Phillips Gordon: That's exactly right. It's like I tell my children a lot of times. They'll fuss at me for canning stuff. I've done it all my life. My husband, whenever we were first married, the year we married, then you couldn't go out and buy a cook stove. You had to have a permit in order to get one, in order to buy one [stove purchase certificate, part of World War II rationing program]. I could have bought it at the company store right here, but I didn't have a permit. So we waited until his sister moved, and they were going to Baltimore. And she give us her cook stove. And I started making kraut and canning, stuff like that. Back when I was first married, didn't have any children, '43.

My husband always raised a garden at his mother's, and he'd go down and bring me huge heads of cabbage this big. And I'd say, "What am I going to do with these?" And he said, "We're gonna make kraut, Momma." And we'd make kraut and can it in cans, or we'd have big jars we put it in till it krauted and then we canned it up. Canned apples, everything. And see, I've done that all my life. Frank fusses at me, and Janice does too [son and daughter-in-law, who live with Nannie], "We don't need that stuff." But it comes natural for me to do it. I've done it all my life. Now we've got two boxes of apples out on the porch that we're going to get into this evening.

We've really had some rough times, you know what I'm saying? I can remember when they first organized the union here. My dad was a big union man. And he walked these roads. At this time, we lived over across the mountain. We lived there, being that my daddy walked these roads with the union members organizing the union. Then it all went union, and he got a job

55

in the mines. He worked in the mines up until he retired. He had a letter of recommendation from—at that time it was Clinchfield Coal Company, it wasn't Pittston. I've got the letter my dad had as a recommendation letter from Clinchfield Coal Company of how good he worked and what a good worker he was.

And Mr. Long fought the union, oh yes he did. And at one time, my daddy almost got fired for joining the union. But you see Daddy joined the union and belonged to the union a long, long time until they went to sending out union cards. And then that's when Mr. Long found out about my daddy. But after that, he wrote my daddy that letter, stating what a good worker he was, and how he worked, and really give my daddy a good recommendation.

At one time my dad was a loader, and then he went on as a brattice man. They had this brattice cloth that they had to put down for the men to work in the mines. I seen my daddy come home from work many times wet up to here where he waded in water in the mines. He was a brattice man; he loaded very little coal. Now brattice cloth looked like an old grass sack, only it come in rolls. And they had to hang that in the mines ever so often, or ever so far. To direct the air. He went from No. 3 to 53, as over across Trammel Mountain. And he worked there until he retired in about—I can't even remember when my daddy retired. But I've got letters of recommendation that my daddy got from Mr. Long who used to be president of Clinchfield Coal Company.

The worst mine disaster we had: six men was killed in the bump [roof fall described by Matthew Kincaid in chapter 11]. Now my daddy got hurt in mines a couple of times, but not serious. My husband never worked in the mines as long as we was married. He worked at drying sand [for use on rail tracks to increase traction]; he was a sand drier. My mother never worked on public works. She worked in the home, and she did laundry for some of the people, you know, like Dominic. I can't think of his last name. He was just little bitty short; he was Hungarian. My mother did laundry for him, but she never did public works. She raised a big family; there was seven of us children.

Lucille Whitaker: The company paid in scrip, but you couldn't take that scrip and go down St. Paul. You had to put it right back into the company store. No way. Well, when John L. Lewis come here to organize and everything, he seen what the situation was and what the company was doing to the people. Now you could rent a house for $6 a month. Me and Harry when we got married in '46, that's all we paid for rent. And it was maybe $2 or $3 for our light bill. The company furnished power and everything. But John L.

Lewis come in here; he organized the coal miners, you know, and he changed a lot of things around.

He made the company do away with the scrip and start paying silver dollars. You take a boy worked ten hours and maybe get $20, and you had to go out here, and you lined up—all the miners lined up to go get your payday, you know. But you got it all in scrip. He made the company do away with all that. And they was a lot of change after John L. Lewis organized it. And if the company found out you were going to join the union, you got a union card—they run you off. They come to your house; they say, "You leave right now." And you had to pack up and leave. They didn't give you a chance at it.

People was angry about it. They was angry. And they would do things which they shouldn't do. I'm not going to call the gentleman's name. I know him well. The company would get a company truck, and they hauled the men to the mines. Well, the miners would get out every morning and walk up and down these roads here at six o'clock in the morning. I would set on the porch with my mother and watch them go up the road, march up and down the road. And then the company would take a truck and pick up the men that wanted to work in the mines, that didn't want the union.

And one day it rained, and the creeks was up, and everything. We've got a place up here called "Horseshoe Curve." This gentleman got up on the hill, and here come the truck with all the miners to take them to the mines to work and take other people's jobs. Well, he just got him a gun and shot right down into that truck. And so the gentleman that was driving the truck turned the truck over in the creek and liked to drowned half of them. And then they got afraid, you know. The miners done some things that it wasn't very nice for them to do. But they showed the company they wasn't going to get away with it. So they started raising their salaries up when they got organized and everything like that. And we got a health card. Of course, we had the hospital down here. If you got hurt or got sick, the company took care of you at the company hospital.

The company started selling homes when they got the union in here. You live in a house, and the company would come in and say, "Are you going to buy this house?" "No." "Well, you've got to move out. We've got a buyer here. Someone else is wanting this house. You either buy it or you get out." A lot of people did leave Dante. The company officials would just come around and say, "You have to leave." And you had to leave.

I was raised here in this community, been here seventy-three years. We did have our own policeman here. The company furnished the law to keep order and everything. Because the Hungarians and the Greeks, they had a boarding house and they had dances, sometimes they'd have a fight break out. They'd have to have the law there to break it up and everything. Mr. Cox was the law the company had.

Emogene Kincaid: My daddy would come from work, and I've seen him coming down the hill. And they'd holler back at him. And he would come home, and my mother would pack his bucket. And he'd go right back to work on the second shift. Two shifts. Where I lived in Straight Holler, where my father worked at, we could stand in our yard. And my father was a motorman, and we could see him coming around the track. That's how close we lived to the mine.

Matthew worked, we called it the "hoot owl." He'd go in at twelve and get off at eight. He'd work at night and come home in the morning. And years ago, they didn't have a bathhouse. He'd have to come home and bathe and eat breakfast, and then he would go to bed. He came in the house and bathed. Law, we had a lot of arguments over that [bringing coal dust into the house]. Yeah, we did. But I was used to it with my father, and then when I married him, it was just more of the same.

Even I went down in the mine one day. When I went down, you had to hold onto the ropes. I was curious. I wanted to see, you know. All I knew all my life was coal mining. And I just wanted to see what it was like. Uh huh. And I went in there. And you had to hold onto the ropes and go down the slope. Then after I got I guess about a mile and then you leveled off. I was scared going down, but once I got down in there it didn't bother me. I went all the way into the mine to the dispatcher's office. About two miles. I was just curious.

Roy Phillips: Mostly it was Baptist when we moved here, when I was fourteen years old. And we had Presbyterian. Also we had an Episcopal church; we had a Catholic too way back there. Most of them is gone. I belong to the Church of God, down here on the side of the road, brick church. And there's not too many of those. There's some up West Dante.

They call me preacher. A long time I witnessed . . . I never did feel like I wanted to be a pastor. I have been at the Church of God for several years. How come us happen to have that church down there, they run us out of Dante because the road took our church. And the preacher bought a house down there and had church there. They were making too much noise, the Church of God. That's how come the company give us that lot down there to build that church, to get them out of town.

Lucille Whitaker: I belong to a Free Will Baptist church up here at what we call the head of Straight Holler. If they have a revival, different churches go to that revival and help out and everything. When I was a young girl, I went to Sunday school and church down here at what they call the Union Church. Community Church, wasn't it? Any minister could come in and hold service, revival, or whatever. The company built these churches for the people to go to. The church I go to right now, the Free Will Baptist Church, the company built them. They built one in Bear Waller, what we call Bear Waller. They even built a church in Sawmill Holler for the colored people. When the company owned the houses, they separated the colored from the white. They had their own school, their own church.

The company built what the people wanted, the minister wanted. The company built it. And you didn't pay rent on the churches. The only thing you paid was your light bill. And sometimes if you had a furnace, they furnished the coal to the church. Then after they sold the houses, they let the churches go to whatever minister was there. They took the church over and preached.

My husband, Harry Whitaker, was a Baptist minister, and he was the chaplain of the United Mine Workers. And if they had a fatality at the mines, it was his duty to go to that family and see if they was in need of something or if the union could help them some way or another. And he always conducted service for the miner or anything, and it didn't make any difference what denomination that you belonged to, Harry was right there to help that family and do whatever he could. If that family was in need, he would bring it up to the local union to see if they could help that family out. He served them all. Of course, he would ask different men to help him out—the colored or whoever it is, whatever denomination they are. Harry always asked them to help him out if he needed help.

Kathy Shearer: What is interesting about the Union Church is that Episcopalians apparently met two Sundays out of each month, and the Methodists would meet two Sundays, and the Presbyterians got the fifth Sunday. Got shortchanged a little bit. You didn't have to be an Episcopalian to go to the Episcopal service. You went to all the services and participated in the pageants. The company officials brought in the Episcopal Church. It wasn't here already, but several of the company officials were Episcopals who came here from the outside. The local people certainly were not.

And they brought in the deaconesses, who held Sunday school out in the hollers at little elementary schools. In primary schools, they would hold Sunday school services. The deaconesses were a very positive influence here, according to everyone I have spoken to. The earliest one was Maria Williams, and she came about 1912, long before they had a resident priest in the area. Now they had a Catholic priest, but they didn't have an Episcopalian. Most people still to this day think that the deaconesses were Catholics. And they worked with all of the people—it didn't matter if they attended church or not.

They had basically a mission out here in the wilderness. And they taught Sunday school, they taught a kindergarten, they had plays that they had the children in, they provided clothing and food. It was kind of like a food and clothing pantry, which we have today. But they made everybody work a little for it—they had to come and work in the garden or do some kind of community improvement thing. And they encouraged kids to go to college. They arranged for them to go to Berea [College]. They would find transportation for them. They just did wonderful, out-in-the-field work. And because of their activity, eventually an Episcopalian priest did come to live here for a while.[1]

When most of the Episcopalians and Methodists pulled out around the time Pittston took over, the Baptists took over the Union Church, and it was called the Union Baptist Church.

Nannie Phillips Gordon: My daddy was never a church person. He went to church some, but not like you and I would. Daddy was brought up as an unbeliever. All of daddy's people, his daddy, was no-hellers, we call 'em. His aunt Rosie and uncle Andy, they were no-hellers. My daddy kind of believed with them. They didn't believe there was a god; they didn't believe there was a hell, or nothing. They called 'em "no-hellers." I remember one time my daddy went to church, way back on Hazel Mountain. He went to a no-hell church back there.[2]

My mother knew different because she was brought up in the Church of God. My grandparents on mommy's side at that time was real true Christians. Not long after that, they both backslid. They both drank right much. But Mommy kept us children in church as much as she possibly could.

Matthew Kincaid: During that time on Sunday morning, you could know where I was—Sunday school first. And you get out of Sunday school right into church. That was every Sunday. I went to the Methodist, and I went to the Baptist. As long as it was Sunday and church, I was there.

In St. Paul, you have an elected town
council, you have private enterprise.
In Dante, you have no business district
outside of the coal company.

TEN

The Two Towns Interfacing, Diverging

Kathy Shearer: Dante is located eight miles north of St. Paul, and back in
its heyday, Dante was the economic engine for Russell County. It was the
largest town in Russell County. Probably at its peak, it had four thousand
people living here. That would have been around World War I, 1915 through
about 1920, '21. There was still activity going on here after World War I that
involved helping rebuild Europe. They still needed a lot of coal to power
the factories. But sometime in the mid-20s, that started going downhill. The
factories—they still used coal—but the pricier city homes started heating
with oil, and then gas later on. So coal started going out of favor. The Depression hit here in the mid-20s, earlier than the stock market slide.

This was the coal boomtown, and it was much larger than St. Paul. People really didn't need to go to St. Paul. People didn't need to go anywhere,
which was good because most of the coal miners didn't have cars. They could
take what they called the ten-cent bus to St. Paul if they wanted to go down
there. But here they had everything that they needed. They had a company
store where they could buy all of their clothing, their food. They had a pharmacy. The company provided a doctor; there was a hospital here. This was
the hospital that actually served the western side of the county. It wasn't just
for Dante people. The miners were able to use the hospital and the doctor's
services in return for a small fee that was withdrawn from their pay every two
weeks. And other people who came in would have to pay their way.

The doctor had clinic hours. There were nurses. There were schools in
every hollow. There were churches for people. And there were activities that
were social in nature. There was a ball field, baseball field. And everybody
went on the weekends to watch the miners play ball. There was a theater
building, and they could go and watch movies every night of the week. So

people were pretty well satisfied here. They came from miles around. This was the center. And as people like to say who can remember back that far, "St. Paul was nothing—no reason to go there. We had everything we needed right here."

All that has changed. I would say the major reason St. Paul still has a population of a thousand and Dante is withering away would be that Dante was never incorporated. And this was the design of the company. Clinchfield Coal Corporation, followed by Pittston, they never wanted this town to be incorporated. They didn't want them to have their own government. They didn't want to pay any more tax burden. And in fact, they put an end to all of those efforts through the years. So consequently, people in Dante relied upon Clinchfield. Even though it changed names later on to Pittston—became a successor company—people still called it "the Clinchfield." People relied on the Clinchfield to provide everything for them. Clinchfield made all their decisions for them.

This was interrupted certainly by the UMWA in 1945 when they finally signed a contract under great duress. Clinchfield held out longer than any other coal company in Virginia. The other companies allowed the organization to go through in the '30s. Clinchfield held out because they had an iron grasp of the people here. They provided everything, and in return they wanted complete loyalty. So town governance and local decision making was not in that plan. It's been told to me that they told people how to vote. And the vice president of the company, Mr. Long, most everybody thinks was the president. But the president was really absentee—he was in New York. And Mr. Long was like God or the king. He was a very strong Democrat, and everyone knew that. And if you wanted to get along, you voted that way too. You helped him out. And he made all the decisions, and the people who came after him were somewhat like that too.

But at that time up till the union came in, all the managers and the vice president lived right here in the town. They knew everybody, and if you had a problem with your boss in your particular shift, say, and you didn't like what your boss was doing and you couldn't get an answer you wanted, you just went to see Mr. Long. It wasn't like today, where you can't go any higher, you have certain appeals steps. You went right to the top. And Mr. Long would handle your problem. Mr. Long was followed by Rush Adams—same thing. You didn't like the answer you got, you went to see Rush. This worked two ways. If Mr. Long didn't like you and Mr. Adams didn't like you, you were out. It was very paternal. It was much like a family. People talk fondly about "the good old days when we knew everybody." But the good old days prevented this town from ever becoming independent while the coal company was here.

I think the company provided well for the needs of the people, given that most of the coal miners and their spouses had very limited education. Some of them may have gone to school for a few years. Now we're talking about in the '10s and '20s typically. A little later on, they generally got up through seventh grade. So given their lack of education, like a formal education, and their inability to go somewhere else, just pick up and move, and their strong ties to the area, Clinchfield Coal Corporation provided more or less steady income for the workers that it liked, and all of the necessities for fairly comfortable living. Dante would not have been a model coal town, given that there was no indoor plumbing provided by the company. And in the model coal towns, that was provided. But it certainly was better than average.

The Depression, which started here earlier, say about 1922 or so—the Depression lasted from then until World War II. So it was twenty years of Depression, and in those times the coal mines might run just one or two days a week. And they rotated men around. They would send them over to other mines within their jurisdiction to try to get them work. They wanted them to have enough work to be able to pay the house rent. It all worked in together. And they would keep charging at the company store. If they were good miners and were receptive to the company and did what the company wanted, they could keep on charging. And apparently there were debts that were just written off afterwards, that were never paid off. But that was a very tough period. As I said, unlike some of the smaller companies or even some of the larger companies, Clinchfield—to its credit—did not close up and go out of business. They really had an obligation to their workforce. And they felt that it was going to come back. Coal's going to come back. Eventually it did, because there was another boom after World War II—well, during World War II there was a boom, and afterwards too. So they did, in fact, provide for people.

But while they did that, they made very sure that there was no competing private enterprise going on in this town. Whereas in St. Paul, you have an elected town council, you have private enterprise, you have people who have a history of owning and operating businesses, and who have a real interest in keeping the business district going. In Dante, you have no business district outside of the coal company.

LeRoy Hilton: There were seventeen established saloons. There's many old rooming houses, bordellos. When the miners needed a little recreation, it was here in St. Paul. But there was still nothing but a wagon road going to Dante. Now right down here on Fifth Avenue, there is a big line of garages. And these company officials would leave their cars in St. Paul. The road went to Bristol, when they'd leave for the weekends or whatever. When they come to work on Monday morning, they come to St. Paul and left their car. They caught the train to Dante to go to work. At the end of the workweek, they'd come back by train to St. Paul, pick up their car, and go from here. In the early years, 1910 or whatever, the roads were not there to accommodate the cars. But the good road was into St. Paul. So therefore, all these officials would come here to trade centers and whatnot.

Plus, the company stores, they charged one price, and these people . . . "owe your soul to the company store," which was true. My daddy had a business here. These people would come up to the company store and buy a carton of cigarettes. They'd bring them to St. Paul and trade them, not only to my dad but many, many other people, they'd trade them for cash. They got no cash when they worked for the coal company. They got scrip. You would have got scrip, or they took in merchandise. They'd get their merchandise and come and sell it in St. Paul and get the cash so they could do what they needed to do here. That's one reason kept the town going.

Plus, there was a big wholesale business here, Dickenson-McNeer Wholesale. It supplied all of Dickenson County, Russell County, and all back into Buchanan County. Even by horse. But Dickenson-McNeer Wholesale was one of the biggest wholesale companies in the country at that time. It was a wholesale grocery. And it supplied all these communities all the way back. George Albert Lee and a bunch of people—they had salesmen on the road, and they traveled all the way through Dickenson, Russell, and Buchanan counties, supplying them with all their many needs. They were selling to little stores all along everywhere. They furnished everything from there.

In the early '30s, my daddy had a contract with Armour and Company, and that's when they had to finish the road through. I was, like, a fourteen-year-old kid. And he had a truck, and I would walk into the company store and deliver meat. And Dante, the commissary at Dante, I delivered meat there. We delivered to all the commissaries, wholesale meat. And then, of course, they redistributed it.

Tom Fletcher: I knew Mr. Long. He passed away when I was just a young kid, but he and my dad were big, avid gun people. My dad went on in during World War II in the navy as a gunnery officer. He and Lee wrote each other many times because they hunted together and had a great interest in guns. Lee apparently was a well-versed coal person and one who knew the people and the community and got along well with everybody. As legend would have it, they allowed him to operate the coal operation pretty much and determine who was hired and fired and what the conditions were and just manage the community and the business as they were so closely knit.

My dad was mayor during the later "Western Front" years. He understood the free spirits that existed in the people at that time. He understood them, and I thought was probably an appropriate type of person to deal with those people at that time. I think he did it in a friendly but fair, firm-type approach. There was guidelines, there was limits as to where a person could go. I think if a guy was out of order, that was one thing. But if he was causing problems with other people, that was still another thing too. Lots of those people were brought over to the police station, and they would call a relative or something to come and get them. Some of them had gotten into fights and everything, and that kind of went over the limit. They locked them up and allowed them to work their fines off working for the town. You can imagine, everybody was working hard, working five days a week. They kind of liked to say, "Let's go to St. Paul and get a beer and have some fun." So that's kind of what they expected to do on Fridays and Saturdays. I don't remember people coming down and bringing weapons and getting in that kind of deal and having violent fights. We had rowdiness though.

LeRoy Hilton: Many of the officials and many of the people who worked in the coal mines didn't live in the coal camp. They lived here in St. Paul, Coeburn, Cleveland here just up the river. The president of the company lived here in St. Paul up on top of Gray Hill. As they changed presidents of the company, they called it "the Clinchfield house." One president would move out, and another would move in. He would move into the company house.

Kathy Shearer: The real president of Clinchfield Coal Corporation lived in New York. He never lived in Dante. He came to visit on the train ever now and then. And James Mabry would carry his suitcases. There were different men, of course, through the years. As long as it was Clinchfield Coal, it was always an outside board of directors and president. And then you had the local superintendent of the mines, who was a vice president. Lee Long lived in Dante, lived in a house where Kareen Couch now lives right on Roanoke Hill.

In 1945 when the union came in and Pittston took over the company—and ironically it was Pittston who said, "Let's sign the contract and get back to work"—they were the ones who decided that they would sell the houses to private individuals. Up to that point, the company officials lived on Roanoke Hill, and they paid very little rent. They had nice houses with indoor plumbing and furnaces and the whole bit. Roanoke Hill is the highest point in the community, very nice area. So at that point, the officials had to choose whether to buy their home and stay there, or move out. Everybody had the same choice. They were offered their houses at reasonable prices. But as the company was changing, a lot of them decided they didn't want to stay with the company anymore because the union was coming in. They were not going to have the power that they had always had. So many of them left the company.

Those who stayed behind generally chose not to stay on Roanoke Hill. They moved to St. Paul. When Pittston came in, Clinchfield Coal Corporation ceased to exist and became the Clinchfield Coal Company, a subsidiary of Pittston. They had presidents locally, and those people may have well lived in St. Paul after 1945. I didn't really follow that history.

Frank Kilgore: After 1959 when all the Dante mines had been shut down, most of the miners who lived in Dante proper—the younger, married men who had families—had to move to other areas. Many of them went up to the Great Lakes states for manufacturing jobs. You had a great exodus from the whole region in the '50s and very early '60s. I've seen estimates of one-third of the population left to find jobs elsewhere. The Virginia coalfields lost over a two-decade period about a third of its population due to mechanization and the drop in worldwide demand for coal.

If they stayed in Dante, they had to do like the St. Paul miners had always done. They had to commute somewhere else to stay employed. Of course, there was shops and stores in and around Dante that some people got to work at. But the middle-class incomes kept being lost, and there was fewer and fewer people to support the stores and the shops. So it was the gradual downturn of Dante, economically.

ELEVEN

Mining Safety

Dean and Terry Vencil: We've got this waterbed downstairs. I went to Kingsport to get it, and the guy was talking down there. And I told Terry I said, "We've got to have this big mirror to go up on the ceiling when we get this thing."

Well, back up just a second though. I wanted the waterbed, coming out of the '60s. He was afraid that the floors in this old house, built in 1918, wouldn't support the pressure. And I was saying, "No now, per square inch, the pressure is the same thing as a regular bed." And he said, "Darling." When he says, "Darling," like that, I said, "I might as well forget it." But I just kept sort of tickling at it until he finally went down and got the waterbed.

June Carter and Johnny Cash.

I graduated from the University of Virginia in '73 and came back to the mountains. At that time, I had a son from a previous marriage, was offered a position at CDC [Center for Disease Control] in Atlanta, Georgia, and did not want to rear a child in Atlanta. So I came back home, and my first job, the boss was Dean Vencil, a rough, crusty old man, and just sort of fell in love with the crust. Med-tech. We worked in the laboratory at the old Dante clinic, which used to be a hospital, and then moved into the newer clinic later.

She walked in . . .

I walked in the first day, you know this poor little girl just fresh out of college, and I bounced in, and I said, "Hi, I'm Terry Kern, and I'm here to start work." And he said, "I'm ready to leave." I don't know if he thought I was there to take his position or a threat, I'm not sure.

She said, "Hi, I'm Terry and I'll be working here soon." And I said, "Yeah, and I'll probably be leaving." Because I didn't think the clinic was big enough . . .

. . . for the two of us.

. . . for the two of us.

Have you ever seen the movie *Shrek*? He is Shrek, and I am Donkey. I'm always the happy one, and he's always the one taking care of his buddy. I came in October, and I guess . . . December?

December.

Wasn't long. Our laboratory was, how big would you say?

The one at Dante wasn't much bigger than the kitchen in there.

About fourteen by twelve, maybe.

Yeah, something like that.

Very small laboratory and two people working in it, you soon bond.

Yeah, you rub cheek to cheek every once in a while.

At that time, I guess I started making less than $5,000 a year, in the early '70s. And you might have been making what?

I was making ten.

Big money. And Dean had a son by a previous marriage, and I had a son by a previous marriage. We knew we had these two boys that we were going to have to take care of. And so one of us had to get a job that paid. So Dean went into the coal mines. We both worried about it.

She told me after I retired that she didn't think I would ever live long enough to retire. She thought I'd get killed. And I told her one time—aw, it was fifteen years before I retired—"If I get killed, don't wait until my body is cold before you sue Clinchfield, because I'm not going to be doing anything wrong. I'm not going to be doing anything unsafe. It's their fault. And don't you let my body get cold before you sue 'em."

And I know that there were a lot of days that I would watch him—it was the typical woman watching at the door—I just wondered, "Is he coming back?"

. . . . .

I was a mine examiner for a long time, and the last few years I worked by myself. And I've been in places that no one else went. We started bringing coal out of McClure 1 in 1978, and we stopped mining coal in 1995, April of 1995. And there's more coal left in it than what came out. And we pulled twenty-eight longwall panels, which is anywhere from 3,500 feet to 5,000 feet in 600-feet-long panels . . . one block at a time. The continuous miner just goes across and cuts 600 feet at a whack. It's called a longwall—it just goes right down that panel, and it cuts about 3 foot all the way and keeps cutting.

By mine examiner, what do you mean?

You examined the whole mine. You checked the ventilation. And you went into remote areas that no one else went into. And you were by yourself. Of course, you had all kinds of equipment with you. You had your rescuer, self-rescuer, that would last for an hour or so. You had instruments to check the methane, oxygen, and all that stuff. Still that didn't do anything with the top and the ribs.

And too, how far down was McClure? How far down did the shaft go?

We got on an elevator and went down 600, I believe, 608 or 610 feet.

And then out how far would you travel?

Oh, two, two and a half, three miles.

Kind of scary in the dark, by yourself.

And I've walked every inch of it. One section we had was about fifty-eight hundred feet, and you only had two places that you could stand up. And it was walked three times a day, had to be walked three times a day, had to be checked three times a day, on each shift. And I had gone on up this section and down on one that had been shut down and had to go over and check it. We had pumps set up, pumping the water outside, and we come back. And you have metal doors in a concrete wall, cinderblock wall, called a brattice door. And you open that door, and the hair on the back of your neck will stand up, and we say, "There's something going on here now." And you pull your spotter out, and you've got 5.5 percent of methane. And 5.5 percent methane is one of the most volatile mixtures that you get in there. Once you get above I think 10 percent, you don't have enough oxygen left to do anything. I've been on a section as a section boss, and another guy will come up and say, "Man, you've got 2.5 percent methane out here on the track." And I say, "I've only got six-tenths over here." And he's not thirty feet from me. So we go back down, and we just shut everything down. We go back down the track checking, and we get 5.5 percent down in the corner and have to leave the section.

Shut the whole thing down?

Your cousin was superintendent, and he told me that I didn't have the authority. I said, "Hide and watch me." And I shut it down. The beltline one time—I didn't do this, a friend of mine did—it was on a 17 percent grade, and coal would fall off every day. And it had fallen off so high that the belt was about four foot off the ground, off the bottom, and the coal was higher than the belt. And he told them they had to clean it up, and they said, "We don't have time to clean it up." So he just pulled the switch on them, cut it clean off. They said, "You don't have the authority." He said, "I've got the authority, and I've shut it down." He said, "We're shut down until it's clean." And one of the bosses started to go over and turn it back on, and the federal inspector walked up. And he said, "Nobody touches it." He said, "That's his job, and he shut it down. And it's shut down." And they had what they call a "red tag." He walked over to the portal and hung a red tag on it and said, "It's shut down until it's clean." This was a federal, so they cleaned it before they ever started it back up.

. . . . .

I told someone before I ever went in there that I would be scared to death because I would be afraid of the top. And I watched it all the time. You just have to keep check on everything that you do. I've seen rock fall, and we've put up five-foot roof bolts, and put it in with glue, and it fall five and a half feet. So a six-foot roof bolt would have held it. But a five-foot wouldn't hold it.

Tell about the night of the explosion. The night Covy got killed.

Oh, bad time.

You were supposed to work that night, weren't you?

I was supposed to been the boss on that section. They'd offered that job to me, the section foreman.

You know how little premonitions . . . and I guess coal miners and their wives are the most superstitious in the world. You feel like tonight's not the night; you want to stay home in bed, close to me. And I had just asked him— just tonight—call in and tell them you're not coming. And sure enough, the mines blew up that night. And he was supposed to be on that section. Now why did it blow up? I don't know. I don't know if the venting wasn't right. Do you?

My theory always was that it started with the power unit. The federal inspector said that he thought it came from one of the mantrips. It's kind of like a shuttle car or something that you would transport men from one section to another or from the outside inside. It's called a shuttle car or a mantrip.

Is it kind of like a dune buggy, only lower?

No, on tracks. It's like a locomotive. Everything from when we first started over there was battery powered. All of our mantrips were battery powered, and the locomotives were battery powered. And they said they thought that's where the explosion came from. I think it started up at front and went back out. Ten killed. The first woman that was killed from Clinchfield was killed in that explosion. One guy I had worked with, we worked together running a miner at Smith Gap, was miner operator there on that section.

So we woke up sometime in the middle of the night. It just sounded like all hell was breaking loose, with fire trucks going and police sirens and everything. You knew. You knew something had happened. And the mines was, what, forty miles away?

Twenty-five.

But you still knew, it couldn't have been an accident. Yeah, my paranoia paid off, that particular time.

One premonition she missed. I did not get killed in the coal mine.

That's true. You did not get killed in the coal mine. I never thought he would go in the coal mines first of all. His daddy worked in the coal mines, got his arm mangled in the coal mines and gangrene set in, and he lost his arm when he was . . .

Twenty-four.

Twenty-four. And proceeded to work in the coal mines with one arm and support a family.

About a year later, they came out with penicillin.

And supported the family on a coal miner's income in a coal mine camp.

He raised five of us.

Don't you think the miners of your day were a lot more fortunate because of UMWA and the care that was taken of your breathing? Your daddy, when he was in there, they didn't use water, sprays, mists, or anything. They used soap sprays when you were mining on the long wall.

My dad was called a canary. He was a fire boss, and he would take a mining light. It was a carbide light, and he would go in and burn the methane out of the facement where the workers were going. He would go in and set it on fire and burn it out. I don't know how they did it without blowing themselves up. He never did say. At one point through Clinchfield, he was the only man that they had that had first-class mine foreman papers. Because at that time, you had to have three years experience in a gassy mines, and he was the only one that had it. I didn't have to have that. Of course, when I went in, they considered all mines gassy mines. But they didn't back then.

Frank Kilgore: Thousands of coal miners were killed during World War I. A lot of them opted to go in the military because they thought it was safer. The production was so intense because the whole country ran on coal and steam that coal miners were pretty much very expendable. My grandfather had the option of staying in the mines or going to war. He stayed in the mines, but many, many of his coal-mining buddies took their chances in the war, in the army. Because you had some odds you wouldn't even go to the front. And once you got there, some odds of not getting killed. The odds in the mines were sort of like riding a horse or a motorcycle. If you do it several years, sooner or later something bad is going to happen to you.

What happened was when vegetation was squeezed and heated over millions of years, it emitted methane gas just like it would now if you piled up some compost, and it started rotting, and you dug into it—you would get a little whiff of methane.[1] Unfortunately, with coal it is under pressure from solid layers of rock, and methane can't escape. So it is trapped. As coal decomposes over millions of years, the methane stays inside, and it is sealed inside with the coal. So at times when these coal miners would open up these seams of coal and start mining, they'd hit these pockets of methane. And years ago the way they could see in the mines is they would have an actual flame from a carbide lamp or an old oil lamp on their hat, and that open flame would ignite the methane, which would blow up and kill them.

Even years later when they used battery-powered lights, sparks from coal-mining machinery could set off a methane explosion. Hundreds and thousands of coal miners have been killed that way. So death was all around the coal camps. If the siren went off, you knew if your loved one was in the mines, more likely than not they were injured or killed. So you see a lot of graphic pictures of newly made widows waiting outside an exploded coal mines to see if their husbands were going to make it out or not.

Unlike a roof fall, which may kill one, two, or three miners, a gas explosion would knock out a whole shift. And if you lost twenty to fifty to a hundred miners in a gas explosion, you usually decimated the working-age male population of the entire community. And then you had anywhere from five to fifty people per miner that were emotionally impacted and, of course, several that were financially impacted.

So that was truly one of the reasons that the federal government took over mine safety was because of gas explosions. Just like a war, if they're getting picked off one or two at a time, it doesn't make headlines. You lose a large number in a single episode, and it makes the headlines. If anything really gave the federal government the political willpower and the public support for uniformly applying safety laws in the mines, it would be gas explosions. That was the incentive to pass the Mine Health and Safety Act in 1969.[2] That act imposed uniform safety regulations throughout the United States for coal mining, and that was the first real step toward saving coal miners from some of the more obvious problems.

The original major Mine and Safety Act on the federal level addressed methane, it addressed roof falls, it addressed water problems, impoundments, and that sort of thing. So it was pretty comprehensive. They addressed methane by requiring more air ventilation, requiring modernized testing. And also they had them address dust because a lot of dust circulating, coal dust circulating in the mines was highly ignitable also. So methane might be the kindling that set off the dust, but the dust, which was pervasive in the mines, the coal dust, would explode. So you had a combination of very fine particles of coal dust constantly in the air inside the mines and methane. The two together were extremely combustible.

When they reduced the amount of dust in the air, then they reduced the exposure for black lung, silicosis, another major mining health problem. A Black Lung Act was a spin-off. There is now a black lung program to help compensate miners for the black lung disease, an insidious disease that destroys the capacity of the lungs to properly breathe. Many, many older retired coal miners have to use oxygen tanks. You couple that with some self-initiated health problems such as smoking, and you add those two together, and you have a very high death rate from lung-related diseases. It's not uncommon for someone who has worked in the mines who also smokes to die in their fifties or sixties; it cuts off twenty to thirty years from their life. It's a lot better now than it used to be. There's a lot of enforcement of dust controls and coal dust and rock dust controls so that you have less and less episodes of black lung disease in the newer generation of coal miners.

Kathy Shearer and Matthew Kincaid: What year did you go into the mines?
[In] 1966.
How old were you then?
Thirty-three.
Oh, what did you do before?
Chauffeured for the president of the company for ten years. I drove a Cadillac. They got planes and helicopters then. They didn't need me no more.
Who was the president then?
Robert H. Hughes. He was first president, and he left and went to New York. And George Judy, you know him?
I've heard of him.
He was the last president I worked for. Good man.
And how did you like mining?
Oh, I loved it. I did all different types of jobs. About every job to be done, I done it. I didn't dig. They had machinery to do that, what they call a miner. That's what got the coal. I was a roof bolter, bolting the top up for them to go in there and cut the coal. We didn't use timber, like they used in the olden days. We used roof bolts. And that tied the top in, keep it from falling. They had them from three foot up to eight foot. You put it where you think you need it. That's where experience come in. I've done that a lot of times—"spot bolted" is what they call it. Still, I was on my pattern—four-foot centers, and if I think I needed one in between that, I put it there. It's four foot or closer,

whatever the roof bolter decide on. But you can't go beyond four foot. You can come in, but you can't go out further. And it worked out all right. I never got hurt, and never got nobody hurt. They give me credit for twenty-seven years, but I worked longer than that.

Now with the roof bolter, is that a machine you're riding in or you're pushing or what?

You're riding it . . .

It's just got a hydraulic arm on it?

Most of them has got two heads on them, where two people can work, one on each side. It would drill a hole up in the top, and then you would put the bolt in. What they use now is glue. You'd get a couple of sticks of glue and stick up there in that hole. And that thing raises up in there. And once it's up there, it ain't coming back. It was exciting. It was just fun to go to work. I couldn't wait until Sunday night get here, to go to work.

Did you like the men you worked with?

Sure, sure. For awhile there—the last eight, fifteen years—it was only one black there. And that was me. And I haven't never had no problem with nobody. Everybody's my friend.

Who are some of the buddies you work with?

I don't know whether you know him or not. Snake Fields here on Straight Row, Junior Axsom up Bear Wallow, and a whole bunch out of West Dante. Darrell Salyers and Alonzie Holbrooks and his brother rather. And it's a whole bunch—Burl Coverson. We all worked together there on the section at Moss 2 in Carbo. Bobby Fields. When I started, I was driving back and forth by myself, eight miles. It would take about thirty minutes to drive. So another fellow come off the mountain. And I would ride a week in his car, and then he'd ride a week in my car. Since he lived on the mountain, when he'd ride with me in the wintertime, he'd get in my car and drive, then have to come back and warm his car up. He said, "Just ride with me, and my car'll be warm, and I can go on home." I said, "That sounds all right." So I started riding with him and rode with him for twelve years.

Did you have to travel inside the mine quite a way to get to the face?

Oh sure. Furtherest I've been back in there—now it ain't level—between eight and nine miles.

You were half way to Lebanon [Lebanon, Virginia].

We'd get out around 8:00 and take a shower. And we would leave the mines after the shower at about 8:30, and we'd get home around nine in the morning.

You were on night shift. You would start working around midnight?

At 12:01. I worked the hoot owl for twenty-seven years.

Did they run three shifts then?

Oh yeah. Yeah.

. . . . .

Matthew, did women come into the mines while you were still working?

Sure did.

In your section?

Uh huh.

How did that work out?

Okay, but I'll tell you what. We had one come in there, and they sent her to the timber hole to get some timber. See, us guys, we'd go down and get some timbers like that [indicating a five- or six-inch diameter] and load them up. She'd go down there and get them golly-whoppers, and help set them.

She was tough.

Oh my. Us guys, we'd go down and pick over everything, leave the big ones for somebody else.

When the women first came in, did you give them a hard time?

Naw. Naw. Sure didn't.

What about rookie miners? Was there some kind of initiation?

Oh yeah. Yeah. That's got to come. Well, when they come in there, the first thing they do and especially if they're assigned to that section, they have to bring us some candies or something like that. And on birthdays or if you get married or you have children, if you didn't bring it, your britches leg was cut off. James Mabry Jr., he got married and his wife had a little girl. And we told him, "Bring some cigars out." And he got in the jeep, on the backside where nobody couldn't get ahold of him, stuck his little head out and said, "I ain't bringing nothing." Had on a brand new pair of denims. And the next morning when he come upstairs and leaned down, they was cut off up here, and they was dragging the ground. And we said, "You'll bring us something now, won't you?"

Did you ever try to scare them?

Oh yeah. I'll tell you what. We was on a pillar section. That's when they are peeling the coal back, and the top's falling in. Well, you've got to set so many breaker timbers. And setting up there, I said, "Come on and help us set the breaker timbers here." It starts smoking and popping and going on. Well, he [rookie miner] got scared. And it come a thundering, and you could hear it falling in. I said, "Bring me some wedges up here." And he looked behind the breaker and said, "I'll throw 'em up there."

And one boy, the first night he'd been in there, and I kept telling him, "Big John talking tonight." And it was boom, boom, and going off like that.

And he said, "Who is Big John?" I said listen, and it give another big boom. I said, "That's that top coming in." And he messed around there and finally got enough nerve to help me set the timbers. I said, "Now, we gotta get outta here." He said, "If I make it out of here alive tonight, I won't be back." And he never did show up no more.

That's a scary time to be there.

If you get back far enough, it's no danger because where you set them timbers, that's where the top's going to break off. I've set up there and watched a many a time a pillar fall.

Now when they're working on pulling pillars, do they have engineers or somebody go in there and say, "You can pull this one now. It's still safe. You can pull this one, you can pull that one"? Or is it pretty much up to the men who are working?

No, they know they have to leave one over on the return side and a block on the intake side. They know that, so they work in between.

You've heard about the "bump" in No. 2, back in 1948?

Uh huh. I was in one myself. It's where that top comes down, squeezing the coal out. And it'll hurt you too, kill you too. What happened, I was sitting right there on a pile of timbers, and that miner started in there. And hadn't nobody cut a bump hole. So he was going in there that way. And there come a bump, and it blowed his buddy all the way over on top of him. Blowed the buggy back, and it blowed every curtain down.

Yeah?

It was so dusty, you couldn't see nothing. And it come another bump. I went over there, and one curtain I never did find. We had to get the curtains back up so the air would blow that dust out of the way, down the return air. Them bumps are dangerous. The bottom and the top is squeezing together. We had to get bump experts to come in there. He was good now. He put a thing in that coal, drill a hole in it and put it in there. And tell you exactly when it was going to bump.

That's what I was wondering, if they had experts who could predict when it was time to run. Because they were saying up at No. 2 that they really pulled out too many pillars, took too much of a chance.

What happened in '48 is, they wasn't getting the pillars out clean behind them. And that puts pressure in front of you.

So they were still standing, so it was kind of curving over the pillars.

If you take a pillar, and you don't get it clean and everything, why that pressure is going to stay right in front of you. That's why you should get everything you can while you're there. When it falls, that relieves the pressure in front of you. That's what happened to them. They left too much standing, and the pressure got in front of them. Quite a few people got killed at that bump at No. 2.

Six. That was the worst disaster in Dante that they ever had, that many killed at one time. There's a story in the book [*Memories from Dante: The Life of a Coal Town*, edited by Kathy] about Marion Hardy. He was the motorman for Woody Phillips, and he thought he had killed him. Thought he had knocked him off, thought he had died. He said people were blown every which way. And, of course, like you said, in something like that the dust is thick, and you can't see.

You can't see a thing. You know what I done? I just got out in the middle of the break and set down till it cleared up. Ain't no use to try to go nowhere, because you can't see where you're going.

. . . . .

One night, I quit roof bolting, and I was sitting on the ramp. And I heard a rock fall. It didn't sound right. So I went around there, and shore enough, it was. And it had a man under that rock.

How big a rock?

Oh gosh, it was wide, but it wasn't too thick. We got some jacks and jacked it off of him. He lived.

Break some bones?

No, almost smothered him to death. What it was, he couldn't breathe. He was about to panic there.

Have you ever seen anybody die in the mines, get killed or badly injured?

No, not right off. But I was right behind it. One morning, a fellow lived on the mountain up here, one I used to ride with, young boy. And he worked on this section up here, and I worked on the section down below him. And when we come off the section and come out, we noticed all them lights up there. And this boy—they had these here electric buttons to start the feeder. Well, they were electric then. Anyway the buggy run over it and done something to it. So he had it, and he went around and knocked the breaker on it, what he supposed to do. And he tore it apart. Then he walked around there, put the breaker back in. Went back down and sat down on the same rope, and that's what got him. It electrocuted him right there. Young boy. When he set on that belt rope, that was the ground. And it killed him. His name was Luther McCoy.

Then, one boy I had told, preached to him because he used to help me roof-bolt. And I was always on him about setting the jack, the safety jack. He got off of roof bolting and got back on the miner [continuous mining machine]. Went out there and was pulling some slate down—him and another roof bolter. Went out there and pulled it down, and pulled it down on them. Well, it killed him. And the other one, it had him covered up. So we got him out. And we were looking for the other one. And I was standing on a big slab of rock and looking around. And I was on top of him.

Goodness, Matthew. There was, I guess, a lot more people killed in your daddy's time.

Oh great day, yes. Shore didn't have the protection that they've got now.

What did you think about your boys growing up? Did you want them to go in the mines?

No. I shore didn't. But my oldest boy, he worked in the mines about eight years. He worked right along side me, on the same section and everything. But the other one, Kelly, no way. Kelly said, "That's not for me."

When did you realize you had black lung?

Well, I knew I had it before I even quit working. I worked long as I could, and then I got out of it. So 1995—I applied for benefits, and they said I had it, but they took it after I was on it about a year—said I didn't have black lung. Said my problem came from cigarette smoking. Dust won't hurt you, but cigarettes will kill you. That's the way they figure it. But once you get that disease, it ain't no going back. It ain't getting no better. It get worse. I've had this oxygen here going on five years. And I've got a nebulizer that I've got to use four times a day. With Albuterol and Atropine. And I've been on that two years, And then I use Maxair, Atropine, and Flovent.

You got it roof bolting?

I was right behind the miner. A lot of people don't understand. You don't have to be in a lot of coal dust there where the miner is mining coal. That ain't what gets you. The float dust—what you breathe in, cause it's lighter, it floats in the air, and you're breathing it in. That's the hurtin' part.

Is it thick enough so you can see it?

No, no. Not that float dust. The only way you can see it is get you a light and kind of look up at it. You know how dust hangs in the air? Well that's the way coal dust is in the mines. And you breathe that stuff in, and you work in there twenty-five or thirty years, your lungs are going to get coated.

Well, after you were drawing it for a year, did the company then come back and take it away from you?

Yeah, yeah.

The company went through a period when they challenged everybody.

I had about three or four doctors say I had it, and they had twenty-two said I didn't.

They've always got more doctors than you've got.

Pete Castle: "Black Lung Fever." It's an old coal-mining song that I did for all the old coal miners here in Dante.

Men go to work in the mines when they are young,
They work in the mines and they get black lung.
They got the black lung fever, they got the black lung fever,
They got the black lung fever from working that coalmines.

Go to work before daybreak, get home after dusk,
Working that face, breathing that dust.
They got the black lung fever, they got the black lung fever,
They got the black lung fever from working that coalmines.

Oh, the coal was low, the water was high,
When you worked down on nine, right.
They got the black lung fever, they got the black lung fever,
They got the black lung fever from working that coalmines.

Oh, the boss on nine he was great and oh,
Said I've got to have more coal, boys, and then we'll roll.
He's got black lung fever, he's got that black lung fever,
He's got that black lung fever from working that coalmines.

All I saw was smoke from the tires,
smoke from the exhaust, and smoke
from the gun.

TWELVE

The Strip Mine Act of 1977

Frank Kilgore: Except for a couple of branches of my family, most of them were blue-collar workers. Some of them owned businesses, and most of them had just basic educations. But I did have one branch of my family, my dad's uncle's children, who went to college. A lady, Virginia Kilgore, who just passed away at age eighty-three, I think. And she was in the Wacs [Women's Army Corps] during World War II, and she was at that time the only Wise County lady in the army. Her twin sister, who predeceased her, Victoria Kilgore, went to the New York school of deaconesses supported by the Episcopal Church in order to come back to the mountains and continue the mission of education and healthcare that was provided by Episcopalian sisters. And she was going to be their first native-born, local girl that went to the New York school, became trained, came back. But by the time she came back, the mission, due to the onslaught of publicly financed schools, was sort of abandoned. She was a deaconess in name only, but she became a public school teacher for like forty years.

She and Virginia never got married; they were nonidentical twins. They lived together until their deaths. And their brother, who was a World War II veteran, never married. Their photos are downstairs [see figure 9 for the photo of Virginia Kilgore]. And their mother was very active in the Episcopal Church. She moved to the head of Honey Branch, where I was born and raised, and married my uncle Ben Kilgore, my great-uncle Ben Kilgore. He was my grandfather's younger brother. He married my aunt Carrie. She was very active in the community; she helped get funds raised to build a chapel for the Episcopal Church missionary. She was very educated. She helped bring deaconesses to this region for healthcare and educational purposes.

9. Virginia Kilgore, 1942. Courtesy of Frank Kilgore.

And she and Uncle Ben built on their property a chapel and a school to provide religious services.

And there was another building used for circuit riding healthcare services. I was born in one of those little houses they built for missionary purposes, because after it was abandoned, my dad and mom when they got married moved there. I was actually born at the house. And then we moved down the road a couple of hundred yards to the log house which my great-great-grandfather James Holbrook had helped his mom and dad build before he went into the Civil War. I have a picture of my grandmother Holbrook who lived to be 111 [see figure 10].

Anyway, I was raised on that kind of history. And to be raised at and in the house that my great-great grandfather helped build, that he raised his family in, gives you a real sense of belonging and a real sense of roots. So I was always interested in history, local history. And I was a verocious reader. Is it verocious or veracious? Anyway, I read a lot, maybe a ferocious, veracious reader. And I can remember when the bookmobile would come up Honey Branch, I was the only kid that went down and stopped, and got all the books on lawmen and read them. And when I was in school I would use my lunch money to buy books, through the *Weekly Reader*. And when I was finished with them, I would rent them out to other kids for a nickel a day. So I would get my money back.

10. Frank's grandmother, Elizabeth "Granny" Holbrook, 1940s. Courtesy
of Frank Kilgore.

Aunt Victoria would come to my house every few months and give me reading comprehension tests. And, like, in the third grade, I would be reading on the sixth-grade, seventh-grade level. And she kept up with me all the way through the middle grades to see how I maxed out. She was real interested in that because she was, I guess, our family historian, plus an avid reader. And when she found out I also liked to read, she paid a little more attention to me than some of the other dozens of nieces and nephews and cousins.

And that encouraged me to keep going to school because my mom and dad had quit school in, like, the fifth or sixth grade. And there was no real pressure to finish school because you could always get a job in the mines. If you were lucky, you got one with Clinchfield. If you were not so lucky, you got one at a truck mines or a doghole mines, a non-union company, making a subsistence living. Or you could get a union job and get two or three times that money. My dad always figured I'd end up working in the mines. I thought about it a couple of times. But by the time I thought about it, I had made so many coal companies so mad with my radical environmentalism, I couldn't have gotten a job with them if I had wanted to.

Dink Shackleford: I grew up around the mining industry, been around the mining industry all my life. My father was a coal operator, and I grew up in his shadow, running around following him on Saturday mornings, riding to work with him. And I graduated from the smallest high school in the state of Virginia—Keokee High School, which is now consolidated into Lee High, one of five county schools, a big high school now. And went to Mountain Empire Community College and took mining technology classes there for a while and then transferred to East Tennessee State University in 1982, with one year of credit from Mountain Empire, and got a BS degree in history and political science.

And I continued my studies there and got a master's degree in city management and public administration and worked for about four years as a circuit-riding town manager out of Marion, Virginia, in Smyth County. And I was the town manager of Damascas, Virginia, the "friendliest town on the Appalachian Trail," and Saltville, "the salt capital of the Confederacy." And I learned a lot about public administration and public services and the demand for that and the interaction between people and the need for those services, how you distribute the pie to people. That was '87 to '91.

And I became a lobbyist while I was there and worked on route 58 "for growth across the state," and that road stretches from the Cumberland Gap all the way to the coast, and I was the deputy assistant lobbyist on that. And we got a billion-dollar project my first year up there as a lobbyist, you know, and some of those lobbyists were asking me what I was going to do next. But it's been all downhill from there; I haven't got any billion-dollar projects since then. I'm on a couple of boards, and I have to go to Richmond. One is for the protection and advocacy of the disabled. That was my first forte into the lobbying experience in Richmond, and I've been doing that ever since.

Now I am executive director of the Virginia Mining Association here in Norton, Virginia, in the southwestern tip of Virginia in Wise County. And I've been doing that since '90, late '90. We do a lot of things here. We're a trade association. We publish a quarterly magazine, the *Virginia Mining Journal*, a newsletter monthly on the Web site, and we do a lot of media things. We primarily have the mining industry and people that are associated with the mining industry, and vendor and support industries and supply industries.

So we really have three categories: the miners; and then the people that directly sell mining equipment—hydraulic hoses or something like that to the mining people—and then we have people who are indirectly members. A lot of those people join for the health plan; we have some extra benefits in our group health plan that you can acquire. And so they join, and we've got Bob's Grocery and people like that that join that sell to coal miners. And they're indirectly supportive.

For each mining job that rolls over in the community, there are four to five other jobs, according to chamber of commerce numbers. And we've got about six thousand miners in southwest Virginia now and mine about thirty to thirty-five million tons of coal—it varies from year to year. And so it's a big part of the economy down here. And we're real proud of that and proud that we pay high wages—the average coal miner's salary is about $45,000 a year.

If the media needs a question answered in the coal industry, they call me, and I'll take the guy out on a surface operation and let him see it—those type things. It's not uncommon for the Associated Press to come through like that, give a tour of the mining industry. We also take elected leaders from Richmond and give them a tour of the mining industry, Governor Warner, for instance [Mark Warner, governor of Virginia, 2002–6]. We had Governor Warner come down, and we gave him a tour of the coal mines, and he spoke to our association and the people in our association.

My father, Sam Shackleford, started in the mines at an early age, about fourteen years old, and then he got his high school education completed. His father died in a gunfight, when my father was about five years old, in Harlan County, Kentucky. They were gambling and drinking moonshine, and they got in an argument. And they jumped up and decided . . . a real man in those days, instead of standing back ten feet, they held each other's left hand and drew pistols. And they shot each other and, of course, killed each other.

And my father was really down on alcohol and cards after that, saying it made an orphan out of him, and didn't like to see a deck of cards in our house growing up. But he was an orphan and had six brothers. So he grew up staying with relatives from place to place. And he and his brothers eventually all stayed together and worked hard together and stayed in a little clique. And they eventually got to own the largest coal mines in Harlan County, Kentucky, had about three or four hundred people working for them there at the end.

Frank Kilgore: When I was growing up, my dad taught me to hunt. And I'd be out in the woods, trespassing on coal company land, and strip mining started around here in the '50s, picked up steam in the '60s. And that was my prime hunting ages. So I started seeing strip mining very early '60s. And when I would walk through a strip mine and I see what it did to the forests and the water—the streams—and the wildlife, I just became incensed about how it destroyed the earth. And my dad, at times when he wasn't actually working for Clinchfield, he worked for these truck mines, and some of them were strip mines. So I learned very early on that you had to balance wanting to make a living for the local population versus environmental concerns. My opinion on that was that you couldn't, maybe even shouldn't, ban all strip mining. If it was a necessary evil, it certainly had to be done differently.

And back then I had no vague idea what reclamation would be, but I knew it had to be better than what I was seeing, because there was zero then. Then it was just shoot, shove, shove it down into the creek, and it wash down into the streams and then into the Clinch River and went on. At the time I got active with the pro-federal strip mine act movement, my dad was a UMWA deep miner, and UMWA deep miners were very suspect of strip mining because it was displacing them. Per worker, strip mines produced a lot more coal, and it was causing pressure on deep mine jobs. So a lot of union UMWA miners were opposed to strip mining for economic reasons.

So I used that, and a lot of the UMWA deep miners joined our group— Virginia Citizens for Better Reclamation, that I founded while I was at Clinch Valley College, 1974–77—and came on board in favor of the federal strip mine act. We had conservationists. We had landowners and homeowners who had had their property damaged by almost completely out of control strip mining. And then we had UMWA miners who didn't want to see their jobs displaced. So we had sort of a coalition. It was the first group that had ever taken on the strip mine issue in the Virginia coalfields that was indigenous.

Two or three prior efforts to support federal legislation were promoted by people who were from outside the area, came either to the college or came to southwestern Virginia for other reasons. They saw this devastation and would fight it. But they were always susceptible to the attack "You are not from around here; you're coming in here costing us jobs." And the coal industry would really whip up a wedge between them and local folks. Outside agitators costing jobs, maybe even a little bit communistic. And I was red-baited a couple of times. That didn't take very well because my family had been here for two hundred years. My dad was a coal miner, and a lot of our members were coal miners. So we were able to overcome that previously fatal tag and do a lot of good.

In promoting the federal strip mine act [Surface Mining Control and Reclamation Act, or SMCRA, signed into law in 1977 by Jimmy Carter], our group was the first to testify before Mo Udall's House Interior Committee when it took up the federal strip mine act once again after the previous one had passed but been vetoed by Gerald Ford. I had put together a slide presentation, showed it to local colleges and schools, with mixed results, mostly supportive. And civic groups. That was a tougher sell because those were businessmen. But I got it honed down to a thirty-minute presentation. That's how long Congressman Udall gave us. We made the first presentation, did one for the Senate; we did a lot of lobbying.

And our group was given blame or credit for once and for all showing that the Virginia coal industry was lying through its teeth about the benefits of strip mining in southwest Virginia. We even accomplished getting Congressman Morris Udall to come down and take a helicopter tour and see for himself, because Virginia coal interests, including the state agency that supposedly regulated stripping, was lobbying against the federal strip mine act. I mean Richmond was openly hostile to the federal strip mine act. They said, "This is a state's rights issue."

We not only influenced passage, but we had an attorney come down, fresh out of law school from Richmond, and help the Department of the Interior draft some of the regulations used to enforce the federal strip mine act. And we went out physically with inspectors to different sites. I was still in college. I worked for the U.S. Forest Service full time, went to school full time, and got this group going. So it was a very busy time. And I also worked for the Job Corps as a wrestling coach.

I was real aggressive about the issue in college and elsewhere. And I was going to school with some kids who agreed with me, and some who didn't, some whose fathers were in the strip mine industry. So I had had confrontations with them in class and out of class. I will never forget. There was this one young man about my age—I was probably a couple of years older than him because I went back to school after two or three years trying to raise my family without an education—and, I'll never forget, he was from Buchanan

County, his dad owned a strip mine, and he started challenging me in class. And it wasn't just a philosophical challenge. He was challenging my patriotism. And so we challenged each other physically in front of I don't know how many students.

So we ended up going over to the gymnasium. He said if I didn't like what he said I could do something about it, or he would do something about it if I didn't shut up. I can't remember the exact words. And so we ended up over at the gymnasium, and a bunch of people followed us over there. And I will never forget. This guy, I didn't know it, was a AA state wrestling champion from Grundy. And he thought, although I was a few pounds heavier than him, that he was just going to go over there and humiliate me in front of these folks. And so that's how he chose to settle this—we'll just wrestle. You know, the better man will go back to class, and the other one will shut up.

I said "okay." He had no idea I had ever wrestled. And so I pinned him in like fifteen seconds. And he told me I cheated, I started too early. I don't know how you start too early in a wrestling match. So I said, "Well, we'll do it again." So we got in position, and I pinned him in like ten or fifteen seconds. And he didn't believe that, so I did it again. By that time, his buddies came over there and said, "Can't you see? He's going to beat you every time." And I will never forget the look of surprise on his face. Somebody blurted out, after I pinned him the third time, and they said, "It looks like you got your butt whipped; I don't guess that state championship helped you any here." That's the first time I knew he was a AA state champion—which may have made me tighten up a little bit if I had known that, but I had no idea. So I learned then, when it comes to bullies or something like that, the less you know about their reputation probably the better off you are.

So it was a very hostile situation. We had people becoming multimillionaires, virtually overnight, and they were just running rampant through the coalfields, mining under public roads, mining within five feet of adjoining property lines, blasting rocks through houses. They blasted rocks through the gymnasium and covered swimming pool at Clinch Valley College. They were cracking foundations, rolling rocks down onto a playground at Norton Elementary School. And there was nobody there to stop them. And we would publicize, highly publicize nationwide, all these abuses.

Well, we started out with just sending out news releases at random, pictures, and then different newspaper editors or journalists would pick up on it and call us. They'd come down and do stories. They'd come for themselves. Bill McKelway from the *Richmond Times-Dispatch* did some stories in his early career. Coleman McCarthy out of the *Washington Post* came down, did some stories. Jack Anderson sent a reporter down to do some stories.

So we were giving the coal industry somewhat of a black eye. So when we were getting nationwide press on the issue, at least in the eastern part of the nation, then they started paying more attention to us, saw us as a threat, and started threatening us. But unlike the previous groups who were somewhat pacifist, I was not a pacifist and really shot back. So it was a different kind of group that the coal industry hadn't encountered yet. And that was indigenous people, who understood the culture, who couldn't be red-baited, and couldn't be scared off. And if they were shot at, they'd shoot back. So we may not have gotten the instant popularity with the coal industry, but they understood and had to respect us more because we were more potent.

One night, I was on the way back from work with the Job Corps when we lived in Wise and coming up the crooked road there in my little pickup truck. And in this horseshoe curve it was these three guys in a black Torino leaning up against their car, waiting on me. It was just obvious when I pulled up and my headlights hit them. They saw my truck, and they hopped in their car. And they got in behind me real close and tried to hook my bumper and push me off the road. Of course, I couldn't outrun them in a Datsun pickup truck, but I gunned it best I could. And they were right behind me, within two or three feet of my bumper.

I slammed on the brakes and hit a wide spot in the road and skidded to a halt right against a cliff. Their momentum was such that they went by me, and then they put it in reverse to back up. I wasn't about to let them get out; I knew there was three of them, maybe more. So I had a .357 Magnum in my truck, and I just started shooting through the trunk of that Torino. And all I saw was smoke from the tires, smoke from the exhaust, and smoke from the gun. And they took off, of course. My dad always taught me, the best way to avoid trouble is to jump into it early with a lot of force, if you are going to do it. That way, the people who are truly not wanting to face that will leave you alone. So I didn't see them again that night; I didn't see them for subsequent weeks.

And then I was loading—we moved to Honey Branch; my grandfather died, and we moved into his old house that Christmas—following Christmas Eve, I'm loading presents into the vehicle, getting ready to go get my children. Here comes this black Torino by my house up Honey Branch, and that's when they shot at me. They reached their hand out the window and shot at me while I was loading the car with Christmas presents on Christmas Eve. And the shots went way over my head. Either they were really bad shots or they were just trying to get back at me for putting the bullet holes through their trunk.

And so my wife at the time said, "Are you going to report that to the police?"

I said, "Naw, I shot at them." That's how I looked at it—fair is fair. And it really didn't bother me, and I never thought much about it until I was telling my now, present wife about it, and she said, "My God, I can't believe you lived like that." But it was rough-and-tumble times when I was growing up. And violence was a way of settling disputes. You didn't take warrants out. You waited and practiced and caught somebody. And you had a fight with them.

So that's the way I was raised, and that's the way most of the coalfield kids were raised. It was somewhat lawless around here when I was growing up. And it's part of our culture. The kids had a quarter of a mile drag strip marked off, painted off on the public road. And they would drag race every Saturday night. The police, unless one of them wrecked and hurt somebody, never did bother them. And drunk driving was a way of life on Saturday night. I didn't participate in any of that. I didn't drink, didn't have a hot car either. But I saw it quite frequently, and fights were the norm instead of an exception.

It's not as prevalent now, thank goodness. A kid runs to court now if another kid says a cuss word to him. And it's probably better to have it in court than to have it out in the classroom. So I'm not putting it down. But it was a whole different culture. You know about St. Paul's background—the juke joints and the violence and so on. So that was sort of the way of life around here.

After they got rid of the juke joints—in the '70s—then that culture sort of died out slowly. We had enhanced police enforcement and just a nationwide attitude that finally permeated to this area: drunk driving is not a manly thing to do, and fighting and breaking bones are against the law—better not to do it. It's not a $25 fine anymore. And so the judges started cracking down, prosecutors started cracking down. I think our culture has changed to be less violent. The good old days weren't so good when you look back on them, how we treated each other.

Dink Shackleford: I heard stories—my grandmother thought she had died and went to hog heaven. I mean they lived on a ridge where, if you broke your leg, you probably died. You couldn't get medical help, no doctors, and life expectancy was real low. And the railroad came in, and suddenly you could order anything you wanted from the Sears and Roebuck catalog, you had a company doctor. You know, everything was great. You got water lines and plumbing in the house. She was a little worried about electricity though. When electricity first come in the area, and they put up a coal generating plant and generated their electricity, she was just afraid to cook in that electric stove. She just thought electricity was going to get in the cornbread and kill us all.

Keokee was a coal mine camp. We bought the coal mines. They had had about fifty-three strikes the year before my dad and my uncle Henry and uncle Byrd and uncle Tom and all of them purchased the mines. And my dad had a few shares in it. My uncle Henry was the primary owner; he was the main person. But they were all getting older. They were in their forties and fifties, and they decided they were going to buy that mines and let it go union. And my uncle Tommy was president of the union at that mines, and we kept it close. And I used to laugh.

Because when they would buy a coal mine community—that was the last one, I just got to see the last mines they bought—but they had bought several ones, and they would move all of their bosses and most of their workers with them. And they would move into a coal camp and basically overrun it with their workers. And my dad, I remember him telling me once, "Son, people are going to say that we've moved in here and took over this town and everything and that we are a coal mine mafia." He said, "But we're not a mafia; we're just all real close." And I always remember that and found it to be kind of true.

Well, growing up, I always went to the mines on Saturday with my dad. And I would mess around on equipment with him with me. And I had learned a lot about outside equipment. I can't ever remember not knowing how to run a bulldozer or a backhoe or equipment like that. Or a locomotive. And I went one Saturday morning, and I went that morning in particular to run cross-country back—it was about an eight-mile trip from there to the house. And as I started off the hill, one of my brothers-in-law pulled me to the side to go down inside the mines to look at a new piece of equipment they'd got.

So I went down in there, and it probably wasn't a hundred yards inside the mines. And it was in the fall of the year when the air is kind of thin, and it's a dangerous time to be in there. And I stood beside a new continuous miner, and watching the hand controls instead of being behind it, I stood beside of it, and a rock fell—vibrated loose—and I was fifteen years old. And it made me a T-12/L-1 paraplegic. I went to the University of Kentucky Medical Center and spent about a year in and out of rehab, went to Woodrow Wilson, Fishersville.

My injury was real low; it's allowed me a lot of flexibility. And I've got good arms and hands, as opposed to a lot of people I saw that didn't have. So I've been able to live completely independent, had a pretty good life and went to college. Only thing I hated about it—I went a few years without riding a motorcycle when I got hurt at fifteen because I had always rode mini-bikes and motorcycles. And my dad died when I was nineteen; he basically grieved himself to death over my injury. I always said, "That rock hurt me, but it killed my dad."

And about a year or two after he had died, I had kind of gotten depressed and was in real bad shape. The doctor told me he was sending me home because I had lost the will to live at the rehab center. And it kind of hit me like a ton of bricks. That's when I come home and changed my life. I decided I was going to stop listening to everybody and listening to the way people wanted me to live. So I had rode a motorcycle always, and I decided, "Well, I'm going to buy a Harley since I'm going to die anyway. I'm going to get that Harley I always wanted."

So I bought a 1952 Forty-five Flathead, old service car. And the brakes were bad on it, and I had a friend used to have to ride on the back of me. And he'd jump down and drag his feet, you know, when we'd go down big hills. But we fixed the brakes and got them going. And I rode that for a while, and I decided, "You know, hey, I can ride a motorcycle again; I can do this." And I started feeling alive again. And that's what really brought me out of it, I think. I felt the wind in my face, and I felt alive again. So I went and bought a 1982 FLH Belt Drive Classic King of the Road, they called them then—it's a Road King now—and put about seventy or eighty thousand miles on that baby, and went to college, and sold that one and bought an FXRS with a sidecar. And it was souped up, had branch heads on it from out in California. And I kept the sidecar; I sold it a couple of years ago.

I wanted to go to law school. And I said, "If I sell that motorcycle, that will help pay for it." And my wife said, "You'll never sell your motorcycle. If you sell that motorcycle, you're going." Well, I sold it about a week later, but I kept my sidecar so I wouldn't be plumb out of business this time. I went to law school for a year up in Grundy. And I couldn't do that and keep this job too. I was going part time; I was the first part-time student they ever had. I had to go through the program, and it was really hard because they didn't know how to handle me. But I knew the folks that founded the school, and they about had to oblige me. And I had to drop out after a year.

But I was fortunate in that Virginia is one of the few states you can still read law the old-timey way. And other states have nullified that—it's about three other states that do that. But Virginia, because Thomas Jefferson envisioned the program and put his stamp of approval on it, he saw this genteel farmer society and becoming a lawyer. And he put his stamp on that. That will never go away in Virginia probably because Thomas Jefferson is the thirteenth apostle. And anything he's done in Virginia, it's descended from God. You can hear the angels sing when his stamp's on it.

But a problem we have, I go to the beach, and people say, "Do they still mine coal in Virginia?" And they're kind of shocked. Growing up, people touched coal or wood as they carried it into the house or filled the furnace in the basement. They were aware of the role that it played in the direct heat to their homes. Through the years, it's gotten to where people don't know it. I think about 60 or 70 percent of the people don't really understand where electricity comes from. When you've got man-on-the-street interviews, you'll get things like, "Well, it comes from that plug in the wall, I know that." They're not aware at all that it has to be produced instantaneously and it's transmitted over wires. The light above your head right now is being produced somewhere up on the Ohio River, I think, or down in TVA. And they're just not aware of that.

I tell a little story about that, that kids today think chicken comes from Food Lion. And they just really don't have any idea. When I was growing up and we wanted chicken down at my grandmother's house, we went out in the back yard and killed one. She had this real good craft. She could take a chicken by the neck and spin it around her head like a whip, and crack it. There's two ways to kill one—that way or cut its head off. And she could snap its head right off that way. They'd probably put you in jail for child abuse if you did that in front of a kid today, kill a chicken. But I had six older sisters and brothers, and each trip to Grandmother's house, when my sisters started getting married, I noticed I got a better piece of chicken each time when I went to Grandma's house. So I was real pleased each time a sister got married, 'cause you just kill one chicken and you don't have ten legs like you can go to Food Lion and buy it now. So I had to work my way up that chicken, and as each sister got married—I was the youngest—I just kind of worked my way right along. But I knew where chicken come from when I went to Grandma's house. Kids don't know today, and kids don't know where electricity comes from.

But in this area, not many people work. We have a lot of people on workers' comp; we have a lot of welfare. Appalachia, the little town down here that Westmoreland [Coal Company] closed down in, I think about 70 percent of their population, probably higher since then—their town manager told me about four years ago—is transfer payments. They make their living from transfer payments out of the mailbox. That's now all welfare and food stamps and workers' comp. Some of it's retirement and those type things. But that's an astounding figure for a community to have. And you talk about trying to increase taxes or something on those folks, and you can't do it. But fortunately in Wise County and Lee County both, we've had the mining industry subsidizing the tax base and keep the revenues fairly high and keep the educational system going, and keep the property taxes sort of low. So we've been fortunate in that fact about the mining industry; we've been able to put money back in the community.

Frank Kilgore: When coal seams were opened up, and the coal was processed and brought out and picked through, the slate pickers would pick out the rock that was on top of the coal and was mixed in with the coal, that would be thrown out to the side, and it would rain on it and leach out heavy metals and sulfur and iron. That would leach into the water supplies and water systems. That was one of the major points of water pollution from deep mining. Millions of tons of this slag, this waste, would pile up, and it would ignite sometimes through spontaneous combustion. These coal camps—I remember when I was little, at Dante, there was this smoldering pile of slate two or three places that you could smell sulfur throughout the community, day and night, that would burn for years. All those have been reclaimed under the federal strip mine act that are in the Dante area now.

We, before the 1977 strip mine act passed, had the worst restrictions on strip mining, because basically it was seven counties out of a hundred counties that produced coal, and of those seven, three of them produced 80 percent of the coal produced in Virginia. So it was hard for three or four counties to have any political clout in Richmond. So it took the federal government to step in and rectify that. We are as far away from Richmond as you can be and still be in Virginia, so all that—remoteness and lack of political clout—led to very poor restrictions imposed by the state. Virginia had among the weakest programs in the nation in both mine safety and reclamation. So Virginia has a history of being so pro-industry that they have overlooked safety for miners and environmental issues for the land. And we were sort of the poster child for bad coal-mining practices.

Dink Shackleford: In Virginia, in the '60s, the Tennessee Valley Authority wanted some coal, wanted some steam coal. And they built these plants. And it's kind of ironic that the federal government itself was basically responsible for the demise of a lot of the area. They wanted that steam coal, and it created a little boom. And anybody who could get a backhoe or a bulldozer and a pickup truck could become a coal miner, a surface operator. And there was no laws or regulations—very little—and they used the "shoot and shove" method. They just drilled a hole and shot the dynamite and pushed it over the hill and got the coal, and left it that way. And so you had a real mess. Acidic water was coming off the soils mixing, and that's what makes the bad water, going through different types of soils. That was done up to '77 till the mining act came along. And when the surface mine act came, it changed a lot of things, and reclamation become a mainstay of the industry. And a lot [of] the jakeleg operators got out of business to where now, I'm proud to say, we don't really have any wildcat operators. We have people that are responsible, that the [Virginia] Department of Mines, Minerals and Energy monitors.

And the Department of Mines, Minerals and Energy has come a long ways too. For example, in Virginia in the surface operations, about 80 percent of all surface operations are on abandoned mine lands, which was mined before the '77 act. So we're going back and taking a second, sometimes a third, cut—because equipment is so much bigger now you can go back and get more coal—and reclaiming those sites to modern-day standards. And the Powell River Project's [partnership between coal operators and Virginia Tech ecologists and foresters] been instrumental in that and the Department of Mines, Minerals and Energy. Virginia's the model. As a matter of fact, last year Virginia reclaimed more land through the "abandoned mine lands" program than the rest of the country combined. We're really after it, and it's really making a difference in the water quality.

In the 1970s, the executive director of this same organization [Virginia Mining Association], B. V. Cooper, was real vehement about no laws and regulations, that it was communism, and that the next thing you knew, government was going to be telling you what to do here and there. And I think it struck a chord in the Appalachian independence that we have. I was a kid in those days, and I remember it. There was some wild surface operating going on in those days, and they needed some regulation.

Now B. V. Cooper was real adversarial to Frank Kilgore. And he and Frank went nose-to-nose on all kinds of stuff. Times have changed: most of the jake-leg operators are gone now. And we can live with the environmental regulations. I think we cannot only live with them; I think we can take the land to a higher level. There's two hospitals, a couple of schools, hotels, a Wal-Mart out here—all built on surface mine lands that the money to level those properties would have made them infeasible to construct. But we can go in there and get the coal, and leave level, developable land.

That's why I'm so aggravated about the mountaintop removal opponents. I think their intentions are probably good, but the road to hell is paved with good intentions. And I think they're stopping the opportunity we have to create more level land. They say, "There's not going to be anything way up there." Well, we didn't think there was going to be anything here when we started laying water lines to these places, and you would lay water lines and—poof—development starts happening. So you are precluding that anything will ever happen up there, and I don't know what can happen there. But I know that a hundred years ago, if you had told somebody they were going to get in a big metal tube and fly from one end of the country to the other, listening to a symphony in an earplug, they'd think you were crazy.

And I think a hundred years from now, they're going to have things and uses for things we can't comprehend today. And that we are really stopping the opportunities that we can create for ourselves. And I've noticed the valley fills, when they fill the refuse in the valleys, that used to just have water when it rained. The ones I see now have water year-round because they are like a big sponge—they absorb that water, and they just kind of let it out gradually. I think it's improved the water quality in the long run, and I think they're going to find that in the long run.

Frank Kilgore: Fortunately, Virginia hasn't had as much of that mining method used as West Virginia and Kentucky. I understand why people get very upset about mountaintop removal. When you harken back to the pre-1977 application of the federal strip mine act, though, mountaintop removal is an improvement over steep-slope, "shoot and shove" mining. With mountaintop removal, you can control the sedimentation and erosion much better because you are segregating solid rock from the soil and dirt and doing end dumps into the head of a hollow with the solid rock. The solid rock doesn't erode and create sediment in the streams like steep-slope, "shoot and shove" mining did.

Under the federal strip mine act, the coal company has to pre-engineer where to put the solid spoil. What they will do, they will go in and cut the timber, and they'll take the huge dozers, and they'll scrape all the topsoil and subsoil off, store it on the site, then blast the rock off, push that rock or haul it over to the head of the hollow, dump it into the head of the hollow. It's called a French drain. They just dump it and dump it, and it finds its own angle of repose. Sometimes they have to go down there with their equipment and reconfigure it some to allow the water to flow properly out the end. And then out the end, they'll have a sediment pond to catch the sediment. All the time, they've stored the topsoil and subsoil up on the flat area they are mining. Then when they get through blasting away the rock, putting it in the head of the hollow fill or French drain, and they're done, then they take that subsoil and topsoil and spread it back out atop the flat top of the mountain that they've created, the flat area they've created. And they seed it with grass, legumes, and trees.

Unfortunately, the huge downside is it completely removes the aquifer because each coal seam is its own aquifer for groundwater. When you mountaintop remove, you lower the actual elevation of the mountain. Say you take three seams of coal that are sandwiched from the top of the mountain down. You have a layer of sandstone on top, have trees and rocks and animals on top of that, then you go down tens of feet and that will be your upper seam of coal.

In this area, it might be the Splashdam Seam. And then below that would be the Upper Banner Seam and below that would be the Lower Banner Seam. And sandwiched in between would be a layer of sandstone and a layer of siltstone, somewhat in a stratum. Well, if you go in there and take all three of those seams of coal in a mountaintop removal operation, you have removed three groundwater aquifers from the ecosystem.

So you end up with what was a steep ridge top covered with, usually the steeper and the higher the ridge top, the poorer the timber. And the poorer the soil. So a lot of times they go in, there might be a lot of substandard trees, they cut those off on the very tip-top of the ridge. And then they turn it into a flat area that, if they would plant native nut-bearing trees, they'd probably have a much better situation than they do now where they plant locusts and white pine, which are both susceptible to pests and diseases. There's a move afoot to return mine sites, strip mine sites, to oaks and nut-bearing trees. But where they really do damage to future timber is down in the hollow where they have dumped all this rock.[1]

Dink Shackleford: A lot of people don't really realize they use about thirty, thirty-three pounds of coal a day—through electricity, each person does. So when I hear these people talking bad about coal or talking bad about the energy that they use, I say, "Well, live in a canvas tent and turn off your electricity and don't be a hypocrite if you're going to get out here and criticize the easy life that you have." And so that's sort of a stickler with me. I deal with a lot of people a lot of time that are just against any development. And they use the environmental movement to stop that. And I think it's a real travesty that that's happening. Like I said, I grew up hunting and fishing and have a real keen sense of the land. I kayak. I've got a lot of Cherokee blood in me, and my father brought me up with a real respect for the land.

Frank Kilgore: Dink Shackleford was critically injured in a deep mine accident when he was a teenager, down in Lee County. He was raised in Keokee, which if there is a wilder, meaner town than St. Paul, it was Keokee back in the old days. And Dink is a unique fellow. He is very active in conservation issues, yet he is the executive director of the Virginia Mining Association. And their predecessor, the Virginia Mining and Reclamation Association, fought the federal strip mine act tooth and nail. They red-baited its proponents. Some of their members threatened members of the conservation community. And from that attitude in the '60s and '70s until now . . . and they'd hired outside people—I call them agitators—who'd come in, had no connection here, no sensitivity to the culture or heritage of the area, they were just paid as mouthpieces to shout down their opponents and to influence political leaders. That was their job; they were lobbyists.

And then when Dink took over, he started talking to the coal operators in his group about, "Look, the federal strip mine act is not only a permanent fact of life, but we caused it. If we hadn't throttled the state and kept them from doing a few things to help the environment, the federal strip mine act may not have gotten off the ground. So we traded those heydays with nothing but profit and no reclamation for a future. We made our bed; let's sleep in it. Let's be the best reclaiming coal companies in the nation, go from the worst to the best." And in many aspects, the Virginia coal industry has done that very thing. Many of the nationwide reclamation awards go to Virginia operators. And it's just an about-face that's phenomenal when you have lived with and then lived through it. I credit him for a lot of that, and I credit a younger, more educated set of coal operators and coal officials, many of whom are outdoor enthusiasts—hunters, fishermen, mountain bikers, canoeists, conservationists.

The old guard was guys who just got into the coal business, toiled along, barely made it. The big prices jumped up, they became millionaires overnight, but they were the same people. They lacked the education, sensitivity, and knowledge of the environment as a whole that these younger coal officials have. It's just a generational change too. So the old guard went out, and the new guard came in. And they were used to regulations. They were used to permits and bonds. They were used to inspectors. They were used to planning. And they were used to reclamation and actually took pride in it, take pride in it. I don't believe a lot of them would ever want to go back to the old ways because it was destroying the very area they had come from in many instances.

The rechannelization kept St. Paul from
being underwater.

THIRTEEN

Regional Planning and River Politics

Frank Kilgore: Obviously, the reason that people suffer from flooding is they
build in the floodplain. Lacking a lot of flat, developable land, our early settlers settled close to the rivers and streams. So in doing that, whenever you
have a major flood event, you always had major damage.

Fortunately through FEMA [Federal Emergency Management Agency]
and state emergency agencies, when there is a flood now, rebuilding in a flood
zone is off-limits. You can't get a permit. So that's going to help in the future.
Another flood prevention factor that we are undergoing is we had the Clinch
River rechanneled in St. Paul, which has stopped any major flooding. And, of
course, I guess Grundy, Virginia, was the most devastated in the 1977 flood,
and the entire town's being relocated and the town flood-proofed. But just
the fact that new homes can't be built in floodplains and that old homes, if
they're devastated by flooding, have to be rebuilt outside the floodplain will
eventually cure this longstanding problem.

The '77 flood crested at thirty-six feet; '77 was a hundred-year flood. I guess
it was bigger than any the last century. And it happened to be the same year
that the federal strip mine act [SMCRA] went into effect. Of course, it took
awhile for the federal strip mine act to have an effect on the watersheds because you had so much abandoned land that had never been reclaimed, and
some pitifully reclaimed land under state regulations. So I think all those
factors together are going to slowly but surely reduce the number of flood
problems that we have.

And then we have a weather pattern in far southwest Virginia that's a little different from the rest of the state, particularly Buchanan County, where
it's the head of the Big Sandy watershed. And there are some divide ridges
between them and Kentucky and West Virginia. It appears that the Hurley

region particularly—that rain gets dumped into that region—seven inches at one time just recently, or maybe it was more than that. Maybe it was thirteen inches, maybe it was thirteen inches in seven hours or seven inches in thirteen hours. I can't remember, but people died, and they are still reeling from the effect of that. The school washed out, the whole community washed out.

And that was the result of a traditional weather pattern. That's not just a freak weather pattern, but Buchanan County is hit with floods yearly. In fact just last week, the little community of Council was flooded; nobody else had a flood. So there's something about being at the headwaters of a huge watershed that's creating a little havoc in Buchanan County. I guess it's where the moisture-laden clouds are coming on up that watershed, and then when they've got to go up, raise up to get over the ridgelines of the headwaters, why it just dumps their load. And so they have a particular problem, and they've got the steepest slopes, and they've got the most narrow river bottoms, so they have very little flat land to build on.[1]

And traditionally too, the coal companies have always owned the huge majority of surface land. And what they owned couldn't be built upon, and what they didn't own was already owned by folks along the creeks. So you couldn't buy land outside the floodplain a lot of times. The rechannelization kept St. Paul from being underwater during the '77 flood. St. Paul always flooded before then when it rained. [According to Charles McConnell, houses had been relocated out of the flood zone by 1977 as part of the rechannelization project; however, the channel itself was not changed until 1981.]

LeRoy Hilton: Interesting thing about the river. Where they rechanneled the river, it actually run uphill from there. As it come down through, it made a complete horseshoe about a half a mile. And as it run through the west part of town, it actually was trying to go uphill. And there was about twenty-five feet of water there in a big deep hole, and then as it pushed its way out it was like two feet deep or something, made a big channel in there. And that water would come and, like I say, it was trying to run uphill at that point. And every time you got any kind of water, immediately it would flood, all over this area. All of it would be underwater. And they cut this channel through, and they cut out a half a mile of river actually is what they did.

They were pushing the dirt, and they cut this channel through, and all the water left. And there were deep holes like twenty feet deep. All these fish were trapped in there. Now we talked to the Game Commission to see what they were going to do, and they said it is easier to raise more fish than to try to recover them. We asked permission to seine the river, which is against the law you know. They gave us permission to seine the river. People would come with barrels for their farm ponds. We recovered over two thousand largemouth bass, crappy, walleye pike, and northern pike, drum. We know we recovered two thousand, and took them and put them in other streams, put them at the golf course at Lake Bonaventure. We'd take a pickup truck, put a piece of plastic in there, and fill it with water. And we'd go up after we'd get four, five, six hundred fish. We'd go and just open the bed and dump. We know of at least two thousand we personally put at the lake at the golf course.

Bruce Robinette: I had been in public education for seven years and had a career goal of being a public school superintendent somewhere up in the Shenandoah Valley. We were in Waynesboro, and I had completed my master's requirements at Tech, lacked two courses of getting on the superintendent's list when I would have obtained my five years of administrative experience. And I got a phone call one morning about 6:30 from a gentleman in Big Stone Gap that I knew. And he told me about this regional venture that they had down here. And I had read about hopes of an industrial park at Duffield on the floodplain and through the local county papers. So he called me and told me, "Why don't you consider coming back down here and helping us?"

This name LENOWISCO—it sounded like an Indian name—which was an acronym for Lee County—that's L-E—and N-O is for the city of Norton, and W-I is for Wise, and S-C-O was for Scott. And you put it all together, and they call it LENOWISCO in all caps. And that's been a byword here in development. LENOWISCO was one of four planning districts in the state. There was one at Richmond, and there was one in Tidewater, and there was one in the Roanoke Valley headquartered in Roanoke, and us. And that was all local initiative. There was enabling legislation in the state code. You know, we have to live by the infamous Dillon rule. In Virginia, localities can't do anything that's not provided for in the statutes of the General Assembly. So we had that authority—local units could go together for planning and economic development purposes.

The first director was an industrial critter. He came here from Kansas; he was a native of Appomattox. And he was probably about seventy years old. And he was near retirement; he was getting tired. But he told them, "You don't have infrastructure, you don't have water, you don't have sewer, you don't have roads. In the three counties, you only have one technical school." And said, "You're not ready for me, so I'm going to move on, and I'm going to wish you well." So they hired a gentleman from northern Virginia who was nothing more than a super salesman. And he came in with all his flamboyancy, and the people immediately cast a shadow around him, because they said, "I just don't believe that guy." He was whispering, "We've got General Motors coming next week; we've got Ford coming the week after that." And it was just a bunch of hot air. So he never did gain the confidence of the people.

So the fellow who called me was exactly right: they needed to get somebody locally that they could relate to. "Yeah, I know that boy's brother; I know his dad and his mother; he went to school at Big Stone Gap; he's one of us." So at least they would give me a chance. So I talked to my wife. Her parents lived in Kingsport nearby, and her mother had had a heart attack, and she was not feeling well at all. We decided to come back. That was about 1965. After I had been here two or three weeks, I realized I had made a big mistake. I said, "Good gracious, this is something." They thought the regional effort was basically a communistic threat toward local government. "You all are down here to take over our county and our towns and our city. And we're going to have to answer to another level of government bureaucracy."

Before the '70s, there was no real water treatment, no real sewage treat-ment anywhere in the region. They had a few collection systems but very little treatment, and what treatment, it was just passive, it didn't do anything to it. So either the homes ran straight into the creek—straight-line pipes—and then if it was collected, the towns ran it in a bigger pipe. So it all ended up straight in the creeks. Coal companies, by in large, built a lot of these homes all over this region, and single-family duplexes. And they built them in a hollow where there was a flowing stream, and they would run potable water to them. But all of the bathrooms and all of the in-house water was straight-piped to the nearest creek.

In the '70s, we started getting a few systems. The base systems are in the towns. They've got the sewer plants, and they've got the water plants. And then they go outside the corporate limits to propose annexed areas. We started doing that in the '70s, but I'm gonna tell you in the last fifteen years is when it's really taken off because EPA [Environmental Protection Agency] has started really putting a lot of money in it. It's coming to Vir-ginia through the Virginia Department of Health. We've always had Farm-ers' Home, which is now the new Agency of Rural Development. Being in the central Appalachian region, here where we are, we get the ARC [Appalachian Regional Commission] funds or Appalachian funds. If you are eligible for that, you are also eligible for the Economic Development Administration, known as EDA. They've been concentrating on water. EPA came in and told these towns and cities, small, all over southwest Virginia, you can't continue to dump raw sewage or partially raw sewage into these streams. So they got those people cleaned up, and now they're going to rural areas. The big thing the LENOWISCO people have been targeting and doing a great job with is water, potable water, indoor plumbing, all of which is necessary for any kind of regional economic development.

And in St. Paul, we also got involved in flood control. I had lived in St. Paul for a few months when my wife and I came out of college and just been married. She was a teacher at St. Paul High School, and I was a teacher in the next town west, which was Coeburn. And we lived in St. Paul. Anyway, I went over with a floodplains specialist with the Tennessee Valley Authority. And TVA—other than being in power in a big way—they had floodplain and flood relations responsibilities for all the seven states in the valley that they served power to and eleven counties in Virginia, including our three counties. And they had records and were very much aware of what was going on in the flooding of the Clinch River in St. Paul.

They had just completed a flood project because of all the flooding that took place in Coeburn in '62, '63, and '64. That was the precedent. So TVA after Coeburn took a lot of interest up here because they said these other communities—we've been so successful in Coeburn and everybody likes it what we've done. They did downtown renovation, they did flood proofing, they built floodwalls—it was amazing, all of the things TVA did. They not only dredged a channel on some small streams that went down to the Guest River, they did a little work in the Guest River, so that it wouldn't back up these smaller streams.

So after I became director of LENOWISCO, I went over to St. Paul and went into council, and the mayor was a gentleman named Holland Fletcher— he was the mayor, he was the chief of police, and he was also the fire chief. There's two boys: Tommy, who is now the principal of St. Paul High School, and Kyle, who is retired and he is on the school board. But anyway, a very well-known, influential family in St. Paul. And he didn't know anything about us, and knew very little about TVA. So on public expression, I stood and had a gentleman with me from TVA by the name of Glenn Wall. But anyway I stood and told them who I was and what I was doing there, and hopefully we could do some basic planning in the town of St. Paul and we would do a comprehensive plan, and that we could address the flooding problems that they had and hopefully some relocation of people out of the floodplain because TVA was really high in that. Because we never thought about rechanneling the river at all, you know. This came when the highway department came into the picture.

Mr. Fletcher said, I think he called me "boy," he said, "Boy, I just tell you, we are doing just fine up here now. And if we need some planning done, I'll call you down there in Big Stone Gap." That was where our office was, and so I expected that answer because that was the type fellow he was. Anyway, we left. Glenn and I, we stood out at the car and talked a good while, and I said, "Just keep this in the active file because," I said, "we'll be back in St. Paul." And while I lived over there, there was an MD, medical doctor, by the name of George Cain, and we became very good friends. And he heard what Holland said, and he called me. And he said, "I hope you weren't offended by your reception to the mayor and council." And I said, "No, I wasn't because I know Holland, and he was coming from the right place, and the town is fine, and he doesn't want to make any ripples, and he's running the show, and we're outsiders." And I said, "That's fine."

But I said, "George, I hope one of these days if we both live long enough, I would like to see something of this flooding you've got—every time it rains— I'd like to see that addressed." And it even blocked Route 58—you couldn't get through there. You'd have to go around another route or something. So anyway, he said, "I'll tell you what. I'm calling to tell you not to be offended because I'm going to run for council, I'm going to run for mayor, and there's some other people going to run for council that want to do some things that I want to do." And I said, "George, can you beat Holland?" He said, "Don't know, but I'm going to give it a good try." So, anyway, the next election, which was probably in '69, was the most heated election in a town of nine hundred people. They had people going door to door, and they had people working the streets, and it was one heck of a battle. George Cain did the impossible— he defeated Holland Fletcher. And he beat him on the fact they wanted to do some things in town. They wanted to take on some monumental projects. And they wanted to get all the outside help to come in.

Tom Fletcher: It is fair to say that there was a representative group of the town, meaning a lot of the Hollands, and the Fred Boltons, and the Domer Molinarys, and the various people that made up the town at that time and other citizens probably looked at this like, "Now you're moving along doing this, and maybe we need to sit down and talk about this a little more and make sure that as we move through it that we're taking care and dotting all the *i*'s and crossing the *t*'s as we should." And they would be a little leery of a lot of outside people directing the traffic. They were in essence the people who had lived around here for several generations, classified maybe as the old guard or old-timers.

I think my dad understood the need for the river relocation. I think maybe all the different things that went along with it were not exactly the way he would have preferred they did it. For instance, I remember standing there one day talking to him about that cut that cuts through to the shopping center.

By that time I was gone coaching at the University of Virginia or Carolina or somewhere, and they were in the midst of cutting through the mountain there. And I asked him what he thought about it. He said, "Well, it's probably a good idea. If it had been me and I had that much money to work with, I believe I would have done something different than what we are doing."

Bruce Robinette: So what George did in his campaign, he got people to thinking, "Well, maybe we ought to try to do something about—I mean we're sitting here, and we're just paying the bills, and it's just getting worse all the time." The next day after the election, George called me and he said, "I'm going to be sworn in on this date, and I want you there. I want you to be there because we're going to get that Wall guy, get him up here, and get anybody else up here because we've got a lot to do and don't have a lot of time to do it."

They didn't have any money, but they wanted to do a comprehensive plan. And we got the firm of Harland Bartholomew and Associates—they were a nationally known firm from out of Richmond—to come down. And they had a young man who is now in Richmond, owns his own firm, his name is Ken Poore—he's Ken Poore and Associates—they sent Ken down; we got acquainted with him. And we did a comprehensive plan, and of course the plan spelled out exactly what we knew. They needed to take this section of town and eliminate it, and get people relocated and all these businesses out of here.

Anyway, one day out of the clear blue, I got a phone call from the resident engineer of the highway department [Virginia Department of Transportation] in Wise. And he said, "What are you doing on this morning of a particular day at 9:30 a.m.?" I said, "I'll make myself available." He said the head of Location and Design—his name is Paul Coldiron, a native of Norton—he's coming down. "And they want to meet with you—just two or three of us—we want to throw some things around on four-laning Route 58." I said, "I'll be there."

They were doing some preliminary work on coming from Castlewood—that's across the river—on in down to Coeburn. And they got to St. Paul, and they said, "What are we going to do here?" So anyway, we went up and had the meeting, and they laid out some blueline prints. And everybody introduced theirselves. And he was a very personable individual, which you would expect being from Norton, and a VMI [Virginia Military Institute] graduate. And he said, "Bruce, we got a problem. We don't want to go to the town and get everybody up in the air until we sort of bounce this off of some people. We can't get a four-lane road through St. Paul."

And I said, "You're exactly right." Well, they had a scenario on paper that would just virtually eliminate the town. It was really going the shortest distance between two points. And they were going to put in two pretty high double bridges, and it was going to come right through where the Ford dealership is now, take the high school, the football field, and cut a humongous hole, not a tunnel but a cut, through where Gray Hills subdivision is and then come out on the other side, which is what is known as Virginia City. And when they went through there, they would probably have four or five seams of coal in that hill when they went through it.

And I said, "Naw, you would eliminate St. Paul." I said, "We don't want to do that to get a road through it." And he said, "Here's the loop in the river, just a big, not an S loop, just a big horseshoe loop." The horseshoe was very narrow down at the end where the opening was. And there was a great big hill right in the middle of the horseshoe. And it had a rock on top of it, and everybody thought that hill was solid rock. And even the highway department, without drilling it, they thought it was.

Anyway, the town of St. Paul was in the process of going to bid on a new sewer project that they had funded under Mayor Fletcher's regime. And the engineers were some local folks—the firm of Thompson and Litton in Wise. So shortly after our meeting in Wise, which we left, everybody shaking their head, I got a call one day from a gentleman, a principal at Thompson and Litton named Bill Thompson, and he had just gotten back some core drill reports on the hill. That was south St. Paul. They were going to put a sewer over there, so he had about six holes drilled. And he said, "Bruce, you know what I'm talking about?" And I said, "Sure, I lived over there. And that hill, we think, is solid rock."

He said, "It's dirt and shale. There's one rock up on top, and that's it." I said, "You're kidding." And he said, "No, that's what's so misleading." And he said, "That can be moved very easily." And he is the man who said, "If we could change that river"—and he knew about the road situation—"we could bring 58 across that. And we could take all this material, and it would balance out plus some to fill in the old channel." So anyway, Bill Thompson, being a very sharp engineer, had it all. And I said, "Where do we put all these people?" Had houses on both sides of the road, near the railroad and up above, old dilapidated substandard housing. The best of them were wood frame and just wasn't what you would call first-rate or even second-rate housing. So anyway, he said they needed to be relocated.

So it was in May 1970 we had the first meeting of all parties. The highway department was elated. And then all the TVA—the powers that be there—the experts in flooding, flood relations, and they must have brought about six or seven people because they had a genuine interest because they had all this history on the flooding. And so anyway we started in 1970, and a snail's pace is an understatement, or overstatement, because it was terrible.

Because we were relocating people in substandard housing, we needed to go to HUD [Department of Housing and Urban Development]. Their closest contact at that time was Philadelphia. We got on a plane, commercial—about four of us, three from my office—and a couple from Richmond met us in Philadelphia. And we just ran into a brick wall with HUD. They said, "You know, we don't do relocations. We do a few in New York City, and we've done a few in Boston and all that. But rural areas, we don't do anything in rural areas."

I said, "Well, you've got about sixty public housing units in the city of Norton on what they call their south side, which is their minority district." And I said, "Their grass is cut," and I said, "It's first class." And I said, "They run it with an iron hand, and you all don't know about that." "Norton? Norton? No, we'd have to go back in the records." And I knew right then, we was in trouble.

The HUD act—I don't know what happened to it. Fortunately, from 1970 to 1971, they decentralized from their regional offices and put it in states, state capitals. So for the first time, we had a representative in Richmond—I take that back, our representative was in Charleston, West Virginia. But they set an office up in Richmond; the timing couldn't have been better. And so we made some friends with the people immediately. We got them down to St. Paul; we visited them in Richmond.

St. Paul's planning commission—you're not going to believe the people they put on it. The chairman of the planning commission was a former CEO of the Pittston Company, which was the dominant coal company in that region and has been on up until just recently when it was broken up and sold. But his name was Kyle Teiche, and when he walked in a room, he just sort of turned heads. He looked the CEO part. He was a brilliant mining engineer, businessman, and when he talked to the feds, he put out the right questions. "Well, why can't we do this?"

George Cain, the new mayor, had enlisted all these people: "We're going to put you on a planning commission." And the answer was, "I don't want to get involved; I'm too busy." "That's the reason we want you, because you are busy." And so, it worked. It was the most phenomenal thing you've ever seen.

From the first meeting in '70, we made good progress for about a year, then it got bogged down, and about '72 or '73 we thought we had lost it completely. We started running into funding problems. The highway department had their own: they were ready to go. Fifty-eight was an arterial road, and it was state funded—no federal funds in it. TVA, to do a project, had to go to Congress, and they didn't budget anything, except people. They give you all the manpower you wanted, but they couldn't do construction. HUD had to do the same thing, and HUD was new in Richmond. They had just reorganized and this kind of thing.

Meanwhile, Charles McConnell, who was assistant director at that time of the housing authority, had moved in and assumed the project away from LENOWISCO—me and my staff—which was the natural thing because ever who did the relocation was going to run the whole project. We agreed on that early on. So we had moved out—very much interested and on the sidelines and doing what we could.

Charles McConnell: When I came on board, there was a freeze on monies that could be used to do this kind of project, '73. Tyler Cornett was hired to get this project started. He came from Hazard, Kentucky, and he worked for HUD. And a major part of the funding was HUD, and the other part was TVA, and the other was the highway department to build the bypass. So he was hired to come and do this project. The freeze about killed it, and so Tyler set around from January till we actually got approved in July of '73.

And the way it got approved was Lynwood Holton was the governor of Virginia, and he's from Big Stone here in Wise County, Big Stone Gap. And the town of St. Paul had some incredible political connections. And it didn't matter which party was in power—Democrats or Republicans. Lynwood Holton was a Republican. There was a guy in St. Paul—his name was Fred Bolton— very active in Republican politics. He knew Lynwood Holton personally. Lynwood Holton knew Richard Nixon personally. And so Fred made the connection to Lynwood Holton to make the connection to Nixon someway to unfreeze this money because we got a real problem in St. Paul.[2]

The problem was—there was several problems. One was a major part of the community lived in the floodplain, and so people got tired of getting flooded and got tired of maintaining their houses, so the neighborhood really started becoming very dilapidated. And the people were threatened by the Clinch River. TVA couldn't justify moving the folks out of the floodplain— didn't have the money to do that.

The highway department was looking for a route to get around St. Paul— and there was steep terrain and mountains and the river, which was meandering through town. So they would have had to build several bridges to go the route that it went, and if they didn't do that, they would have had to circumvent the town. There was all kinds of environmental problems and going through neighborhoods and residential areas, and so they really had a dilemma.

HUD at the time had a Neighborhood Development Program, and basically that program was set up to get rid of blight, and when you buy that property turn around and create new residential and new industrial and new commercial space. And another issue the town had, they were straight-piping their wastewater sewage directly into the river, which was becoming totally unacceptable. And so in the design of a sewer treatment facility, there was an area that they possibly could use, but it would be a lot easier to use that configuration if the river was moved.

The Clinch River created a loop in St. Paul. It was kind of the shape of an oxbow or horseshoe shaped, this loop. And it was about a thousand feet. If you made a channel change, it would shorten the river and it would create some open space that would have a variety of different uses. Before this, the loop was a residential and small farm area, a little subdivision, and most of the acreage was two farms. One was owned by two brothers. The consultant, the planner in Richmond, talked to some of these local officials—primarily the mayor, who was a medical doctor, George Cain, and Bruce Robinette, LENOWISCO. And they all started talking about how to get money to get rid of the flooding, the blight, and to create some commercial, industrial space in St. Paul.

If the highway department changed their route and they came down through where it is now—the straightest shot through town—if the river was moved, they could do it in an affordable manner. It would eliminate some bridges; the grading, construction would be really easier. If they could get TVA to dig the channel, that would help the highway department. But TVA just doesn't dig channels to dig channels. Their benefit would be if some way we could get the people out of the floodplain.

So the planner and the town officials and Bruce Robinette started meeting with people with HUD. You know, "Can you do this? If TVA dug the channel, could you buy the residences, relocate them, and then after they're relocated, the highway department could use this route because it would be easier. And part of the highway department grading could be brought over to raise this area up to create commercial and industrial space." And HUD started saying, "You know, we could achieve our goal of some economic development and removal of blight." The highway department said, "If that river is moved, we can go through this route." And TVA said, "If HUD moves the people out of the floodplain, we could justify paying for digging the channel."

So it all started to fit, all three agencies' goals and objectives and what they did at the time. HUD was interested in community development, so if there was some new commercial space and industrial space, they achieved some of their objectives. Certainly if the people got out of the floodplain, that would help achieve TVA's goals. And the highway department, they found a corridor that would be affordable and an easy way to construct the bypass.

We were ready to go. However, you have to submit an application to move a river or do anything in a stream. It's called a 404 permit, that the Corps of Engineers controlled and regulated. They would be the one that would issue the permit. Part of the permit process was, "Let's ask the community. Let's ask all environmental agencies, is it okay to do this?" And when we notified EPA and Fish and Wildlife Service, they had very strong objections. They didn't want to set a precedent.

Bruce Robinette: The Clean Water Act of 1975 comes into play.[3] The Environmental Protection Agency, who we had never had any dealings with, didn't have to have any dealings with, they come to calling and said, "We have to sign off on your construction permits." The gentleman that was assigned the project in Philadelphia did not believe that you should touch anything having to do with water. We met with him on numerous occasions. We met with the Corps of Engineers in Nashville because they had some jurisdiction on the Clinch. And the corps—they were ready to issue the 404 permit for TVA to do the rechannelization. But the corps could not move unless the protocol allowed them, for this man to sign off in Philadelphia. The corps didn't have to sign off at Coeburn because the rules hadn't changed, but when we got to St. Paul EPA came into play. And they said this fellow—one guy—has to sign off. And it's his department.

His big boss was a gentleman by the name of Green Jones, and he was a born and bred native of the city of Norton—went to high school there, went off to college at the University of Virginia, got a job—before it was EPA, it was called Federal Water Quality Management or something—but he would not get involved. He said, "Naw, you delegate these responsibilities to your underlings, and they do the work," and he said, "You really mismanage when you go out and you tell them."

But this guy in Philadelphia was hung up on the fact: "I just don't want you touching that stream." It was full of junk cars and garbage and debris and all this, but he said, "There's some critters there that need to be protected." And I just sat in meetings around these big tables and just listened, but he just wouldn't budge. And we were on time constraints. TVA was going to lose their money on this date and HUD had theirs approved for the fiscal year. And the highway department was the only one saying, "Boys, we're here when you need us; we're ready to go." That was state money. But the two feds were going to lose their funding.

Charles McConnell: And so TVA's environmental department, which was a strong environmental department, started analyzing what effect would this channel change have on the quality of the river.[4] And they determined that it would probably make the quality of the water better in that in the loop there was very slow movement; it was just choked with silt. If you dig a channel, you're going to increase the speed of the water and you get oxygen, so they finally concluded, "We think it will be better; we think it's good." Fish and Wildlife and EPA still strongly opposed it. This was, I think, in the Carter administration. This was '76 through—it took us four years to get the permit. And that was an incredible experience.

We would meet with TVA folks, and they pretty much were sold on it. And we'd go to the corps, and they were sold on it. And then we started having meetings with EPA. We'd tell them all the specifics of quality of water. And I really think they were afraid of setting a precedent: "If we start letting channel changes happen in St. Paul, somebody somewhere else—Mississippi or somewhere—will say, 'You did it there.'" Total opposition. And we had the planners, and we had environmental folks, tested the water. We did an environmental impact statement that was incredibly thick. Then to really complicate the thing—remember the snail darter—they found endangered mussels in the river in St. Paul, where we were. And that we thought would probably kill this thing.

Finally, Bill Wampler, who was our congressman at the time, said, "Let's meet in Washington with not the employees of these folks with these agencies; let's get together the people that can make the decision. Let's talk about this one more time to see if we can get this thing off center." So we had not the head but almost the head of Fish and Wildlife Service, EPA. TVA was there, the Corps of Engineers was there, there was a whole entourage of folks—Bruce Robinette, Bill Thompson, and our planner Ken Poore—and we had a very slick presentation to tell these folks, led by our congressman, Bill Wampler.

We went through all of this, and TVA even supported: "The quality of water is going to be better with this channel than it is now." And we did tell them about the jobs that would be created, get the people out of the floodplain, the threat of being flooded. And it's very unhealthy, just a terrible situation there. And the impact on the town would be very positive. So we told them all this. We had been fighting this for three or four years at this time. And Bill Wampler ended the meeting basically saying, "In '69, I voted for the passage of the Environmental Protection Act [enacted in 1970, in part creating the EPA] and what we're going through here is nowhere near what Congress intended to happen with that act. This is way beyond our intent. And you've just got to approve this." And he set down.

And Fish and Wildlife folks and EPA folks—I'll paraphrase a little bit— said, "With all due respect and from all we have heard here today, we have heard nothing that changes our mind. We're going to continue to oppose this project." And we all—our jaws dropped opened—we really couldn't believe a bureaucrat would tell a congressman, "I don't care what you intended, this is the way we're going to do it." And we left the meeting thinking, "We're dead in the water." And we really didn't know how to proceed.

About that time Senator John Warner was elected to the Senate, and he had not even won the nomination—I believe the guy's name was Obersham [Obenschain], I've really forgotten. Killed in a plane crash. There was a guy in St. Paul, Fred Phillips, that had supported Warner from day one during his attempts to get the nomination, never wavered. Warner got elected and had a meeting in Wytheville to kind of say, "Thank you, and I'm here. Is there anything I can do for you people out here? I'm here to serve you" and all that. And there was probably two or three hundred people in the meeting room. He came in and saw Fred Phillips, walked straight over to him and said, "Fred, how are you doing. I really appreciate your help through all of this. Is there anything I can do to help you?" Fred said, "Well, as a matter of fact, there is." And Warner said, "When we get through here, we'll go back in a room and you can tell me what's going on."

So we did. We had four or five of us—Bruce may have been there, Robinette; the mayor at the time; and certainly Fred. We told him what we had been through for four years and what our intent and goals for this project were and the conditions, as briefly as we could. And he wanted to know more, and we scheduled some more meetings with his staff. Anyway, he said, "I was the secretary of the navy before I became a senator." And he said, "The now secretary of the army, which controls the Corps of Engineers, I've helped that guy a lot. This is where I'm going to collect." So a few days or weeks or months—not long after that—somebody in his office called me and he said, "Can you have the mayor of St. Paul up here Friday?"

I said, "Absolutely." He said, "We'll go get the permit." So we went up and went to his office, went by Bill Wampler's office, and there's a guy, Steve Berry, that worked for him—Steve spent hundreds of hours working on this thing to help us, and I'd go meet, we'd crawl all over Washington. I don't know how many times we went up to pursue this thing—every avenue he could think of. So he was a key part, along with Congressman Wampler. So I went by and got him, and we went over to Warner's office, and we chatted for a while. And he said, "I'm going to call the Pentagon and tell them to come over here and get us." So he or somebody on his staff—he may have himself. Anyway, shortly, two full-bird colonels came in two staff cars to get us.

And Senator Warner was kind of in no hurry. He made us feel very comfortable. Finally he said, "Okay, let's go." And these guys had not even parked in parking places. They had just parked in the street. We got out, and they had blue lights, it seems like, on. And we went flying to the Pentagon. We'd been there several times before, and to get in the Pentagon back then was kind of difficult. You had to get an ID and all this kind of stuff. Senator Warner never stopped at the front door, and he had just been elected and he had been married to Elizabeth Taylor. So he was very very well known, and employees at the Pentagon would stand at the door as we walked by. We tried to keep up with him. He was walking thirty miles an hour down the hall where we were going, stormed into the Corps of Engineers' office and said, "We're here to get the permit."

They hadn't even had a chance to finish typing and they were doing that and said it was going to be a while, and we kind of set there for a minute. And he just reached over and picked up some papers and had a photographer with him. And he said, "Let's go take some pictures." So we went out to the entrance to the Pentagon, and he walked out holding this paper up in his hand and had the mayor and myself and Steve Berry in line as we walked out. And that was in every paper in southwest Virginia. Finally went back in and typed it, and we signed it and got it, and they still resisted some.

Part of what we had to do as a concession to Fish and Wildlife and EPA, and it turned out wonderfully, we had to preserve a big portion of the riverbed. We built a dam over there and created the Oxbow Lake and created a walking trail around it. It's just a beautiful area. They insisted on at least we do that. The contractor dug the channel in the middle and dug out both ways. Then they cut the lower plug, and then one day they kept getting closer and closer, and the contractor finally said, "Today we're going to change the flow of the river." Had a power shovel, an old steam shovel we used to call them, down in the channel, and he kept getting closer and finally reached over and pulled part of the plug out and part of the water started coming through. In one day we changed the flow of the river.

Before the river was moved, TVA came in with divers, and every endangered mussel they could find they gathered those and moved them to other parts of the river. That was another concession. Part of what Fish and Wildlife—and TVA wanted to do it as well—was preserve as many of the endangered species as we could. So there were a lot of concessions. The quality of the river is much better. There's some rapids in the channel. That was a mistake; it turned out to be a good one. The grading was at a flatter level than it should have been, and so we had an elevation change there of three or four feet. And so the engineers said, "Oh goodness, we're going to have to build that up." And the environmentalist folks said, "No, let that oxygen get into the water." So that turned out okay. And that freed up the construction.

While all that was going on, we continued to acquire property and relocate people out of the floodplain. That took several years. We had money to do that, and so we continued with that. Which would have been good even if the river had not been moved, to give people an opportunity and a means to relocate and get out of that threat. We moved almost a quarter of the town of St. Paul. Moving those people was very frightening for some, and some were thrilled to get out of the threat. A hundred families, and each one individually.

I went over and helped a lady hoe her garden. We did everything to try to make them feel more comfortable about what was going on. I hadn't had that much experience in buying or doing that sort of thing. We created a residential committee. The first thing we did was acquire the property. There was a lady there that had no facilities, no running water, no bathroom, elderly woman, horrible living conditions. She went to bed with a bat to beat the rats off of her. That's all she had ever known. And we got her out of that and moved her into a decent home. A lot of people lived in deplorable conditions. With the flood threat, you get to the point "I'm not going to spend any more money. What's the use?" Very low income, the majority of the people that lived down there. And it made you feel good to get them out of that threat. Some of them, though, that was their old home place, and they were opposed to it.

Bob Salyers: The town wanted to annex this property, for growth and also for the channeling of the river. Rab and Dule Couch were brothers. But Rab has passed away, and Dule has too. And these boys were not offered enough money for their thirty-eight acres of property. So they helt fast that it was not for sale. And it went all through the court systems. The court ruled that they couldn't stop the river channel because of the need for it, but the price that was agreed on was far too little.

That was a land grant, and it had never been sold, and no price had ever been established. They had timber on their property that had never been cut. There was oak trees on there that was five and six feet in diameter. Because when they cut them, we took pictures of the stumps. Walnut trees that were so big that the company that purchased the walnut trees even dug up the roots. And the coal reserve where the Couch boys and their granddads had supplied the old extract plant right across the river. They supplied the coal. And that extract plant was one huge plant because the smokestack was something like a hundred and forty feet. It was a concrete structure.

So TVA and HUD had to go back and pay them for the mineral rights, the timber. Those boys went from $38,000 to $218,000. They still didn't want to leave. They maintained that it would never be for sale. But they were evicted. They were country people, worked for the rock quarry here, the Clinch River Rock Quarry, worked there their entire life. You couldn't ask for better neighbors.

The channeling of the river helped me. I'm within three hundred feet of the river channel. The railroad is between me and the channel. I didn't get no money, but as far as never being flooded or being protected under what they call the "hundred-year flood," I benefited from it. I think the town and everybody that was left really benefited from the project as a whole. Until this went through, the town didn't have no place to build a sewer plant. The town of St. Paul had a sewer, but it was all going in the river. So they had purchased X number of acres of property off the Glovers', which adjoined the Couch property. And that's why the town had to have that, because they couldn't build their sewer plant.

Most people were satisfied with how they were treated. A lot of them would have liked to got more money, but they didn't want to go through the court system. So they settled.

Charles McConnell: Initially, we had a lot of condemnation cases, but when they started seeing with the relocation money they really got an opportunity, the condemnations almost went away. It was a major impact on people who had never seen anything like this. There was, I think, $25 million spent, counting the highway bypass and all the grading. That's a tremendous amount of money to spend on a small town. I certainly think it was worth it. It was a lot of benefits there—the impact that we had on those folks getting them out of that threat.

Tom Fletcher: This whole area that houses all these buildings, the river went right through the middle. It is a shopping center, which features both Food Lion and Food City. It has a bank, a Hardee's, a Pizza Plus, a Dollar General, a Family Dollar, Rite-Aid Pharmacy, Riverside Medical Clinic. We have a space here that we use as a softball field for our high school team. We have a Chevron, an Exxon, another pharmacy, a Burger King. There is a plaque in the bank where the center of the river used to be.[5]

Everything you wanted was right here
in Dante. . . . And now we don't
have anything.

FOURTEEN

Company Town with No Company

Kathy Shearer: Right now, and we're talking about October 2003, this is what
was once a bustling coal town. And right now, it's almost a ghost town. Not
in terms of the residences—there's still probably three hundred houses here.
The ghost town aspect is the downtown section. You've got the empty office
building of the coal company, which vacated in May. You've got a post office
and a little general store. You have the concrete platform that used to be the
foundation for the old theater, and another office building and barber shop,
newspaper stand—all that was torn down. You have a large green grassy area
where the company store used to be, one of the largest company stores in the
area. You've got an old depot, what used to be the Clinchfield railroad depot.
It's now owned by CSX, and it's vacant and falling down. And you've got a lot
of other buildings that are just gone. You have vacant buildings, or you have
just the foundation of the building that's been removed. So there can't be a
business there now. It's a pretty sad-looking downtown.

The old bank building is still there. It's in pretty bad shape, but it was built
around 1908. It's one of the two original Clinchfield Coal Corporation buildings, the other being the old steam heat plant next to it. And the bank is the
focus for a new community revival group which is just getting going, and they
hope to become the owners of the building, fix it up, and make it a cultural
center.

Dante was the headquarters of the Clinchfield Coal Company, which became a subsidiary of Pittston in the '40s. But in 1972, they built a brand new
building over in Lebanon, which is several miles away, still in the same county.
It's not clear to me exactly why they did that. They had plenty of space here, I
think, for what they needed to do. But they wanted to be in Lebanon. So they
built this new building, and the Dante building became simply a building for

the field force, the people who would go out and supervise the operations, and the engineers. So that was a big bump for people, when they realized this was no longer the headquarters; this was no longer the main office.

But still they had people coming and going. So they hadn't lost it all. They tore the store down in about 1975. That was a blow to the community. The hotel was torn down in the mid-50s to make room for the office building. And people who can remember the beautiful hotel still really are sad. They miss the hotel, but at least it was replaced by the office building. When they tore the company store down, it was simply grass. So that was the first major building to be removed without anything going in. So by the mid-70s, I think they were getting the idea that something major was going on here.

Now the mines in Dante all closed down by 1959—that early. So miners at that point—people here who still were mining coal—were sent out to other coal mines in the area. They had Duty, they had some mines north of here—Clinchco, Clintwood area. So it was obvious—certainly by the mid-70s, maybe late '70s—that things were not going well for the coal industry, for the people here. They said actually at the end of World War II, when the mining equipment came in, for every piece of equipment that came in, ten men came out of the mine because they weren't needed anymore. And that must have been a big dislocation.

So I guess all along there have been these bumps, little hints that things were not going well. Dante's population is now around eight hundred, we think. We're guessing. We don't have any census figures to base that on, but based on the survey we did ten years ago, that would be about right. In 1930, to give you a comparison, there were thirty-eight hundred people living here, and this was the largest town in Russell County. People have just had to move away to find jobs. And then as they retire, they want to stay here, but eventually poor health intervenes, and they've got to go somewhere else.

As I said before, people could not make their own decisions here. The coal company made every decision for everybody in the town. And as a result, once the coal company pulled out, Dante was left totally on its own, without a lot of direction. So people are inventing a process now, but you don't just leave nearly a thousand people with no hope. A lot of them are elderly, on fixed incomes. Many of them are widows of miners.

But we do have young people in the community. We have people who live here with their children. They may be the grandchildren of people who came here. But there is not a big youth population. There is no active school in Dante anymore. There used to be a white school and a black school—high schools. There were all the little neighborhood elementary schools. In every little holler you had your own school. And you see the schools just disappear and be shut down. And so it's a difficult problem.

Shirley Glass: It's just hard to believe we had a hospital and a company store. Everything you wanted was right here in Dante—the doctor, the stores, and everything. And now we don't have anything. And now everything is gone, and it really just breaks your heart because our town is dying. And along with that, so is everything that we own. Our houses are losing their value because Dante's not a bustling town anymore.

I live in the upper Bear Wallow section of Dante. I've lived here all my life. I was born and raised in the house—it just recently was tore down—here in Dante. My father worked for Clinchfield; well, he retired, or really he got disabled, from Clinchfield. He had black lung. And he worked for them like thirty, forty years, up into the '80s. It used to be, above where I lived was the tipple [structure where coal is screened and loaded into trucks or railway cars]. And they would wash the coal, and the creek would be black as coal. And we'd be playing, and sometimes we'd fall in the creek and get black as coal.

When I got out of high school, one of my first jobs was working in the company drugstore. And they had like a restaurant in there, and they would serve food every day to the people that worked in the office building. And they would come over every day and eat. And they'd have CPAs and different officials that come in from New York and different places. They would come over, and they'd always give us tips. That was real exciting for us because nobody gave us a tip but them. So we'd always count their money to see how much money each of us got. That was a thrill. My sister-in-law used to work in the company store, and my cousin. I would catch a ride down with my cousin to work, or sometimes I'd even have to walk home. But it was real exciting working over there, especially when the officials from up north come, so we could get some extra money. About $90 a month was all you made; that wasn't very much. We got a little discount, but it really helped.

When I was a little girl, we used to come to Dante to buy our groceries, furniture—anything that you wanted was at the company store. And at Christmas time they had a special place, and they'd open it up with toys, and you looked forward to that. And now that we don't have nothing, it's just really sad. Like grocery shopping, you have to go to St. Paul. Or most people go to Bristol or even to Norton or Wise to the Wal-Mart, but we don't have any shops like that. We have a little grocery store which you can go in and get emergency things, like milk and bread and smaller things. But Mark won't be here long, I don't think, if the buildings don't stay. Well, if the buildings don't stay, he can't stay. But I don't think he'll be here long either. Then we'll lose our little store. To get your hair cut, you have to go seven miles. Or you can go to Hanging Rock to a doctor.

I was born at home. Dr. Davis, the company doctor, come up. He would come by and deliver all the babies on the way up—there was a boy he delivered on the road below me; then he come on up and then delivered me. So he had two on that day.

Terry and Dean Vencil: Dean worked with him much longer than I did.

He was a basketball player from the University of Kentucky. He played for Adolph Rupp. He would stand in the old hospital. He could stand on the floor and take his foot and kick the top of the door.

What. Fifty years of age.

He did home deliveries, made house calls, took his nurse with him. Delivered babies, and they paid him with chickens and hams. He came there in '48, I believe.

He had people who were from Castlewood over there going to Dante.

I came to work in '73, at the clinic at that point. The hospital had closed down.

When I first came there green out of college, I had never done an EKG in my life. And that was one of the responsibilities of med-tech. So one Saturday I was there all by myself, and Dean wasn't with me to hold my hand. I had to do an EKG on a woman, and it took me about an hour to do that EKG. And Dr. Davis came out and said, "Well, hell, Terry, if you didn't kill her, she ought to live." He was one of those people that was bigger than life, sort of a John Wayne–type person. And everyone loved him.

Pete Castle: There used to be trucks hauling coal through here, mines work three shifts a day, miners running up and down all these hollers here. Tipples in Bear Waller, tipples in Straight Holler, a small tipple in what is known as Tunnel Holler. And now Dante is just a dead town. In the last three or four years, the company has tore down the old theater building, which was a historical site, and other company buildings adjacent to the post office and the Dante store and the old Clinchfield building. And not one newspaper out of the whole area here ever came and made a picture of the old town being demolished. Or no county officers ever offered any help to help save or restore the old theater building, which I consider an old historical site.

My dad was a coal miner. My grandfather brought him off of the Big Moccasin section, the Clinch Mountain area, in 1926 when he was sixteen years old. And put him to work in the mines when he was sixteen years old. This was here in Dante. The mines down through the years run three shifts a day, and in 1959 all work here in the Dante area was phased out and closed out at that particular time. The miners that the company wanted to keep, they sent them to the Moss 2 and Moss 3 area over at Carbo and Cleveland.

And then there was some miners that was instrumental in the union, and the Clinchfield Coal Company thought that they was hotheaded and what have you. And even though my dad was a mine committeeman, he was never rehired because of his interest in the union. And being a mine committee-man, the company said he was a troublemaker, and he never worked again for the Clinchfield Coal Company. That was in 1959. There was some they went ahead and transferred out of these mines; they let them come to these other mines and work. But the ones they termed as troublemakers was never able to be worked again.

I worked twenty years here in the Dante, Virginia, post office. And then the company in the early '70s, the Pittston Company, moved up to Lebanon, Virginia, and it hurt the Dante office because they didn't need as many em-ployees, and a rural carrier out of Dante, Nora, and Trammel at that particular time retired, and I started on a rural route in June of 1973. And I run a mail route out of Nora and Dante and Trammel for twenty-one years.

They said there was two men—Jim Camicia and Nick Camicia—they came out of Prestonsburg, Kentucky, where the mountains are so steep you have to lay down flat on your back to see the sun, and they said Dante wasn't an exciting enough place to have Pittston headquarters. And so they went up and bought twenty or thirty acres of land—it was in Russell County, but it was in the Lebanon city limits—and they built Pittston headquarters in Lebanon, Virginia, at that time.[1]

All down through the years, my brother Bill Castle and myself, Pete Cas-tle, and another band member or two, we've had a country and bluegrass [band] and played old rock music since back in the '60s up to the present time. Down through the years while they had the Dante Elementary School here in Dante, we've played fall festivals, spring festivals, and raised a lot of money for the Dante Elementary School. We took our band and played cakewalks and sessions for the fire department and rescue squad to help raise money, before the county ever give any monies to rescue squads or the Dante Volunteer Fire Department, which we started in 1969. I play rhythm guitar, my brother Bill played lead guitar, and then his son Dave played the bass, and his son Chris played the drums.

And then I played in a bluegrass band with Rick and John Phillips down through the years, and we went to Ralph Stanley's—a prominent musician here in this area—to Ralph Stanley's festivals. We have played on sessions between Ralph Stanley and Bill Monroe, and our band got as much ovation as Mr. Stanley and Mr. Bill Monroe. Ralph Stanley is out of the Nora area, back on the ridge between Nora and Coeburn. They have what they call the old home place back there. Every year they still on Memorial Day have a three- or four-day event back at his place back there.

I wrote an old blues song about my dad working in the coal mines in 1926 when he was sixteen years old.

Dad went to work in that coal mines, sixteen years old,
Dad went to work in that coal mines, sixteen years old,
He'll make a living for the fam'ly,
That was to be his goal.

Loading coal in a coal car, loading coal down on his knees,
With a pick and shovel, a carbide light so he could see,
Working in that coal mines,
Loading that old black gold.
Working in that coal mines,
Loading that old black gold.

My brother was a foreman, son of a coal miner too,
They worked in that coal mine trying to raise their fam'ly too.
Working in that coal mines,
Loading that old black gold.
Aye, working in that coal mines,
Loading that old black gold.

Loading coal in a coal car, loading coal down on your knees,
With a pick and shovel, a carbide light so they could see,
Working in that coal mines,
Loading that old black gold.
Aye, working in that coal mines,
Loading that old black gold.

When they have a revival, they say—that's the format for Free Will Baptists—"anybody got anything they want to say or a song to sing?" Usually, I take my old guitar and I get up just by myself, and the church will have a piano player, and then there is some churches has a church band, and they will play. Sounds great. My theory is a one-man band is like a one-legged man at ass kicking. You don't do much with just a one-man band.

I don't belong to no one particular church. Family and what have you entices me to visit different churches because the family, I've got different members that goes to different churches. And playing country and bluegrass music down through the years and singing gospel music too, and then I accepted Jesus Christ as my personal savior back several years ago. I attend church, not on a regular basis, but from time to time. Usually when I go, everybody in the area in the churches I go to always says, "Hey Pete, come on up and sing a gospel song." I do that and enjoy playing in church or out of church.

Catherine Pratt: The town's changed drastically. Years ago when I was little, we were very self-sufficient. We had a theater and a hospital and a doctor's office and the company store, had anything you wanted. It was a big thing in November to go down for the Santa train and all that. When we were children, that was just a big experience in our lives because we didn't really travel that much outside of Dante. Occasionally, mom would go up to St. Paul to trade and stuff. But the biggest part of it was done right there. But now since the mines pulled out, it's affected the railroad, and then we've just went down to nothing. There's just a little post office and a little store.

I was born and raised in Dante. My dad was a coal miner, and I married Jim Pratt. We went to school together all of our lives, through Dante Elementary, went on to Castlewood High School and graduated from there. His dad is a railroad man from Clinchfield Railroad. We've lived in Dante all of our lives, raised our children here, have two children. We live in a part that is called Ervin Holler, Straight Holler. So we just made our home there, and that's where all our friends and family originated from.

These hollers around here are very narrow. All the houses are built similar because it was a mining camp. On the backside of the houses was a creek, and then the row of houses and the road, the track, and another row of houses. So you just fit in right between two mountains. As kids, we just played in the road and on the tracks. That was our entertainment, to walk the rails and stuff. We knew when the trains come by you had to watch for them. You climbed hills and swung from the trees and played. It was just a way of life to us. We used to slide down the hills on shovels, pieces of tin. We made our own entertainment.

We didn't stay in and watch TV like the kids do today. When it snowed, we all got together and come off them hills and found us a path. We'd stay outside sometimes, twelve or one o'clock. Some of the parents stayed out. We'd build us a big bonfire and burn a few tires, stay out late, and sleigh-ride all day. We didn't freeze to death. Sometime we'd have as many as fifteen or twenty of us out there sleigh-riding. Mom sometimes would have hot chocolate, and we'd all go in and warm up a while, go back out, and hit it again.

Mom and Dad's house, there was a big trestle went right across the top of the house. So you laid in bed at night and feel the vibrations of the train and the house and pray nothing was going to fall off on top of you.

FIFTEEN

The Pittston Strike of 1989–90

Dink Shackleford: I remember strikes growing up, and there was picket lines, and it was tough for me at school. My dad used to tell me, "Pick one side or the other." There's no middle ground on this: "Which side are you on, brother?" the old song goes.[1] There's no straddling the fence. But as long as you picked one side or the other, people respected it. You had an admiration, and it was okay.

Dad's mine was union, but Uncle Tommy was the president of the union at that time. Really, my dad and them saw the union as a way that all their workers could get a retirement plan, and enter the union and work their final days, final fifteen, twenty years, get that union retirement. My uncle Red, on the other hand, was an outlaw in the family. He used to go company thug awhile, and then he would go union thug awhile. And, boy, he was just looked down upon in the family circles. Culturally and socially, he was just unacceptable. But if you picked one side or the other, it was okay. Some of my uncles picked the union side. As long as you picked one side and stood by it, you were okay, that was respected, and everybody knew where you stood.

My dad when he was little one time—I told you he was an orphan—they grew up in this coal camp, and there had been a big gun battle. Virgie, I think, was the name of the coal camp over in Harlan County, "Bloody Harlan" Kentucky. And there had been several people died and got killed. My uncle Dink, who I'm named after, crawled out of the house and crawled down the road and stole a machine gun from a dead guy and got back to the house. And after the gun battle, they sold it the next day. And he said they paid the rent for three or four months with that machine-gun money and stayed there for three more months before they had to go live with a relative. So he was kind of creative.

And my dad, for the orphan that he was and started working in the mines when he was fourteen years old, went to Berea for a year and a half and had to come back home and work. He couldn't make it on his own. So he was a pretty well educated man for the '30s, 1930s, and pushed education on me. Of course, he didn't think my sisters needed to go to school. They were just women and why do you need to go to school? You were just going to get married and have kids, in his mind. And they never pushed school.

My mother didn't want me to go to school. One of the hardest things I've ever done, I was getting in the car to go to East Tennessee State, and she was holding my arm saying, "Please don't go." And I had to kind of pull away from her and go to college. That's one of my worst memories I have is doing that. It was the hardest thing I ever done, and yet it was the best thing I ever done, because it opened doors for me and the opportunities for me to go on and achieve and develop a career.

But my sisters really had it rough. My older brother and sister, my brother Joe and my sister Sue were on the bus, and the school bus driver was going to put Joe off because my dad was a company man and put Joe off the bus, and my sister Sue hit him in the back of the head with a baseball bat, and knocked him out. There's a few stories like that in the family.

I'm the first one in my family to not look at John L. Lewis through a high-powered scope. That was a big thing for some reason. My dad and his brothers, when John L. Lewis would come to town to make a speech at any coal mines they were at, they would just fun around, you know, and look at him through a high-powered scope and say, "Boy, I could kill him right there." But never did, of course. And my wife's father was a union district representative and things, and I'd go to their house—and he was a big Republican—and he's got a picture of John L. Lewis and Ronald Reagan on the same wall, which I think is an odd combination. But, you know, it's kind of neat.

Frank Kilgore: During the strike, lifelong friendships came to an end, at least temporarily, because striking miners would be confronting the replacement workers and also particularly truck drivers who were trying to cross the picket line to haul nonunion coal. And there were some very bitter moments, and some shootings occurred. Fortunately, nobody got shot. Overall, during the Pittston strike of 1989 in southwestern Virginia, we were all very lucky in that no one was killed.[2]

There were a couple of people hurt, but no one was killed. When you compare that to some other strikes in the coalfields in the past, and even fairly current—with those strikes in West Virginia and Ohio—people were killed.

And then I remember the Greyhound Bus strike occurred right after the Pittston strike. And actually some of the money raised for legal defense fees in the Pittston strike was donated to the Greyhound Bus drivers' union. But one or more people in that strike were killed. So I think we are very lucky.

The miners were trying to save their jobs, benefits, and had gone for months without even a contract, which is the first time in the UMWA's history they had ever done that. So Pittston meant to have a strike, because they kept provoking the union until they ultimately had to strike. And they did it, I think, in an attempt to try to cut down their costs and recoup some money. And I think they did end up getting some money from the union, or concessions that saved them some money. And both entities were declining—the union was declining and Pittston was declining, at least its coal-mining sector.

I guess the Pittston strike was the last big UMWA national strike. The UMWA has gotten smaller and smaller as coal operations have used fewer and fewer people. And have become more nonunion throughout the nation, particularly out west. Out west, strip mines can produce huge amounts of tonnage with a lot less problems. You have forty- to fifty-foot-thick coal seams out there that are not the same quality as they are in the East, but they are so huge and have so little overburden that they can be strip-mined relatively cheap. So that has taken the place of a lot of steam coal from the eastern U.S. And Virginia has the best metallurgical coal in the world. And that's the real deep mine coal, the seams that has been here many millions of years longer than the younger seams closer to the surface. And because of its purity, it is used for coking. This is a process where you take coke and get the impurities out and use that coke that's left over to heat raw material, raw iron ore and so on to make steel.

I think this was one last attempt on Pittston's part to try to survive economically, and it certainly was the UMWA's best effort to keep together their organization. And that organization was much more cohesive than anyone imagined it would be. With a few phone calls, you could have from two hundred to five hundred people in one spot the next day. And that is power in a democracy.

That manifested itself in the write-in campaign of Jackie Stump in the House of Delegates. Jackie challenged the veteran delegate, Don McGlothlin Sr., whose son was the circuit court judge that had fined the union up to $64 million. Of course, that fine was eventually overturned by the U.S. Supreme Court. But if it had stuck and the union was forced to pay it, it would have bankrupted the union. So there was a lot of tense times.

Jackie Stump: I grew up in Russell County; I grew up in Honaker. It's a little community about thirty minutes from St. Paul and Castlewood. I live now in Buchanan County, which is about six or seven miles from where I grew up. From Honaker, we went to Buchanan County. My dad was a minister, and he took a church over there and went to full-time ministering. It's the Trinity Pentecostal Church there in Buchanan County, and he's still preaching. He's seventy-eight years old, still preaching. So I'm familiar with the area, traveled a lot in the area.

I had already signed up to go into service when I got out of school in '67. I went into the air force, spent four years in the air force. Came back, drove a coal truck for approximately, I'd say, about six months. And in April of '72, I went to work in the coal mines. I worked at VP [Virginia Pocahontas] 1, which at that time was Island Creek, later bought out by Consol [Consolidation Coal Company], but I worked at VP 1 in Buchanan County, up from the coke ovens in Buchanan County. I worked there until I was elected full-time secretary-treasurer of the district here. I was elected in '79, in May of '79.

So then I spent the rest of my life, I guess, in the UMWA. I spent time as secretary-treasurer; then I was elected president of the district. And then when the international executive board member retired, President Trumka appointed me international board member. I was elected to that my remaining time. And then they combined the districts in 1999, combined us with Alabama. So by [them] eliminating my job, I was eligible for early retirement. That happened in 1999.

At the time the Pittston strike started, I was the district president. The Pittston strike actually evolved and came about because of their decision to cut off healthcare to our pensioners and disabled people. And really when we were negotiating on the contract, we weren't making a lot of progress. But that was a decision the Pittston Company made, and that was the breaking point. And you know, we negotiated for, gosh, about two years it seems like even going into it, and also we kept working it seems like right at a year before we actually went on strike. But the final blow came when they cut the healthcare off to our people.

We had a rally in St. Paul every Wednesday night, and we had crowds, unbelievable crowds down there and from all over the United States, foreign countries. That was just the thing that everybody looked forward to on Wednesday night. We'd go down there and have our rally and keep our people pumped up and let people know. One thing that our leaders did—Trumka and Roberts—they kept the people informed. And I think that's one of the reasons things worked as good as it did, keeping people informed, letting them know what's going on, letting them know what to expect.

A lot of people wonder why Pittston did what they did, and I'm convinced in my own mind that it came down to a decision by one gentleman—Joe Farrell. I think he was vice president of coal operations. You'll never wipe that out of my mind. He was an old military guy, and he thought, "Give 'em a month or two and they'll be coming back, they'll be crossing the picket line." And after about the third month, he realized that he had made a mistake. He had misjudged it.

He was the one that came down—there for a while we wasn't at the table— Judge Williams had us all down to Duffield, both sides. Joe Farrell came in, and the judge wanted us to get back to negotiations. Well, we were willing to do that. Joe Farrell, instead of being in negotiations, the media caught him as he was going up the steps, and he was going up to watch a golf game.[3] Well, that played big. The judge at that time realized, "Hey, you know, the UMWA is not the problem." They had to enforce the law naturally.

All during the strike we won out in the media because if I was before the camera or Marty or Cecil or whoever who, we told the straight of it. We told what was going on. Pittston had a guy named Mike Odom [then president of the Pittston Coal Group]. And Mike's a good guy; I know Mike. But Mike wasn't the guy they needed on the TV because he didn't come across real good at all. And everybody just said, "He's lying, he's lying, he's telling lies." And nobody believed him. Like I say, I know him. He's a good guy. But he didn't come across good on the TV, and Pittston will tell you that right now, some of the old people still around. Mike just didn't come across good on the TV, so we won the media battle easy because we got on there and told what was going on, what was happening.

So the media picked up on that real quick, and everybody that was watching the news that had me on there, Marty, Cecil, whatever, and then they had Mike Odom. There wasn't no question about who the people believed. So we were winning that. Plus we were winning all of the support of the communities because the communities knew that if we weren't around, business and things for them was bad. But the thing about it is, down here, you take St. Paul, for instance. You go down there, and you meet ten people on the street. Out of that ten, at least nine of them is going to have some direct relations to coal mining, UMWA. So we won that. I think we all did a good job of telling it like it is, and not trying to create things or make up things—just telling it like it is. And I think it won out.

The strike as it came off was a surprise to everybody. We set down the night before we knew it was going to happen. Just like taking over Moss 3.[4] Well, we set down and worked out our plans, and each one of us was sent to different areas to hold a local union meeting. The guys that came to that local union meeting, little did they know that they was headed to Moss 3. Without stopping, see, we came in convoys, and we all hit there about the same time because we had to time our distances. So we hit at Moss 3 at the same time, then just took over. So everybody was informed. Nobody was told where they were going. And everybody was just told, "Get in your cars, and you follow me." And they did, and little did they know when they got there, they was going to be staying two or three days.

We had to do something. They were continuing to run the plant and things like that. So we just had to have something to really draw the attention to them. That was pulled off and nobody got arrested. Took it over and then Cecil Roberts, when he made the decision to bring them out—I remember when we went over there to tell them—they weren't happy. But he said, "We've got to do it; this is the way we do it." So that night we had a big rally, they mingled out in the crowd and came out and nobody got arrested. The leadership, like I say—Cecil stayed down there with us, and he was part of it. He was vice president at that time of the United Mine Workers. And when you've got somebody that high—he didn't have to, he could have instructed me or Marty or whoever who on what to do and keeping us up to date—but he came down and lived with the people. He was part of us.

So I think that's the reason he's got so much respect from the people because he didn't sit there in Washington and say, "Do this." He came down and was right here, everything that happened he was right here with it, knowing what was going on. And Cecil's one that's kept up with all labor issues. He's kept up with the issues, the things that the blacks had to go through with, things like that. And he's always been a believer that you could make a difference.

The goal that he had this time was to do civil disobedience. And it was a little hard to get that across to the coal miners. Coal miners are tough. Coal miners are sometimes headstrong. It took all of us working on it; we each had certain areas. Of course, Marty and I covered the whole area. But we had different people that was in charge of different areas, and they worked their people. And if they needed help, we'd go over there. But it took some time convincing people, because a lot of times people had never worked beyond a contract around there either. So we had to do that, and I think we done a good job—I'm talking about from the top on down to the last individual, we done a good job of telling them, say, "If you'll listen to us, if you'll do like what we say, we can win in the end."

And it took time to convince them to work without a contract. And then we came to the civil disobedience. Some of them didn't buy into it right off. A lot of them was reluctant to want to get arrested. And others, you couldn't keep them out of the road. They didn't care how many times they got arrested—they were there for a cause, and they were willing to do anything, go anywhere. But the civil disobedience was something that Cecil worked on, and he said, "I think we can win if we stick with it." And ultimately in the end, I think we won out.

Frank Kilgore: Our law firm represented the UMWA strikers in 1989 during the strike. When I was first asked if we would represent them, I asked the union how many clients do you expect we will have, and they said thirty or forty. And we ended up with sixteen hundred clients and three thousand charges to defend. Three hundred and fifty of them were felonies, everything from blocking the road to attempted murder. We tried cases in all the surrounding counties—Washington, Dickenson, Russell, Wise, Buchanan. So we literally shut down our civil practice and did nothing but criminal law for those two years. Even after the strike ended, we still had cases to finalize. It was about a year after the strike was over that we finished the last cases.

We had 428 people tried in one day in Russell County General District Court for blocking the road. Under Virginia law, if you are a police officer, to arrest someone on a misdemeanor you have to have, through your five senses, witnessed the crime. What they did, these people were laying in the road, the strikers and their sympathizers, and they had sets of state policemen, the biggest ones they could find, would carry them because they would just lay there limp. Carry them and put them on the bus, then took them to Blackford to process them. And then they were placed under arrest by a separate officer. So when they were putting on evidence through the officer that he arrested these people, we asked him did he see them block the road. And, of course, he had to say, "No, I didn't." So we got 428 cases thrown out in one morning.

I remember walking down the hall with my partner and the prosecutor. And 428 people were stacked in there, out in the road, and everywhere waiting on their cases. We came out and said, "We got you dismissed." And they all were cheering. And they were leaving, and I told my partner, "That must be a record for the most cases tried in one day in the United States." And that prosecutor said, "I don't know about that, but it's got to be a record for the most a lawyer's ever lost in one day."

The huge majority of the cases were "impeding traffic," "sitting in the road," "failure to disperse," but we also had those 350 felony charges, which were all either "damage to property" or "attempts to injure someone" or "injuring someone." So not everyone bought into the nonviolent advocacy. And, of course, the coal company said that the union approved it with "a wink and a nod." I never did hear the union advocate or union leaders advocate or approve of violence. And they had a whole separate entity set up that handled the defense; it was not the UMWA International that paid the attorneys' fees. They had a separate entity that took in donations and paid out for legal defense.

I think what made it easier for many local miners to buy into nonviolence, number one, there had been some changes in attitude—and we are talking about people who are the fabric of the community. UMWA members who were making middle-class wages, who were Little League coaches, deacons in their church, Boy Scout troop leaders, helped out with the school proms and every aspect of athletics and academics—they were the backbone of the community. And so by nature, by raising their children not to be violent, raising their children to pursue higher education, they themselves did not want to be seen to be violent.

Then you always have another element that believes in direct action, so that was that three hundred or so charges of violence, throwing rocks, and occupied buildings, cars—one time they rocked a state police cruiser—but most of those, and I'm not just saying this—were from West Virginia and Ohio, who came down to show the Virginia boys, who were a little too pacifist for them, how to really have a strike. And so we represented them too—they were from Alabama, Ohio, Kentucky, West Virginia. When they would show up, there was a lot more rock throwing and a lot more violence.

I'm not saying the Virginia boys didn't do any of that. I'm saying once the Ohio guys and the West Virginia guys started doing it, it was sort of a matter of pride that the Virginia boys had to sort of pitch in and help them. And so I saw a lot of that, and a lot of those landed in federal court through the criminal process because they crossed state lines.

There were a few funny things that happened. One that I remember specifically was this young man who came down to help the strike. He was from Pennsylvania, and he didn't know where the coalfields started and where they ended. And it's very abruptly marked by the St. Paul fault line: you go out of limestone country directly into the coalfields. Well, he hadn't even made it to Russell County. He was in Washington County, which has no coal, but he happened to see a coal truck drive by, going in the other direction. Those were truckers who happened to live in Washington County and came all the way to the coalfields to truck coal. And while they were trucking coal, they had Plexiglas over the windshield, over their side windows, to keep the rocks from coming into their cab that had been thrown by the striking miners.

When they got to the Washington County line, they felt safe enough to take the Plexiglas off because it was hot, and they couldn't get any air in there. So they took the Plexiglas off, and they were driving along. And this kid from

Pennsylvania sees this coal truck, and so he turns around and drives past them towards Abingdon, stops beside the road. And as they were coming up the hill there at Holston Mountain, you have to gear down, he threw a full can of Coors Light at them. And it went in one window, went across their noses, and out the other window. So he was arrested in Washington County with a felony charge of throwing a missile at an occupied vehicle. And so we had to try his case in a little bit of a strange territory that wasn't coalfield country. And I was a little bit afraid that the judges there may not be so accommodating or understand the culture that had developed over almost a century in the coalfields.

So we go before that judge, and he's real stern and real strict. And this kid from Pennsylvania had been held over for his preliminary hearing, held in jail. And we hadn't even gotten over there to get him out on bond because we had hundreds and hundreds of cases. So they bring him out of jail, and he's there, and we're trying a preliminary hearing. And I made a big point out of this driver of the truck and the passenger said it looked like a Coors Light can. And so I asked the judge to make them produce it. And he said why do they need to, and I said, "Well, they accused him of throwing a missile, and you should be able to produce the missile. We don't know. It wasn't in the truck, didn't hit the glass, didn't hit the truck. So all we have is two guys saying something went by their eyes, and it never had any impact. So I would like to know what it was; I think they have to prove that."

Well, the judge bought that argument. And he told the prosecutor, "You have to produce the missile." Well, they had no idea where it was at, or what it was. All they had was these guys saying, "I think it was a Coors Light can because I've seen many of 'em." And so the judge gave us a little break to go back and talk about it. And the prosecutor said, "Now, I'm not dropping this charge; I'm not letting him walk out of here with nothing." So we had it reduced to "littering." So it started out as a felony with a two-year minimum sentence and went to "littering," with a $25 fine. And when we paid the $25, that young man from Pennsylvania just grabbed me and hugged me right in front of the judge. And he said, "I'm going back to Pennsylvania." And he had never set foot in the coalfields, had never made it to the strike, he had had a felony charge against him, had his trial, got released, and went back home. I have always told people that we had every charge imaginable from "attempted murder" to "littering" in the strike, and that was the littering case I was talking about.

And we had some real rough guys on the strike line. Thirteen of them had been so aggressive that when the union and Pittston agreed to sign a contract, it was with the exception of these thirteen could not come back to work. And the union, I think, put together some makeshift work for them for a little while. And there was one guy in particular—his name was "Big Foot"—and I don't remember his real name, huge guy. He thought it would be a good idea to stand at the top of Hazel Mountain, which is probably the steepest primary road in Virginia, coming down into Dante from Dickenson County. And these overloaded tractor-trailer trucks carrying nonunion coal would come through there, about five, ten miles an hour, and then they would start down the steep side. And he walked over and ran along side the truck as it was just topping the hill and cut their brake lines with a pair of metal cutters.

Fortunately, this guy had a more modern truck that, as soon as the air pressure was lost, all the wheels locked up. Otherwise, he would have gone on over the hill and down through there, almost surely killed himself and whoever was in front of him. It took us awhile to get that case out of the way, because the judges were really upset over that. We set down with the prosecutors in a sort of end-of-the-month volume disposition of other cases, got his thrown in with the lot, then got him taken care of. We tried always to keep his in with a group of lesser offenses, so we could kind of compromise and get his taken care of. But he went out and got in trouble again.

What the judges did, which was very good, the first two offenses—if they were nonviolent—they took under advisement. The third one, they would try them. The reason I had to try to keep everybody's criminal record clean is under federal law, even if the NLRB [National Labor Relations Board] found that Pittston had caused the strike and had performed unfair labor practices, and they were ordered to take these striking miners back to work, if they had a strike-related criminal conviction, Pittston didn't have to take them back. Well, every one of them could have been in that situation. And so we tried desperately to always keep their name clean so they would be called back to work if the NLRB found unfair labor practices on the part of Pittston, ordered them to take them back. And so we worked feverishly to keep their criminal record clean. We didn't have any felony convictions of people we represented.

There was someone who did dynamite a coal facility, but the union wouldn't represent him. And he did go to prison. And some of the strikers got hurt. One nonunion trucker ran into four or five strikers with a pickup truck and hurt several of them. And we were very upset when the state police would not arrest the truck driver. We contacted the AG's [attorney general's] office, and the AG's office appointed someone else to look into it, and he was eventually arrested.

The UMWA was fined $64 million in contempt violations by a circuit court judge [Donald McGlothlin Jr.] whose father [Donald McGlothlin Sr.] was in the general assembly for twenty-something years. I was with Jackie when he was told by Cecil Roberts that he was going to run as a protest candidate in a write-in campaign for the general assembly three weeks before the election. So they just wanted to put together a protest so that they could emphasize to the public how rough things were in the coalfields. And it surprised them that the response was overwhelming. So they used their striking miners to go door-to-door to help Jackie campaign.

Jackie Stump: It's just like in coal mining. When we get a young guy in the coal mines, we like to tell him all kinds of war stories and kind of shake him up, and the troopers—the senior troopers—did the same thing to the young guys there. They had a lot of them scared, but I'm still friends with a lot of them. I met a lot of people during that strike. But they had them, and they were nervous. They hadn't faced crowds like they faced, so they were always quick to want to run to the trunk of their car and grab their shotguns, some of the younger ones. The senior ones, it didn't bother them; they knew how to react. But they had some of the younger guys, had them scared up pretty bad.

As far as the local police, we couldn't have asked for any better treatment. I got arrested and put in jail in Russell County. Well, I hadn't been in jail probably twenty minutes there, and the sheriff made me a trustee and put me out in the parking lot picking up cigarette butts and cleaning up everything. That way I got to talk to all the people that came in from all the different states that was in there, and all them came by there to see us. So I got made a trustee and was a trustee for seven days there in the Russell County jail.

They didn't overreact. They had to do what they had to do under law. They had to come and arrest us there for blocking the entrance to the courthouse. But they knew that they were going to be around forever here, working with us. So they knew how to treat. And most of the senior troopers did. I think, and I speak only for myself, I only ran into trouble with a couple of troopers. One of them was a lady that was twisting everybody's ears. And that was kindly uncalled for. And then I ran into one situation where a trooper didn't like the idea that a guy had called me up on the side of his truck, wanted to talk to me—he was a guy I knew. He got kindly upset about that there, and he was going to give me a hard time there, so we worked through that. And that's the only problem I had.

Because my job was really to try to work with them and to try to assure them that it was a different type strike—civil disobedience. If they were going to let us control all our people and have them in one area, between all of us that was working it, we could control them. But I'm telling you just like I told them, told the judge. If I can't have everybody in an area where we can try to control them, I can't control what somebody does a mile and a half up the road. And a lot of the incidents happened that way. And we tried to explain to them why we wanted everybody in one area, but they didn't want us to do that.

I'd never been in jail before. Being a preacher's son, I always got accused of being the meanest, but I never had any trouble with the law at all. The first time that I got arrested was when we was blocking traffic over there at Moss 3, stopping the trucks. I think there was something like 560 of us arrested that one day. And as I said, I was arrested one time for blocking the entrance to the courthouse over in Russell County, spent seven days in the Russell County jail.

And then naturally when we went to federal court over in Abingdon there, the judge asked us if we would go out and ask the people to stop picketing, which we couldn't. We were there for a cause, and we had to see it out. So we left Abingdon with U.S. marshals, in their custody, and went to Roanoke, spent thirteen days in the federal facility up there in Roanoke. So I called my dad on that night before. Our lawyers told us, "Pack your toothbrushes; you're going to jail. There's no way of getting around it." We had had a lot of meetings before we would be in court because we were in court a lot, and we'd always ask them, "What do you think?" "You'll be okay, no problem."

But that particular afternoon when we met and talked, they said, "Pack your toothbrushes; you're going." Me and Marty Hudson, who was another leader during that period of time, we and there was another gentleman, C. A. Phillips, that ended up going with us. So three of us went to federal prison up there and spent fourteen days. I called my dad the night before, and I said, "Dad, don't be surprised if you read in the paper tomorrow that I'm in jail." So I tried to prepare them for that because it was tough on everybody. You have to prepare people for everything, but he understood what I was out there for and was fully supportive, and said, "Okay."

When you go into jail, this was the thing about it. We knew that we could get out of jail, the lawyers could probably get us out. But I would hate to think I had to go to jail and didn't have a way to get back out, a ticket. Because I tell you, it was something that was interesting. The first night we were dressed in suit and ties, and they took us up there. And naturally they took anything—our belts and everything—but they put us in there. The first night we spent just on an iron crate-like thing. You laid on that—it was nothing except metal. And that wasn't too good.

But then they put us in the pod, and we were in there with the hardened criminals. I guess one of the best friends that I made up there, he taught me how to play spades and cards and things because that's about all there was to do. He was in there for shooting his father-in-law. You just meet different people, different walks of life. It was a place I wouldn't want to be. It's tough. There's guys that are there that are still there that we met. I'm sure they're still there. There was no chance of them getting out. So it's a little bit different in our case. We knew that at some point in time that we would get out.

So I see why people try so hard—it's a great thing—to turn kids around and catch them when they're early because there was a lot of those guys that we were in prison there with us that were young guys in their twenties or thirties that are going to be spending life in prison. It seemed like a real waste.

Matthew Kincaid: I got put in jail twice. I got put in jail over at Clintwood. And then around June, July, it was hot, and I got put in jail over here at Moss 3. I was blocking the roadway, blocking the trucks. They arrested me. I mean that courthouse was full. I'll tell you what. Thirty guys got away. Somebody got a rope upstairs in the courthouse—it was on the top floor. And they put that rope down the window and shinnied down the rope, and got away.

Now I'm gonna tell you. I'm gonna say it, now it's over with. But I threw a few jackrocks [two nails, sharpened at both ends, bent, and welded together such that when thrown on pavement, one point always sticks up]. A state policeman was sitting there watching me throw them, but he didn't know what. We was over here at the Chaney Creek, up in that holler. And the state police was following us; everywhere we go, they come. So we got to throwing snowballs at each other. But I was stacking mine up with jackrocks in it. When that tractor trailer come by, I throw it at the wheels. And when I do it, he would run over it. And you could tell.

Funny thing. State troopers was over here in Dickenson County. One was telling on the radio, telling state troopers not to run over no dead animals. He said, "You ain't gonna believe this. Here comes a terrapin across the road pulling a bunch of jackrocks, got UMWA wrote on it."

You can believe it or not. You've got talent in a coal miner. Have you seen any of the things they made during the strike? [Matthew finds a couple of small wooden shoes and a wooden cage with a wooden ball carved inside, all of which he made during the strike.] I carved that ball in there. You can't get it out.

One man had a chain. It was about as long as here to over there, that he carved out of a piece of wood. And made a chain out of it. One boy—we call him Knob, I don't know where he lives, he lives around here in Dante somewhere—he carved a rifle, and it looked like a Winchester, lever action. Looked just like one. And about got arrested too. Almost. Thought he had a gun.

Dean Vencil: I was arrested for sitting in the middle of the road. There would be fifty, seventy-five setting in the road. Virginia State Troopers arrested us. I was arrested twice, and I was put in a bus both times. One time they took us to Clintwood to jail, and the other time they took us over next to Honaker, over at Blackford over there to the state prison. They kept us over there, processed us, fingerprinted us, and turned us loose.

I went to jail a couple of times. Civil disobedience. That was our main objective to the whole thing, civil disobedience, and we were fined for doing it. But it was never paid. Frank was one of the lawyers and I can't remember— what was the guy's name? Mullins, I believe it was a Mullins. He left and went someplace, got married and left Frank. He was the last lawyer I talked to.

During the strike, I went to work for Fornier [factory brought to St. Paul as part of river relocation plans; later owned by Bush Industries and closed in 2003], at that time the furniture factory that was going in down here. And they sent us to Minnesota. And I went up there to Minnesota for a week and came back and worked for them until February. And when the strike was settled, I went back with Clinchfield.

And the strike affected the whole community. A lot of people in St. Paul stopped trading at the Food Lion because they were nonunion. None of their stores in the United States are union. We went around taking up donations from different businesses. Food Lion said they didn't give unions anything. So they just stopped trading there for a long time. And Food City wasn't here at that time. It was Piggly Wiggly.

And the oil company in town, he fired one of his drivers because he wouldn't go across the picket line. So the guy went home, and he talked to his lawyer. And the lawyer called Dave Buck, and Dave went to his house and gave him his job back. It's federal law; you don't have to cross the picket line.

Pete Castle: I was a mail carrier during the Pittston strike. There was areas that the state police, even though I was a postal carrier and had no affiliation with the union whatsoever, the state police blocked the road and wouldn't let me carry the mail on my route. I would have the police to write a statement so that I could take it back to the postmaster and show, because I had to, in carrying the mail, I had a specific route that would be covered with all roads and extensions numbered. And if there was a route that I had to deviate from, I had to have some source to say why I couldn't run that particular route on that particular day. And the state policeman, and we had, oh, hundreds of state police in at that time, and from time to time they would say, "Mr. Castle, you can't run this area today because we've got it blocked off."

I would have a group of miners that would cut a tree down across the road. And they would say, "Now here you are, the mail man, if you won't go through—you just stop and sit right here and let the traffic pile up behind you." See what they was a doing—it was coal trucks transporting coal from the mines or from a stockpile to the tipple, which they was trying to block. And from that standpoint, I would say, "Listen fellows, I don't have no quarrel with you people. My dad was in the union. I am union; I am with you people. Most of you are my friends, and I know you by your first name, and you know me."

"But I ain't got no dog in this fight. I have to deliver the mail." And there's been times when I took this old truck and put it in four-wheel drive and run over twelve inches high—bump, bump, bump—to get over it to go on to deliver mail. And jackrocks, they about broke me up because the route I was running wasn't a real high-scale-paying route no way, and they did put jackrocks out, not just for me but for other people, because I've had to run through them areas. From time to time, I would get a great big jackrock. And then I would have to, at my own expense, go to a tire company and have another tire put on. The government wouldn't pay for that.

Terry Vencil: There are emotional problems when you have strikes. You can't get your life settled. So schedules were a problem. When you take a very strong, independent individual—coal miners are very independent—and you strip him of his job or he doesn't have a job, his self-worth goes way down. We saw a lot of abuse within the family during strikes. This man didn't beat me, but a lot of coal miners took their frustrations out on their families. So you've got scheduling problems. You've got strike problems and emotional problems that go along with that. You've got financial problems. If the breadwinner is on strike, the family uses up their savings. We went through several small strikes where we would use up all our savings, and then as soon as the strike was over and he went back to work, we immediately started putting it back in savings. You know he's gonna come out on strike again. So there's this constant fear that the money's just not going to be there.

During that time, our son had already gone to college, and Dean was on the picket lines at night, so I was at home by myself. And the company had guards—Vance Security—that they hired to bring in teams of men who carried guns, and they would patrol our streets. They would ride down in front of our street to see if he had gone to work or whatever. And at that point we bought a black lab just to stay with me. And thought about naming her "Umwa." She ended up being Emmy Lou after Emmy Lou Harris, but hey, you know, saner minds prevailed. I was teaching at Abingdon High School at that time, and I was told point-blank if I was arrested on a picket line I would lose my job.

And I think, as the company brought in executives from far away, then the harsher they became because they didn't have roots in the community. So they tried to strong-arm a little bit harder. I know Debbie Penland, our librarian, her husband is in management and then a brother or whatever was in the union. So there was a big rift there. Yeah, families would have trouble. You talk about St. Paul and Castlewood having trouble [sports rivalry]; you can imagine a UMWA and a nonunion person sitting down at the same table.

Debbie Penland: It was a very difficult time for us at family gatherings. My father wasn't as civil as my brother. My father is still not very civil and friendly to my husband. Still, after all these years, I don't know whether he thought Tommy should just quit work or what he thought. A lot of hard feelings started then and weren't healed over the years. When we had family gatherings, Tommy usually just stayed away because that's what people talked about. And my brother went to jail a lot. My brother-in-law went to jail a lot. There was a lot of things that happened. One man's car was blown up in his garage at his house. I know they were scare tactics, but you never know when someone could be injured. And just like Tommy, he had an older car that he rode to work that my grandmother had given him. When you're throwing a rock through a car that's as big around as a baseball or larger, you don't know when you are away in the bushes, you don't know whether it might—they never did injure him—it could have gone through the driver's side instead of the back window. You never know.

My husband's vehicles were totally destroyed by rocks and bullets. And these were his friends that he had worked with for years and years and years. And relatives. I was always very supportive of my husband because I knew he had a job, and I knew what was expected. I did get annoyed with my family some. I did get annoyed because they didn't try to see that he had a job to protect and he had to go to work. When the strike was over and they got their contract, they'd go back to work. And he would be without a job. And many of the union men would call him and say, "Tom, you're going to have to stop 'em from working. You're going to have to do something." And he would talk and tell them, "There's nothing I can do."

Even on our vehicles at home, when we started to church lots of times we'd run over a jackrock. He'd always check the driveway and things, but they knew where the foremen lived. And so they put them around in the road everywhere. Several times when we started to church, we had to stop and get out, and he would have to change the tire. The company provided us with tires anytime that that happened, but it was still annoying and aggravating, especially when it happened to you every time you tried to go somewhere.

Our kids had a very difficult time at school because at that time in the '80s the majority of the kids' families were associated with the coal industry. Now the coal industry is depleted so that we have very few families here, even here at the high school, that have parents that work in the coal industry. But then the majority of families were associated with the workers, with the union workers. And then a few people were the salaried people's children. Our kids, my son, was in high school. He was in about the eighth or ninth grade. He was in several fights, people talking about his daddy. "Going to work anyway, he's a scab." But really, that came from their parents. And their parents knew the salaried people, they had to go to work. They knew that if they didn't go to work, they wouldn't have a job.

Jackie Stump: I hadn't really been involved that much in politics, not much other than just helping candidates and things. Cecil Roberts stayed on me and stayed on me. People had asked me before to run and get into it in the nomination process. Well, I didn't want to. I wasn't really interested in politics, wanting to do that at all. But Cecil stayed on me and stayed on me and stayed on me. And he didn't give me any relief at all. He said, "You got to do it." So I went to a rally out in Illinois, and one of the legislators from out there, and I don't remember his name—but he was there; he came out here one time—but we were talking, and he said, "The only way that you can make a difference is you got to be on the inside." And he said, "We can all be on the outside." And he said, "Unless you're on the inside, you ain't gonna make a difference."

Well, that kindly got me to thinking a little bit, you know. So when I came back, of course, Cecil was still on me to run. So finally, twenty-one days before the election, I said I would. The election was 1989 during the strike, November 7. I remember that because it's my mother's birthday, and my slide was number 7 that you had to push up to write my name in. So we ran a twenty-one-day campaign. I mean it was a write-in campaign, and we had plenty of people, we had issues, I had name recognition. I think when they was doing some of the polling, my name recognition for an individual was probably up in the low nineties. Everybody pretty much knew me. A lot of them knew me anyway. But being on TV, being involved with the strike, I have high name recognition. We had plenty of people to work, plenty of people to go out. So I had to do a write-in; it had to be a write-in campaign. But we had meetings; I traveled all around the area.

We had about 300 or 350 senior citizens at the John L. Lewis Building in one day. A lot of people have never dealt with a write-in. Most of your senior citizens are voters, so we were trying to get the feel, "Would they do it?" And I'll tell you what. I left there with a great feeling because they said, "Aw, we can do that. That ain't no problem." So the senior citizens, I felt comfortable with that, and then getting the other people out. There were so many great stories that came out of that, that I still run into people today, they'll tell me things that happened. I guess one of the best things I can remember coming out of that, there was a gentleman in Richlands, a Raven, I believe he was a Raven, and his mother cannot read or write. And she was in a wheelchair. But she practiced for two weeks on how to write my name, so she could go do it. So that is one of the things of why I'm so tied to the people. And I work for the people hard because stories like that—good things have happened to me since then and before then—but you know just to have people that will do that for you.

And then they all kid me, they said, "Most politicians go to office and then they go to jail. Jackie went from the jailhouse to the statehouse." They say, "He done served his time in jail, so he don't have to go." But we beat the opponent, a twenty-six-year veteran, beat him better than two to one. It was Donald McGlothlin Sr. Now his son was one of the judges dealing with strike cases and putting miners in jail, you know. And naturally I got a lot of votes that way. People were mad there. But as time has went on, I have realized a lot of people went out and voted because they felt like we could make a difference.

Even if I'm a politician, I'd go back out there. That's just the way it is; that's just the way I believe. My dad, being a minister, the only advice that he's given me as being a politician—he's told me two things. He said, "Always do the right thing, no matter how popular it is—if you do the right thing, you'll be all right." And he says, "Take care of the senior citizens and the kids; the people in between will be able to take care of theirselves." And I've tried to live up to that, but if I had to and knew that it meant going back out on the picket line if they cut healthcare to our people again, I'd be back out there with 'em. It wouldn't bother me.

I think what should have happened as far as unions altogether, we should have done this back when Reagan fired the air traffic controllers. That's when it really should have happened. Everybody should have joined together—our union would have done it. But some of the others weren't that . . . when we had this strike, and I give Cecil and Trumka the credit, they were able to draw in all unions from everywhere. And it made for something that showed that if everybody sticks together, you can win out. Now do you always win in a strike? Well, sometimes there's no winners even though you achieve what you set out to achieve.

I think there is no question that it had to happen because we couldn't leave those people sitting on the sidelines. Most of them had been the ones that had worked for our union and give us what we had. And just like my father-in-law, wasn't my father-in-law then, he had just gotten disabled over at Moss 3 in an accident, almost took his life. He was bedridden at that time but later was able to come out to the strike. And I met his daughter—and we ended up getting married—because they were out there picketing for him.

Terry Vencil: And there was wonderful music during the strike. Of course, you have a lot of gospel in the mountains anyway. Gospel and union songs, a lot of music going on.

Jackie Stump: I know the numbers of active workers are down. But as far as the union, the union is still strong. We're going to have a fish fry Saturday. There'll be all kinds of people. The numbers, like I say, of the working people may be down, but the union is still strong. Right now, in this area—and I represent union miners, and I represent nonunion miners—I wish they were all union, but I understand that a lot of people working today are nonunion because they have to work. They're scared. They've got a job and a lot of companies—not all of them—will say to them, "If you join the union, we'll just shut down."

That scares the individual if he's got a job and a family he's feeding and things, and so right now people are scared. But still in my own mind as I go out there and I travel and stop and run into people, the union and the sentiment of the union is still strong. It's just that right now our working numbers are down. The ones that are working in the coal mines, the ones that are not fortunate enough to be under a UMWA contract right now, they're scared, and I can understand. They're not going to take on losing their jobs.

I deal with coal operators all the time as being their delegate—there's issues out there that we all work on. I know if I can keep them working, then I got my constituents a working. If all the coal mines shut down, I ain't got nobody working. And some of them that's in these low seams are just making it, barely making it. So I think there's some reality to that. And naturally when people go into a mines, they want to make a profit. The companies that does good are the companies that makes a profit and will put some of that into their employees and equipment. They're the ones that's able to stay in business and do good. Now, not all of them are like that, but they are the ones that do the best. They are able to keep a steady work force and good equipment and make a little bit of money. If they're making it, they're keeping people working.

I was the person who introduced the coal tax credit in the state of Virginia. Well, a lot of people didn't understand why I did it, but it's plain and simple. We had to have an edge to keep our coal operators being able to operate. And we did it, and it passed. I'm pleased to think I got a hundred percent in the house and one vote against it in the senate, if I can remember—it was some time back. And they've come to me to make sure during the budget cuts that I'd go to Governor Warner and say, "Let's keep the tax credit off the table" because everything was being looked at. And I think Mark understood that this area he wasn't going to hurt the coal any.

So I think operators will tell you that I've been tough, but I'm fair. I hope they all say that. I think that's how I've tried to be. They don't hesitate to call me if they have a problem, and that's the way it should be. If you're their delegate, their representative, you've got to try to help them. Because if I keep them in business, I'm keeping people working.

Debbie Penland: My husband's granddaddy gave a 1954 Ford 150 truck to Tommy. And he and my son, they completely rebuilt it from chassis up, took it apart. They started on it right after the strike, and they finished up in about '96. And he and my son, they completely rebuilt it from chassis up, took it apart. It's in the garage, he shows it to everyone. It was a wonderful bonding experience for my husband and my son. And my son, I remember he was just about thirteen or fourteen, one whole summer he sandblasted it out. They bought a sandblaster, and he worked on it all summer long out in the heat. He'd have to wear long sleeves and a helmet and long pants because when you work that sand, it beats you up. They started going to car shows too and looking at other vehicles people had created. It took them about seven or eight years to complete it. My husband's granddaddy got to see it before he passed away.

The survivors are doing much better by getting along.

SIXTEEN

Changing Attitudes

Frank Kilgore: When we had the thirty-some beer joints and all the fighting, that was in the '40s and '50s and early '60s. And then after the last ones were closed down in the '70s, and as those people who really liked to yuck it up and have hard weekends, after they got older, they became more mature and their children didn't have a place to hang out and get drunk and fight. So the violence and lawlessness sort of left with that generation.

Plus, that generation was hard working—they worked in the mines, they worked in logging, they worked on farms. And the weekend was time to cut loose. They didn't drive to Bristol or down to Knoxville, and go to a ballgame or go out to Damon's. There wasn't anything like that available, so they clustered around St. Paul because it was wet, and they brought with them their tribal instincts from their community that they were going to fight somebody from another community. And so they'd clash here. This is where they met, this is where they fought, and that's how they entertained themselves. And back in the '50s and '60s, in the mountains, there was fewer things to do, to occupy you other than to hunt, fish, work, and fight.

And my contemporaries back then, we didn't have very many outlets. And we'd get together, and there would be words exchanged, and the next thing you know you are out duking it out. Now I see these young guys and young ladies at fifteen, sixteen, seventeen years old, they go on trips together, they go down to tri-cities. Their parents take them on trips together; they just seem a lot more relaxed than we were.

When I was growing up here, it was probably ten, twenty years behind the rest of the nation in attitudes towards sex. And so you just didn't have the opportunity to do anything but go out and have a war. Or a lot of time, you were fighting over a girl, who was sitting at home while you were out here

143

duking it out. And she was kind of, I guess, in the catbird seat waiting to see who won. But even if you won, you went to her house and sat down with her parents and courted and sparked a little bit, and that was the end of it. Be frustrated and go back out and fight.

I've tried to explain this to my wife [a juvenile court judge], and I think she finally understands that young men, when they are driven by their hormones, are going to fight, they are going to do something when they get together. Now, I am afraid that drugs have sort of replaced fighting, Nintendo, and, of course, you don't have all the inhibitions about sex that you had back then. And people say that's good or that's bad, but I think, looking back on it, I had rather had a girlfriend than fight.

I guess in spite of all the roughneck things that went on on the weekends, the core of citizens in St. Paul itself had a pretty good idea about organizing the town for civic purposes and having a good school, and churches are strong here. And we have a pretty cooperative attitude, even among differing political forces. And if we have a difference with, say, the mayor or town council person, we know each other so well, we can just say, "That's just so-and-so; that's just the way he is." Instead of saying, "We're not going to work with him" or "He's no good" or "She's no good" or "She's stupid" or "They're arrogant" or whatever. So what?

So it's a pretty progressive attitude, and we have some very progressive citizens here, some of whom have moved into the area and brought some fresh ideas, have a different perspective, and they have taken a lead role in the community development. And then we have a lot of native folks who are proud of the history of the area, and of St. Paul in particular. And so I think, overall, we like to work things out.

In recent years, our entire middle class of wage earners has been decimated by the decline in the coal industry. Coal miners, because of the UMWA and the other efforts, were the middle-income wage earners in the coalfields. They spent money for recreation and pleasure and things that make an economy go. That has declined radically since the '70s and '80s with the overproduction of coal out west and, worldwide, the lowering of use of high-grade metallurgical coal. All that has really hurt Virginia. Plus, because Virginia had such lax standards in the past, coal operators concentrated here and got out the best coal early on. And now we are running out of good coal reserves.

It's just a quadruple whammy. So we can't rely on coal very much in the future to support our general population or middle-income needs. What we have now, we have a lot of workers who have left the coalfields and gone to other states or other parts of Virginia, and we are left behind with very little middle-income class structure, and that's what's hurt our economy. We have a lack of disposable income circulating through the local economies. And that's why our coalfield governments, our regional governments, have put together economic development projects and initiatives to try to give us an alternative to coal mining.

In fact, the attorney general [at the time of the interview, Jerry Kilgore] has appointed an energy advisory committee that is made up of roughly equal parts coal and gas producers, union representatives, and people from the conservation community. And they're sitting down together. Those are leaders in the industry who believe, now it's engrained in them, that the environment, quality of life, are important issues, and actually take pride in how well they are doing. That is a huge improvement over the 1970s and prior to that. It used to be do or die. And now the survivors are doing much better by getting along.

One conclusion I've reached after decades of community involvement is that people—particularly of central Appalachia, but Appalachia overall—have been stereotyped by the national media and international media in such a negative way for so long that some of our residents actually buy into that stereotype and feel like they can't accomplish great things. On the flip side, we have a lot of folks who are very intelligent who leave the area. And what we have done over the years is export some of the nation's brightest entrepreneurs, educators, military personnel, and they have gone into other communities and helped build them. But one instinct that most Appalachian people have is a yearning to come back home at some point. So we have a high rate of people, after they retire in their chosen field somewhere else, coming back.[1] And we are encouraging our young people to stay and help build our economy from the inside out.

But I've also noticed that our region is much more welcoming of people not from the region coming in and wanting to help than we used to be, because I guess the old fear was that most of the time folks coming in were here to rip off the coal or the timber. Not to say we weren't willing, greedy sellers of our heritage, because we thought our ancestors, and today people still think, "I'm gonna make money from this; why care about the environment?" So we have our own problems with some of our own natives about that attitude, get the money and run. And that's true across the world; that's just human nature.

But I'm seeing a turnaround in the attitude. The Nature Conservancy had a lot to do with that, coming in in a not-intrusive way and pointing out to us what a unique treasure we have here with the Clinch River. I was born and raised here and didn't know it was the most biologically diverse river in North America, or continental North America. It used to be full of trash, full of black water from the coal processing plants. And how these mussels lived through that I don't know, except north of the coalfields are the sources of the Clinch River. I guess the mussels just held on there until they could gravitate down the river as it cleaned itself. So we're still struggling with that, getting people to keep it clean, quit throwing out trash, quit putting petroleum out where it goes in the river. And our group, Mountain Heritage, has taken a very forceful position on that. We've sued people for it.

Lou Ann Wallace is the chair, and it's made up of some community leaders. We've gotten funding to eliminate straight pipes in the Lick Creek watershed, which is Dante, Honey Branch, and that area. It's one of the most polluted major watersheds into the Clinch River. We figure if we can clean it up, then any of it can be cleaned up. So we are eliminating straight pipes, getting more people to hook up to the sewer line in Dante, cleaning up dump sites. That watershed had the largest illegal dumpsite west of Roanoke. And we got it cleaned up.

Some people threw their garbage down there anyway. We found out who they were, sued them, and got a $6,000 judgment against them for throwing down four bags of trash. And we highly publicized that, and now there's not a candy wrapper on it. So our group believes in a carrot and a stick. And when the carrot doesn't work, you take it off and use the stick. And you have to do that. We'll put in the paper, "We've got this money to replace straight pipes; come see us." Well, if you don't come see us, and you're illegally letting it go into the creek, we're sooner or later going to the health department and say, "Make 'em do it."

That's where most state agencies, federal agencies, and nonprofit groups draw the line. They don't want to force anybody to do anything. Well, if the money's out there, the opportunity is there, the incentive's there, and you still won't do it, then you're a butt hole. And, you know, I'm tired of coddling people, and they just set around and say, "We're helpless, we're helpless." We're making it easy for them. And if they won't go drink the water that we lead them to, then we're going to do something about it. Because I'm tired of people saying, "I'm poor, and I can't do it."

Well, I was poor too, and I understand that. But we're not asking them to pay for it; all they've got to do is sign up. And if they're too hardheaded or lazy to sign up, and they're breaking the law and they're polluting the river— which is the water supply for the municipalities up and down the river—then I say it's time to get tough. And so our group has been very aggressive, and it shocked a lot of people.

People always talk about TVA coming down on them, EPA coming down on them—we've got an instance here in St. Paul where we have an auto junkyard right across the park in the floodway. Every time it floods, water gets up in the gas tanks and crank cases and floats petroleum products down the river right above the intake for St. Paul's water supply. I've called TVA, EPA, the water control board, DEQ [Department of Environmental Quality], the Corps of Engineers, and nobody claims jurisdiction.

It is an old folk story. It's a folk tale that the environmental agencies are so hard-core and so pro-enforcement. In the thirty years I've been involved in environmental issues, I have yet to see an environmental agency really take the bull by the horns on very serious, imminent threats to the water and the community and do something about it.

> We started to work with a couple of
> towns, . . . one of which was St. Paul, . . .
> not just for the town, but also for the river.

SEVENTEEN

Women, Conservationists, and the Economy

Debbie Penland: When you look at St. Paul, you think, "The population's a thousand. It probably couldn't support businesses." But the thing about it is, we're a mountain people. The people in Dante all buy everything here in St. Paul unless they want to go to Abingdon or go on to Bristol. And if you go on past Dante to Nora and to Trammel and all the way across the mountain over into Haysi, people from all those communities and all those hollows and all up in there in those mountain areas all come here to buy groceries. That's where they come. And that's why we can support a larger base. And then the Castlewood area, the people in Russell County and that Castlewood area and all the farms and mountains and people who live over in there, either they come here or they go to Lebanon.

They will come to St. Paul to eat. And that's why the Burger King and Hardee's and these restaurants have been supported so well. They'll come to the doctor. You can't get into the doctor at St. Paul hardly. You have to wait for hours. We have two medical facilities right here in the community, clinics. Our banks in this area are well supported by people that live in the mountains around. We have three banks in St. Paul and two banks in Castlewood. And they're all well supported because people want to bank in the community closest to them. And any other service would be well supported—lawyers, any professional people. People from the mountainous areas would rather come to home, to St. Paul, than go to a larger place like Bristol or somewhere they don't know.

Mountain people want to do business with people they know. I know because I'm one. I'd rather do business with someone that I can talk to, that I can see, than someone over an automated system.

LeRoy Hilton: Used to, we used mussels as fish bait there was so many of them. We'd set trotlines and catch the red horse and what not, and the river was just teeming with fish. Used to, you could legally shoot fish. And I've seen twenty or thirty men stand on the car bridge, Bickley Bridge that runs across the Clinch River, with high-powered rifles shooting fish. And the state record is something like sixteen pounds for a walleye pike. Clinch River and the New River are two of the rivers in the state of Virginia that carries an abundance of walleye pike. And I've seen a man carry up the street on his back—he'd have a twenty- or twenty-five-pound walleye pike. Now the state record is like sixteen pounds. And this was common—the many varieties of fish that you could find in Clinch River.

And in 1957, they had an acid spill from the coal company. And it killed everything in the river—turtles, everything you could think of, there was nothing left. Since then, they've restocked it, but the river's not like it used to be. I could go catch any number of bass, red eyes, walleye pike. It was a common thing. If you wanted a mess of fish, you didn't have to store them up. You'd just go every afternoon and catch you a mess of fish. There were that many.

Well, I got up yesterday morning. It was sixteen degrees. I was missing fishing, so I went fishing at Whitetop [Mountain] yesterday morning. It was sixteen degrees. You throw your line out—I'm telling you the truth—when you'd wind it in, and the water would get in the guides of the rod, it would freeze. You'd have to swish it in water to get the ice out of it. And I caught trout, you know. We go fishing at Whitetop Mountain. I may be eighty-one years old, but I don't even know where a senior citizens' center is. I just don't have time to fool around with them old folks. I've got things to do.

Bill Kittrell: We came here because the Clinch River has more rare species than any other river in the United States. It's the number one ranked river for biodiversity. So what we are trying to do is conserve the river and the freshwater mussels that live there and the fish and all the other critters that are there. What you are looking at there are the freshwater mussels. There are about five or six in that box there that are federally endangered species. And one or two of them occur in this area, and it is the only place in the world where they are found. Some of these will live to be about seventy or eighty years old. In Mississippi and Alabama and some parts of Tennessee, some of the more common ones get to be about the size of a dinner plate, get to be very big.

And they have found that nothing makes such a perfect pearl as the seed from a freshwater mussel shell. Now these—the ones we have around here—

are so rare that it's actually illegal to collect or harvest or even have any of these without a permit. We have a permit to have those for educational purposes. So what we are trying to do is protect the rivers and the things that live in the rivers.

The Nature Conservancy is a nonprofit organization, and our mission is to preserve rare plant and animals around the world. We used to do that primarily by buying land and setting up nature preserves. We have around two million acres of nature preserves in the United States. We have, I think, about thirty-five preserves in Virginia. And so what we've done primarily is acquire land or use real estate to protect and set up these preserves and manage them and do research and so forth. And we've got ten preserves here in southwest Virginia, various islands and preserves along the banks of the river.

In far southwestern Virginia, we are sitting in what you might call an epicenter of biodiversity. Of course, nothing compares within the U.S., nothing compares to Hawaii, but here in southwest Virginia we have more rare species than anywhere else in the continental U.S. Not many people know about that. And that extends all the way up, up the mountains on into Bath County [Virginia] and further on up toward Maryland and West Virginia. So we opened an office here in 1990.

But obviously if you own an island in the river, you don't really control what goes on upstream of that island. Maybe we can protect that island, do research there; maybe we can keep the trees from being cut down or so forth. But certainly if a truck turns over upstream, there's not a whole lot we can do about that by owning that island.

So several years ago, we started to work with a couple of towns, a couple of places around here, one of which was St. Paul, to work with the community to develop programs for economic development and community revitalization that are good, not just for the town, but also for the river. And it so happens that we have a couple of preserves not too far down river from St. Paul. So we got interested in working with the town there to help them promote economic development and community revitalization that's good for the town and also good for the river too—things like a canoe access launch, like the Sugar Hill and Clinch River trails, things like a river festival, the Clinch River Festival that they will have in May.

The problem that we have around here is that southwest Virginia— whether we like it or not—has one of the highest unemployment rates anywhere in the country, and one of the highest poverty levels too. So what we are trying to do is protect these rare species, but a lot of people don't have a whole lot of concern for that when they don't know where their next meal is going to come from. So how do we combine those two things together? We certainly can't expect people to not want to have jobs, sacrifice their jobs and their lifestyle in order to protect the river. So our mission is to figure out ways to promote economic development that's good for the people and good for the environment.

Lou Ann Wallace: My mother and father saw that I had a high school education. But after that, we girls weren't really encouraged to go on. Not that my mother would say, "No, don't go." That just wasn't encouraged. I married young. I like to say that I was a child bride, but I wasn't. I married at seventeen, had my first baby at twenty, so I was too busy being a mom and raising children. So the three children came one right after the other, just get out of diapers and go right back in. And then after my children got big enough to go to school and take care of themselves and that sort of thing, I started thinking about doing something as far as college education.

My mother was an environmentalist and didn't realize it. She is just one of these people that has a love of nature, a love of the birds, a love of the butterflies, just a love of her surroundings. And it just bothered her a whole lot when we had a lot of trees that were being cut and they were being logged, and my mother would go, "This is tragic, this looks awful." And all through that time, she was telling me things that I guess it was kind of registering. And she felt like she couldn't make a difference.

And she instilled in me that I could, I think, just because she was upset over things. She wasn't real outspoken, but just little things that she would say along the way kind of made me realize "Maybe I can make a difference." So in a roundabout way I met up with Bill Kittrell, director of the Nature Conservancy's Clinch Valley program, through a really wonderful project that he had brought to the Chamber of Commerce of Russell County in '94, somewhere in there, maybe '93, '94.

St. Paul Tomorrow was kind of my vision for the town. I think it was '98 or '99. I was talking to one of the councilmen here in town, and kind of voicing some concerns and some opinions that I had, and telling him, "This has possibilities; we just need to further this." And I was in Yellowstone Park, and my mother and I were talking on the cell phone, and she said, "I'm reading in the local paper that you have been put on the town council." And I said, "No." And she said, "Yes, you've been put on the town council while you've been gone."

So by the time I got back into St. Paul, I was on the town council, and we were ready to have a meeting. So we went to a couple of meetings—this is a once-a-month deal—I remember this just as plain as it was yesterday. We kept putting a roof on the fire hall. And so I would go home, the first night, and my husband said, "What did you do at town council?" And I said, "Well, we were working on trying to get a roof on the fire hall. And we talked to contractors and bid it out."

And so the next time I went to town council, we were putting the same roof back on the same fire hall. And I was going, "You know, there's needs here. There's store fronts that are standing empty. There's people that are moving away. There's property that needs to be addressed." And at that time we had some logging practices done over at the Oxbow Lake, and it was done by the Forest Service. But it just looked—awful. And a lot of people were going, "Gosh, that looks awful." It was a big clay mud hill over there.

I thought, "Get over it; move on. Let's do something to really change the place." To work on what we have, to address the needs of the poor, and to address the needs of the people who are affluent and want to leave. Bring the two together somehow. So I came home, came back to the office that next day after the meeting, and I picked up the telephone. And I called Bill Kittrell, and I said, "Do you have any money anywhere for anything?" I said, "We have put a roof on the fire hall for three months, and I'm sick to death of it. Can you help me?"

And that's exactly how I put it to him because he and I knew each other well enough that I could just say that. And, lo and behold, he came up with some sort of a little program where there was five communities, and it was "compatible economic development." And so he came up with that, and we had to apply for it, we had to write a mini-grant. And we were one of five communities chosen in the entire United States to receive a $10,000 grant. And from that, we had to pull leadership together, had to have visioning projects. So St. Paul Tomorrow was officially launched.

And we have progressively gone from $10,000 and nothing, as far as no organization or anything, to a nonprofit organization. We have our 501c3 [nonprofit, tax-exempt status], we're legal and all that good stuff, and we can apply for grants ourselves. I can't tell you exactly how much money we have been awarded over time, but I'm thinking it's real close to $200,000. We got about $75,000 to renovate what we consider to be the first and oldest house in the town of St. Paul. And that was called the Brown House, which is now called the Railroad Museum. We haven't officially named it; we just lovingly call it the Railroad Museum because it's still a work in progress. The interior of it has been finished as well as the outside. A small committee is working to put railroad paraphernalia in there or have traveling art shows.

LeRoy Hilton: I used to walk through the woods and the streams, and it was so pure and beautiful. When I was hunting, I could walk in the woods and

I'd get thirsty and lay down in any little creek and get me a drink of water. Now, you can go all day and not even find a drop of water in the mountains. And that's the big change that's happened now. The environment is absolutely being destroyed by the timbering and the mining.

Well, there now are regulations for the coal mines—they now have to try to put the contour back as it was, and they do have to fertilize and seed it and put the vegetation back. It is a lot better now. But the biggest thing I see is this clear-cutting. The erosion—they have done nothing that I can see because I can go and see a mudflats now in the streams that I used to see beautiful clear water and fish in, and I don't see that any more. You can't stop the erosion if you cut all the trees. There's no way of doing it. Some of them do select cutting now and leave some of the fruit-bearing or the nut-bearing trees for the animals and whatever. But mostly when they let you clear-cut, there's no way of keeping that mud from washing out of that mountain and destroying the streams. And that's where it's going to go—into the streams.

Bill Kittrell: A lot of private people—folks like you and me—own land around here. We own farms, we own timber. For many people, that's a source of income in order to make a living—harvesting timber and trying to get the money from that. But a lot of folks don't want to do it unless it is done exactly right from an environmental standpoint. So we created a forestry program, which is called our Conservation Forestry Program. The idea is that a landowner can enroll their forestland into this program with the Nature Conservancy, and we appraise the value of that timber. When they enroll it, they then receive a dividend payment—4 1/2 percent of the value of the timber.

It's kind of like a savings account that you might have in a bank. If you've got a hundred dollars in the bank at 4 percent, then you are getting four dollars a year off of that. The same thing applies to this timber bank, to this forestry program. They enroll their forest into our program, and if they have, say, a hundred thousand dollars worth of timber in it, then they get four thousand dollars back a year. The interesting thing about it is that the Nature Conservancy will actually, in order to be able to make these payments, we are actually going to be out there harvesting timber on some of these properties in a way that is very sustainable and very carefully done. Our thinking is that we are going to do it in a way that's probably more environmentally friendly than just about anybody else that's out there.

If somebody wanted to harvest the trees themselves and do this themselves and not do it necessarily in an ecologically minded way, they might be able to get more like 10 percent a year if you average it out. So if somebody is interested in making a whole lot of money, they're probably not going to go with this. But if they want to make some money and have it managed very well, then this might work for them. And so for people interested in getting a little bit of money off of their timber land in a regular way every year, having it managed very carefully and very sustainably, and protecting the environment at the same time, this might be a program for them.

In general, most people around here own maybe 150 acres, and maybe 75 or 80 of that is in farmland, pasture—maybe they grow a little tobacco—and then the other 60, 70, 80 acres is forest. And most cases, they don't have the time or ability to really manage that forest well. And so that's what this can offer to them, is better management, a kind of liquidity, in other words annual cash that they can use instead of just somebody coming in and cutting it down at one time. They get this every year, and so they can count on that.

We have a forester on staff. We have guidelines or a manual that we use, which tells what's allowable and what's not allowable. It will also be certified by a third-party organization called the Forest Stewardship Council, which is kind of like the green label for forestry, kind of like organic forestry. So there's going to be somebody else kind of looking over our shoulder to make sure we are doing it right, doing what we say we're gonna do.

Frank Kilgore: Virginia is one of the few states in the nation that does not have mandatory best management practices for timber. I can give you an example. If I want to disturb a quarter acre of my own property, and by disturbing I mean tearing away the overburden other than for agriculture, if I want to excavate a quarter acre to add a room or build a garage or put in a tennis court, whatever it is other than gardening, I have to get a soil erosion control permit. Or I could clear-cut five thousand acres in Virginia and not have a permit or put up a bond. And literally, I don't have to water-bar or grass-seed the roads. I don't have to plant any of the trees back. I don't have to put any sediment ponds in. All I've got to do under current Virginia law is not run my equipment up and down the creek and not leave huge amounts of scrap timber in the creek. And that is unacceptable.

One of the major sources of erosion in the coalfields right now is logging. Coal operators have to put up huge bonds. They have permits. They have engineering, pre-engineering permit plans. They have sediment ponds. They're under bond for ten years. A timber operator can go right next to that bonded, permitted site and tear the holy hell out of the piece of land, crisscross it with roads, not water-bar, not seed them, no sediment ponds, muddy the creek for weeks, and not answer to anybody. So it's a disaster. The steeper the slope, the more it's a disaster.

And I've been working for years trying to get the voluntary best management practices made mandatory, because a voluntary BMP is like a voluntary speed limit. Nobody's going to pay any attention to it. So we're working on it. In fact, next week I'm taking a VISTA [Volunteers in Service to America] volunteer with me, and he's got a calendar made up of one of the worst jobs around here, worst logging jobs. We're going to hand it out to all the legislators, let them know what's going on over here. It's a long process in Virginia. Virginia never changes laws overnight, or over decades. It's just a long, long process. You have to be tenacious, persistent, and patient.

So I'd like to see us get a handle on that before we really push a wood-based industry because it's been a major source of pollution for our streams and watersheds. But that is an economic potential if we could ever get a handle on how to do it correctly.

Bill Kittrell: One of our partner organizations is called Appalachian Sustainable Development, and it's a local nonprofit organization that works in two areas. One is sustainable agriculture and organic farming. And the other is sustainable forestry. And just outside St. Paul, they have a solar wood-drying kiln that they built recently, and it will process and dry boards that are sustainably harvested. It will dry them using solar power rather than regular electricity. So we are planning on working with them to process a lot of what we harvest locally, so we are creating jobs locally and adding as much value locally as we possibly can. And then we hope to be able to funnel the boards and the wood into local furniture makers and other people who are trying to make a living.

A lot of what we are hoping to be able to do with this wood is to develop partnerships with a couple of furniture makers around here, and there are several who are making very nice furniture, handmade furniture. In fact, we've got one guy who's going to be making a table, a conference room table for us, out of some of the wood that we harvest. But we think we might be able to tap into some markets that we think we have because of the Nature Conservancy membership. Perhaps members might be interested in or willing to buy a piece of furniture that was made from wood that was sustainably harvested.

We will be harvesting, not for what people want, but we will be harvesting for what the land needs. And so it's kind of different in the sense that, if we have five thousand people wanting kitchen tables, we are not going to go out and cut down necessarily enough wood for five thousand tables because people want those. We are going to harvest what we think needs to be harvested. Maybe that's a hundred tables, maybe it's five thousand tables. It's more driven by what the forester says the management should be, not based on what people want.

All along the Appalachian Mountains is a major eastern corridor for migrating hawks and raptors. And you can go out there on an October day, and you will see thousands of hawks, broad-winged hawks especially, just flying down the mountain range on any one day. They follow that all along there. I moved here from Washington, D.C. I was living and working there. A lot of my friends there said, "Why are you going to southwest Virginia? There's no culture there, there's nothing to do."

I was coming from Washington, where there is a different meaning of culture there in terms of museums and so forth. And I had always wanted to move to the mountains, the Appalachian Mountains. And when they kept saying that, I would say, "Wait a minute. There's probably as much or more culture, really, here—it's just different. It's more raw, and it's more in its basic form in many ways." Music is extremely rich around here. If you've not spent much time in the western part of Virginia in the Appalachian Mountains, then that's part of what you will pick up.

EIGHTEEN

Education and Youth

Terry Vencil: We have been working on the Estonoa Learning Center proj-ect—small wetlands about three minutes' walk from St. Paul High School. And trying to make people aware of what wetlands is and what it does. We don't find a wetlands in the mountains very often. And most of the people in this area don't know what a wetlands is. They look at it, and they think it's just a boggy place that you need to drain and make it productive. And they are precious. Estonoa is a liver for the river.

It collects all the water runoff from the mountains around us. St. Paul sits in a karst valley. Originally, we were one great big limestone block, and this wa-terway cut its way through this limestone block. That waterway is our Clinch River. And over time it eroded out this limestone block until you had a cave, nice little cave with a stream running through it. And then over time the top of the cave fell in, and we are situated in the bottom of that karst river valley. So all the water comes down off the mountains into our little karst valley. Well, Estonoa is a small place where a lot of water comes into. It sits there and then slowly filters into the Clinch River, our water source.

So it keeps a lot of particulate matter from rushing real rapidly into the river. Now this is good for us because you know where we get our water—the Clinch River. And it's also good for the mussels that live in the river. Those little guys are sitting there, they're filter feeders, right? So if they get all that particulate matter rushing down into the river, they end up dying. Estonoa collects all the particulate matter that would end up in the Clinch River, not all of it but a whole bunch of it. A lot of the pollutants—the fertilizer runoff and pesticides and all that—so it really is a "liver for the river," absorbing all the alcohol and other stuff that you put into it.

LeRoy Hilton: St. Paul High School is still one of the smaller schools in the entire state. They've got less than two hundred students, and they're very competitive in their sports. And their PACE [Partnership for Academic Competition Excellence] team—we call it the brain trust—is very well known for just about defeating all the consolidated schools in the county. It's a matter of record that St. Paul nearly always wins the PACE teams competition every year. They have moderators who will ask math questions, science questions, English, so forth and so on. And it's like the quiz shows you see. And St. Paul, the brain trust we call it, they have just about defeated all the other, larger schools.

I honest to goodness believe that the smaller schools give more time to their students. I think you give more attention to the smaller classes. I really think it contributes to a better education and a better understanding because you are giving more of a personal touch to the fifteen or twenty than you would on a forty or fifty basis.

Tom Fletcher: Being SOL [Standards of Learning] accredited means we have met the required testing grades for accreditation as described by the state across the board in the various curriculums. The first year we were fully accredited was two years ago. They did some advanced testing for a couple of years, and we met the criteria then. And then we met the criteria as it continued. But the first time it counted for accreditation was two years ago. And we were, if I'm not mistaken, one of five or six schools the first year west of Roanoke that was accredited. We are also one of the very, very few where the high school and all the schools in the community—in other words the high school and the elementary—are fully accredited.

We get a lot of kids from Castlewood and Dante, and so they're bringing them here by choice. They're not in our school district; they're not mandated to come to school here. They choose to come here; they pay to come here. Over 50 percent of our student body right now in the elementary and in the high school come from outside the mandated districts. Of the thirty-one students in last year's senior class, there was 60-some percent, maybe closer to 70, were going to some advanced school.

The Estonoa project has been nationally recognized, state recognized, locally recognized. They've presented at the local community clubs, at the town council, at the Wise County Supervisors. They presented at the state government in the House. They presented in several forums outside the state. It needs to be said that this represents a lot of different students because it continues from year to year. The one fixed highlight of that group is Terry.

She's the one that's been there through the entire project. And she gives all the credit to the students, and that's another reason for its success.

Terry Vencil: The Estonoa Learning Center project started in the spring of 1999. It wasn't even a project at that point, just an Appalachian ecology class at St. Paul High School. When we went to block scheduling, we were allowed an extra period. And Jim Short, my principal then, came to me and said, "Terry, if you could teach something you wanted to teach, what would it be?" And I said, "Hmmmm, let's do something easy, let's do an ecology class." So we set up the ecology class, and I didn't have a clue what I was doing. I'm a chemist-physicist.

And what do teachers do when they don't have a clue what to do? They assign their students projects. So I said, "Everybody's got to have a project." This one gentleman chose a forgotten lake, a little mud puddle about a three-minute walk from the high school. And he did an eight-slide PowerPoint on it and did basically the history. And his whole thing, he wanted to turn it back into its pristine self. He wanted to get it back to a lake where people could swim in and fish in, a community focus. And so after that semester, he graduated.

The next semester, a young lady by the name of Nikki Buffalo was in Appalachian Ecology class, and I still hadn't learned a whole lot. And I said, "Okay guys, everybody has to have a project." Well, she had learned a lot. Her brother's best friend is the one that started Estonoa. She said, "I'll do Stevie Sabo's project." She thought it would be easy. And I looked at her and said, "You've got to have more than eight slides. You've got to expand this project."

So she was on the Internet one day, and she looked up at me and she said, "Mrs. Vencil, we can't do this." And I said, "Oh no, another project bites the dust." And she said, "We can't turn it back into its pristine self." And I said, "Why?" And she said, "Right here on the Internet, I was investigating ponds versus lakes. And it has the three earmarkers for a wetlands. It has cattails, it has weeping willows, and it has peat." And she said, "It is a wetlands." And I said, "What are you going to do if it's a wetlands, Nikki, and not a lake?"

And she said, "We have to get it protected. We have to get it federally protected." Because at that time, our principal Jim Short wanted to turn it into a softball field. She found out she had to go to the Corps of Engineers to get it federally certified. And so she hounded the Corps of Engineers. She hounded the lady everyday for three months. She called her; she e-mailed her. She called her; she e-mailed her. And finally she got the lady out here. I'm sure the Corps of Engineers didn't want to certify a little one-acre wetlands.

It is more hassle than it is worth, I would think. And she finally got out here, and she certified it as a wetlands, and now it is federally protected.

The next semester, which is spring 2000, Nikki had so many things going on she needed help. By that time, she was in the physics class. So she talked the physics class into adopting Estonoa, but they agreed to do five days of physics in four days. And the fifth day was reserved for Estonoa. And they adopted it, and "Team Estonoa" was born. And from that point on, there hasn't been a director of Team Estonoa, and it has truly been a team effort. They come in here, and they just slug it out.

Somebody might say, "We need this money to put new rails on the floating dock." And somebody else might say, "No, we need the money to put gravels on the parking lot." And they decide. Just like in a family, where does that money go? They write their own grants, they have their own budget, they deposit their own money—with the town. Everything we do, we do at the pleasure of the town council. They go to the town council and ask if they can do such and such. So the kids run the project. I'm on the sidelines cheering.

The first thing we did with Nikki's Appalachian Ecology group—that was fall of '99—we tried to walk around it. And by the time we got around it forty-five minutes later, we had tagalong burrs all over us. We had to cut a path literally all the way around it. Nikki called the Job Corps over here to cut a basic fire path for us. And then we started with gravel donated by American Electric Power and some money from the local Lions Club and put down a hundred and eighteen tons of crusher run. The kids did that. The next thing they did—they wanted picnic tables. And they bought the lumber for the picnic tables, and had the Job Corps make the picnic tables and install them. The town donated trashcans, and the kids installed them. And benches, the kids installed them.

About this time, they decided they had to do something productive with Estonoa, science-wise. So the kids decided to get involved with GLOBE, Global Learning through Observation to Benefit the Environment. And it's an arm of NASA. There are over ten thousand schools worldwide that collect data according to GLOBE's protocols and then submit it on GLOBE's Web site so that scientists and educators all over the world can use it. So the kids investigated and found out about GLOBE, became certified, and now we do water, weather, land cover, and soil.

But when we were trying to do water down at Estonoa, every time they tried to get a water sample out, they'd get peat in with it, and they couldn't get a good water sample. So they came in here one day and said, "You know what we need; we need a dock, a dock out there." And I said, "Okay, investigate it." And they went, "Don't want to put poles down in there, don't want to drive them into another cave and drain Estonoa." So they thought about a floating dock. They investigated what kind of docks they could have that were EPA approved. You can't put Styrofoam in a wetlands. They designed their own dock, and the funniest thing.

One of my big senior boys, James Hensley, came to me, and he was on dock design. And so they decided they needed thirty-three floats to go under this thing. He came to me, and we had $3,000 in the bank. And he had a check for $1,800 of it for the floats. And he said, "What if they don't work?" And I said, "This is the real world; you have to make them work, one way or the other." We got them in, and they were so excited when the floats came in, built their dock, put it out there. And they used all but one float, and it worked beautifully.

Then we had a flood. When it rained so hard and the waters were coming up, we were out of school for a couple of days, and some of my big guys in physics came to me. They were worried that I was going to be upset that it was so torn up and everything. And I looked at them, and I said, "Guys, I'm not worried. Because that project is not that mud puddle. That project is the lives of the students that it has touched, and where you go with it." When you live in a wetlands, you expect to get wet. She did what she was supposed to do: she kept the water out of the basements of some homes around there. So, hey, we just go back and put those old handmade bridges back up and try again.

We have right at $136,500 to build a learning center building next to the wetlands. The kids wrote a grant to USDA—rural development—for $100,000 and received that. And then they wrote an ARC—Appalachian Regional Commission—grant and received $29,600. American Electric Power heard about it, and said, "Could you use $8,000 more?" And we said, "Sure." And so they donated $8,000 more. At the present time, we have the architect hired. And the plans are in Richmond for them to approve. Once they approve it, we can hire the contractors and start building. The kids chose a log structure for the design. It will be one main, large meeting room with bathroom facilities. We will have tables to facilitate the learning of twenty-five active learners. Or we can fold those guys up and lecture to fifty. And it will be green metal roof, rock basement. They have budgeted for a TV, laptop computer. They'll have sinks, refrigerator, stoves.

We'll use it as a learning center to do workshops. We already have DEQ [Department of Environmental Quality] coming in for two workshops in the spring. And ARSI—Appalachian Rural Systemic Initiative—coming in for two workshops in the spring, bringing adult learners from all over the area. Plus we have students that come in from all over the area. Tomorrow, as a matter of fact, we will have 40 fourth- and fifth-grade gifted students from Bristol city schools coming in. And the kids will be doing a workshop from ten in the morning until two. We have adults coming from all over. We've had people from Ferrum College down four times for work weekends.

The kids have been to San Francisco and presented to the Kids Who Know And Do Conference. And the Kids Who Know And Do Conference called us and asked us. We didn't say, "We think we'd be a nice fit for you." They actually tapped us. We were selected by the Coalition for Community Schools as one of fifteen schools nationwide to highlight in their latest report that came out in spring as one of the schools that does community and school involvement very, very well. And they chose St. Paul High School because of the wetlands Estonoa Learning Center project.

The kids—going back to GLOBE—as of the last report in June, they had entered 4,119 data points on NASA's Web site. That's just phenomenal. We presented at ARC's national conference in Knoxville last fall. We'll be presenting to a group in Clintwood—it's the Committee for Dickenson County Improvement. And what they want to do is highlight Estonoa as a group that works with community. And they want to get their teachers from Clintwood in to listen to what St. Paul has done as far as community and schools working together.

I've had graduates come back for work weekends. We have one past student who is on our board of directors. As a matter of fact, we have a student coming back tomorrow who will be helping with the fourth and fifth graders. And the students say the greatest impact on their lives has been their ability to communicate with other people and their ability to think across lines. This project has so many different areas—government, science, English, media, whatever it happens to be. They don't think now strictly in science. They think about how can that be used in literature or some other way. So it has diversified their thinking.

And it has also honed their skills as far as grant writing. You know, how many high school students write grants? The student who is writing grants now, she is on her second grant, ready to put it to bed. And it has to be out on the twenty-sixth. Today's the nineteenth. And I said, "Do you want to send it in tomorrow." She said, "No, let's not rush anything. Let's wait until after six weeks tests so I can look at it with a clean eye." And I thought, "Are you the kid that started in this class?"

Dean Vencil and Terry Vencil: That's part of my life. That is her life, and so that's part of my life.

He was working with a young man the other day who's had a hard time at home. And this child just gravitated to him, just worked with him. We need strong males and females both in education. And frequently I don't think we have the strong males in high school and elementary that we need.

Chelsea Salyer and Jason Boone: I've played basketball for the majority of my life. And I'm on the PACE team, which is just an academic team that competes with surrounding schools. I'm on Team Estonoa. I like to run; I do track and cross-country. And one activity that I'm really involved in, I drive like an hour three or four times a week to a dance studio in Kingsport, Tennessee. It's about an hour away. As far as future plans, I'm really set on going to UVA in Charlottesville. And as far as occupations, I'm completely undecided. I really do not know. Academically, I feel fine, but I'm really close to my family. That will be the main obstacle, getting used to being away from home.

I participate in football and am a member of Team Estonoa. I love collecting cars. Me and my father, we love Mustangs. So we have four or five Mustangs. For my career, I would either like to go into architecture—if I did that I would have to go to college at Virginia Tech or UVA—they have some of the best architecture programs there. If I do that, I probably wouldn't be able to get a good-paying job around this area. I would have to go to a bigger city, a bigger place to get a good job, a good-paying job. Or I would go into my father's field—he puts in heat pumps. And he has a business in St. Paul— been here for over thirty years. So I would possibly like to do that. He's well known throughout the area.

. . . . .

In this area, the main things kids do for fun is just to cruise around in their cars 'cause there's really nothing to do—just talk to your peers. We usually drive like thirty minutes to an hour to go to a movie because those are the nicer movie theaters. To go shopping, the best malls are like an hour and a half away. Bristol, Abingdon, we go to see the movies, and Johnson City has the nicest mall. We're just the same as any other kids. When I go to Kingsport, I see everything, and there's really no difference. It's, like, our proms and dances and things—they're just so much smaller. There's, like, half the kids that they usually have, if not even less than that.

Things to do around here—there's really not much to do. If I'm ever out in town, I always go cruising, just ride around and talk to my friends. Basically just be on the computer or play video games is the only thing really to do around here. If you want to go out to eat, like, a nice restaurant or go to the movies, you have to go to Bristol or some other place that's further. That's forty-five minutes to an hour away. Going to Coeburn, they have a theater there, but it's nothing compared to the bigger places.

. . . . .

I listen to a lot of Broadway, but I listen to a lot of rap music. I listen to, like, everything. Bette Midler is, like, my all-time favorite singer. Recently, I'm, like, really into the *Chicago* soundtrack and, like, Catherine Zeta-Jones. I really listen to her a lot. As far as the names of the rap musicians, I don't really have one particular person. I just like one song from each person. I find around here we don't seem to listen—at least my friends—don't listen to as much country as, like, the people in Kingsport. They seem to listen to country more. Which is kind of surprising, I think, because we're considered more country than they are.

As far as music, about anything. I usually listen to rap. I have a sound system in my car, so anything that's loud I'll usually listen to. Personally my favorite is Cent [50 Cent] or Eminem. Usually don't ever listen to any country or anything like that. Doesn't tickle my fancy too well.

. . . . .

I'm just really proud to be from St. Paul because of our academic standards. We just do so well, like, with SOLs and stuff. I definitely think it's 'cause we have small classes. And the teachers—they can see how each kid is progressing. The teachers in particular that have really pushed me are Mrs. Vencil, obviously; Mrs. Frances Wall, our English teacher; and probably my math teacher, Mrs. Kelly. You don't hear of many kids trying to save a natural resource. It's not big, but it's not so little. I mean it's a pretty big thing. I just think there's not enough—especially around here—of kids getting really involved, I mean into nature and preserving it and stuff. And I've heard my cousin who is in college now—she's a freshman this year—and she said that you'll be so thankful the way Mrs. Kelly teaches calculus. It makes it so much easier. And I've heard another girl that graduated a couple of years ago—she went to UVA-Wise—and she was in her calculus class and on the first day they had some assignment and she knew exactly what to do. And the girl beside her was, like, "How did you know how to do that?" And she said, "I went to St. Paul."

Personally, I really like how it's well known for academics. Helps you to get into colleges because colleges know about that also. As far as the reason why, I think it's more of where we are a small school. It's just more personal. Like the teachers can actually get to know the students a lot better than at a bigger school, which makes everything a lot easier and makes you actually want to learn, I think. You feel more of a connection with your teachers so you don't want to let them down is the way I feel. It is that way with Mrs. Vencil, definitely. Mrs. Wade, our other science teacher, acts like a mother to me. She takes up for me if I ever need anything said for me. If anybody's ever putting me down, she'll speak up for me, be more than happy to, get angry with them or anything.

. . . . .

I personally would never try to disregard where I came from. I'm really proud to come from here, but at the same time I don't see my future here. My parents have taken me to New York and stuff. I've been around a little bit. I just want to go on to bigger things. But I also think that it is a great place to raise a family, so I'm not for sure if I would want to come back, if I decide to start a family. I just don't feel like we have enough opportunities here in the area. My mom's a teacher, and everybody knows about the wages for teachers. But I also feel like you should love your job. So wages aren't necessarily as important to me. So I could see myself coming back here later. But for now, I just don't think so.

As far as me, this place—if I took over my dad's business—I could make it pretty well, get a living here. It would be a great place to raise a family because it would be one on one. You would actually have family time. The furthest place I've been is probably Cincinnati, Ohio, but I don't feel isolated at all. Feel like I have just as many advantages as anybody else does. If you went to a city, might have to drive a good ways to get to work or anything. And I just don't think you would have, like, a connection with your son or daughter as much as you would if you stayed here.

We kept building shell buildings. Until
just recently.

NINETEEN

Changing Strategy for Regional Renewal

Frank Kilgore: We're about what people call "mined out." There's still lots of
coal, but in the central Appalachians, a lot of it is too hard to get to or, until the
technology changes, you can't get to it because previous mining operations
have either caused it to be backed up with water, or the top will be cracked
and it's too unsafe to go in. So that within itself—just bad mining practices
and bad planning—has locked away a lot of coal reserves for the foreseeable
future because you can't get to it. It's too deep to strip-mine, and it's too
dangerous to deep-mine because of what's happened there before.

So a lot of people left for manufacturing jobs. And then the coalfield leadership and the state leadership decided that they would diversify the economy through shell-building projects. Unfortunately for the coalfields, they
thought of it a little late. We got lots of shell buildings that are empty now,
like all across the United States. But we got into the game late, and we didn't
get out early enough. We got into it late because a lot of other places that were
better situated near interstate highways had gotten into it before we did. So
by the time we got into it, the cream of the crop had already been gotten
by the Roanoke Valley corridor, North Carolina, different places that were
aggressive with shell buildings to attract industries. So we got the second-
and third-tier level. We got garment factories and other kinds of mass production, assembly jobs or low-paying jobs in the whole area. And St. Paul
had lots of garment factories in and around it—St. Paul Shirt Factory they
called it, but they made lots more than just shirts. The very building my law
office is in now was a shirt factory at one time. It wasn't built originally to be a
shirt factory, but it was converted into one. And just up the road between St.
Paul and Dante was a garment factory that was there for thirty or forty years.
Like everybody else, we lost those jobs. But we kept building shell buildings.

Until just recently, shell buildings were still what our economic advisers were planning and doing.

And just recently have they changed their position to embrace tourism, which I think is the third biggest industry in Virginia.[1] As you know, the Clinch River runs through the most biologically diverse watershed in the continental United States, and that to me is the hook or calling card for attracting folks to enjoy the Clinch River. And we have some national forest land that is well underknown and underused, so we have a lot of hiking trails and canoeing opportunities—outdoor opportunities—and they're being developed as we speak. But far southwest Virginia is somewhat remote from the traveled paths of tourists, so eco-tourism is probably about the best draw we have. Like, the Breaks Interstate Park on the Kentucky border gets about a half million visitors a year. But the Breaks is hard to get to. When the Coalfield Expressway is built from southern West Virginia down to Route 23, there will be an off-ramp to the Breaks Interstate Park, which will make it much more accessible. So all those things are being planned and developed as we speak. I think tourism will be fairly significant some day in far southwest Virginia.

We have also diversified into higher education. The Appalachian School of Law is what I think convinced economic planners that those jobs created by higher education, by knowledge-based industries or entities, were not only good-paying jobs, but they were ever-expanding jobs. The Appalachian School of Law, been in existence six or seven years. It has peaked out at 340 students, has about a $12 million per year economic impact. So when I went to the Coalfield Economic Development Authority with a proposition for a pharmacy school, I got $3 million from them. And nobody really argued about it much. And I think two or three things had occurred. First of all, the law school had paved the way to show that higher education within itself is an economic development tool and engine. Secondly, we had the advantage of not telling people we wanted to create more lawyers; we are going to create pharmacists. Thirdly, pharmacy schools by its very biotechnical nature brings in more spin-off jobs than law schools do. So we had all three of those things going for us. The School of Pharmacy, under the umbrella of a new University of Appalachia, is going to emphasize community service, require our pharmacy school students to do more community service work than any other pharmacy school in the nation, just as the law school requires more community service work than any law school in the nation.[2]

Our pharmacy school students will go out in the community teaching preventive healthcare and drug awareness, two of the biggest problems facing the coalfield region. Drug abuse, prescription drug abuse, and very poor healthcare are a lifestyle. In fact, our region is number one in the nation in a lot of bad health statistics.[3] And we want the pharmacy school students to go out in the community and teach young people. I think most of the older generations are lost, too addicted to whatever lifestyle they have chosen that's bad for them. We want to teach the next generations how to avoid harmful lifestyle choices that create a lifetime of bad health. As a region, we are number one in obesity. As a region, we are number one in diet-related diabetes. We are toward the bottom or top, whichever you want to call it, in lifestyle-induced hypertension. Heart disease. Lung disorders. Infant mortality. Cervical cancer. Just about any bad health statistic that you can come up with other than sickle-cell anemia, we've got it worse than anybody else.

I attribute it to . . . at the very baseline of it is the fatalistic religious attitude that we have in this area in that somewhere in the sky in a book, there is a date you're going to die. And you can't change that, so why not yuck it up and eat what you want and drink what you want, smoke what you want. Because it doesn't matter. You're going to die that day anyway. I guess it's the Calvinistic viewpoint of religion. And we're eat up with it. So if you talk to somebody especially in the older generations about "you should quit smoking"—well, "something's got to kill you." Or "you should quit smoking"—well, "I'm gonna die on a certain day so it doesn't matter." I hear that. When I was growing up, it made perfect sense. Right now, it doesn't. So it's sort of a self-fulfilling prophecy.[4]

But these pharmacy school students are going to be able to show technically and graphically instead of morally and criminally what drugs, overeating, too much sugar, not enough exercise does to your young body. Maybe it won't work, but I think if you reach them in late grade school and middle school, you have a chance to head them off. I think once you are in high school, the die is cast. And I think public school students will pay much more attention to somebody they think is going to be a doctor or pharmacist than they will a preacher or a law enforcement officer. And that program, when we're up to 300, 350 students, and they go back out into the central Appalachian community where they come from, it will impact the whole region.

They chose the name the other night—Dante Lives On. With or without the coal company.

TWENTY

No-Company Town Fights On

Kathy Shearer: There were 350 houses served by the sewer. So there were almost 330 houses that did not have approved sewage disposal. There were a few septic systems in the community which may or may not have been functioning. The sewer cleared up that problem for 350 houses, so it was a major, huge project. And a lot of grant money and loan money were put into that. If the people of Dante had chosen not to accept the sewer, EPA would have shut down the town. At first, when I came here as a community worker, there were a few people such as Frank Gordon and Lucille Whitaker who understood that we had to have a sewer, but the majority of the people said, "We have a sewer. We have Lick Creek, had it all these years. What's the big fuss?" And the government—EPA—thought differently.

Lucille Whitaker: Me and my husband we worked on it and everything to get the sewage in—because the creek would get real low. It was terrible. I mean you had such an odor around your home. And we knew we had to do something. But a lot of people said, "We don't want this sewage in here; we've got enough bills to pay." I said, "This is our health problem; we need this sewage in here. We can't go with all this." And a lot of the elder people didn't want to leave. And some of them wanted to sell their home, move out of the community. They couldn't do it; they couldn't sell their home because they didn't have the sewage in here. That was the situation we was up against.

Kathy Shearer: That was a major decision that everybody had to make at the beginning of the sewer project because some people said, "Why don't we just take the money that we could get to put the sewer in and move everybody out, because there's never going to be coal here again." But in reality, you can't get money—at least we didn't know how to—to get money to move people out. And in meeting people like Frank and Lucille and Jimmy Mays and other people, that was the furthest thing from their mind. You and I coming into this community see a community at its ebb. And we're thinking, "Boy, who would want to stay here?"

But they have all these memories built up over all these years and this history and these very tight bonds that form in a community, I think, where people work in a very hazardous occupation. And they've grown up through good times and bad times. And they've seen people die, and they've seen people suffer. And they've all fought together and worked together so hard to support each other. They don't want to lose that. They don't want to move to Castlewood or St. Paul, where they won't know their neighbors. I interviewed two twins who have moved to St. Paul, and they said they see the same people they used to see in Dante, but they don't speak to each other the way they did when they lived here. In St. Paul, it's as if, "We're formal now."

So we came to realize that. The community made us realize that. And we all agreed that we weren't going to talk about that anymore. Dante needed a sewer; these people needed to stay here. There were a thousand people, I guess, between Dante and West Dante, whom we could serve with this new sewer. So we went full steam ahead for the sewer.

Kathy Shearer and Frank Gordon: In 1993 we started meeting over in Lebanon at the office of Cumberland Plateau, and Frank Gordon was a member of the community committee. We had somebody from each holler, and Frank was sort of representing Bunchtown, downtown, this area, and Bear Wallow.

There's also Straight Holler and Sawmill Holler.

And then we included West Dante too. We had representatives from each community. And we met, and we talked about the problem and what to do about the problem. And Russell County had known about it for several years but had not made any effort to alleviate the problem of raw sewage going right in the creeks. And finally the federal government said, "You either fix it or we'll fix the community, and people won't have power anymore."

The whole community knowed that we needed to clean the creeks up. But we couldn't do nothing about it as a community. So we had to go to Russell County and People Incorporated and Cumberland Plateau.

And so Russell County ask me and several other people to come and help. And that's how I met Frank. And we eventually started going door to door throughout the community. Frank and I were a team, and then Jim Baldwin [senior planner for the planning commission district of Cumberland Plateau] went with Jimmy Mays some. Each of us went with one community person, because otherwise we wouldn't have gotten in the door. We had to go in everybody's house and sit down with them. I think Jimmy Mays probably recruited everybody, didn't he? He was a wonderful leader in the community.

He was a good leader in the community. He's dead and gone now. Cancer killed him.

I had experience in indoor plumbing. I ran the indoor plumbing program for our agency. In doing that, I had helped people get connected to sewer. I had never worked on a project before where we had to actually get the sewer in the ground. Usually I went in when the sewer was already there; we just ran a little pipe. So this was a big deal. But I think Jimmy understood first that this is what it was going to take. And he recruited people like Frank, who understood. But it took quite awhile for the rest of the community to understand, because, remember, at first we just said, "We'll have a sign-up day here at the fire hall, and everybody will come and sign up." But hardly anybody showed up. So we sat there, and a few people came in. And that was about it. That's when we realized it was going to take a whole nother year, and we would need to go door to door, take our time, and sit down like we're doing here, sit down in everybody's living room and explain to them why this really had to happen.

Me and Kathy went into a guy's house up here. He said, "I've got all I need. Over my dead body, there'll be sewage in this community." He's dead now, and we've got sewage in the community.

I don't think he lived to see the sewer, did he? And we had to ask them a lot of personal information. It wasn't just us telling. We had to write down what their income was, who lived there, what their ages were, the condition of the house, did they have any problems with the house, did they have indoor plumbing. And we had three that still only had outhouses that we had to fix first when we got started. By the time it was finished, everybody had to have a workable indoor bathroom. And we're talking about three hundred houses, so really it was a very small fraction who were still living without indoor plumbing. So when you think about it, all those houses had toilets, and all those toilets were going right in the creek. The outhouses were not nearly as big a problem for the water as the toilets were. And there was a few who absolutely refused to connect to it, but Frank Kilgore, who watches these things, he's found out who is not connected. And he's bulldogging it.

Matthew Kincaid: Glad to see them get it in. We come a long way, because I remember when the people on this side [of the road in Sawmill Hollow] had to carry their water. Didn't have no pipes over here for no water to come in the house. And just a few people on that side. They had one of those hydrants right out there and had one down there, and on down the road there was another one. And at the end the hollow there, as you go around the ballpark there, it was one on the corner there. People had to take buckets and carry. I carried many a bucket of water.

Shirley Glass: I think the idea that the water was going in sort of made us get together and start doing some things. In June of 1999, Eileen McIlvane talked to Kareen Couch about some money being available to do some projects in the communities to build the community up, to revitalize the community. We set up a community meeting, and everybody decided we were going to try to do a few projects. Some of the projects were like naming the streets, so people would know when they come into town, somebody new, they would know where to find you. Or rescue squads—if somebody was sick, they would know where to go. And another project is we would like to have a place for people to meet and have picnics together and have community gatherings. The gathering place would be up West Dante at the old ballpark. And then we had a project for the Coal Miners Memorial because there was one, I think, in Clintwood or Grundy someone had seen, and they thought it would be a good idea.

We decided we needed a name, so we decided on the name PRIDE. It stands for People's Revitalization in Dante's Economy. Once PRIDE started going, we started having these community meetings. Then everybody went on their separate committees. And as a result of that, the Coal Miner Memorial is in Dante. And there's, like, close to two hundred names on them. Then the other project with the picnic tables, they got some money, they run some electricity to the shed, and they put a shed up, and made tables. A lot of the men up there, they did the work. And they had their picnic shed.

But the street names, that was the committee I was on. It fell through because the county was planning on doing the 911, so they wanted to do that on their own. I guess after we got our projects finished, everybody just lost interest. And we didn't meet anymore. But we still have money that we had made that we use to take care of the Miners' Memorial. We are going to dissolve the PRIDE organization and give what money's left over to our new group in Dante.

Kathy Shearer: The oral history project also grew out of the sewer project. Once we had the sewer in the ground, then I started the oral history project. I work for People Incorporated of Southwest Virginia, which is a community action agency [with offices in Abingdon, Clintwood, Grundy, and Lebanon,

11. Lee Long, general manager and vice president of Clinchfield Coal Corporation, 1911–1944. Among photos Dante residents collected for their display and book. Courtesy of the Dante History Project, Collection of Mary Elizabeth Thompson Wilbourne.

Virginia]. And we typically don't do projects like the oral history project. It's the first one that has ever been done by us. We are more in the line of Head Start, senior centers, weatherization—all the typical community action programs—there's a thousand of them around the country. But I started hearing stories and seeing wonderful photographs as I traveled around and met people.

And Jimmy Mays was actually the first person to bring in photographs of how Dante had looked. And I thought, "Wow, there's some great stuff here which needs to be preserved." And I was aware through our committee meetings that the "elder people," as Lucille called them, were passing away, and these stories were disappearing. So I proposed to my boss that I do something, and I was thinking of something small, to kind of record the oral history, just do the recordings, copy a few pictures, and make a display. And he said, "If you can find some grant money to help you do that." Because we didn't have anything. So that's what I did. I really wasn't thinking about saving the town then. I figured the sewer had done the saving part. They're pretty much on their own at that point. And of course the company was still here working, so it wasn't as desolate as it is now.

I guess in looking for money, I hit upon the Virginia Foundation for the Humanities. And that seemed like a really good fit. I talked to David Bearinger,

12. Mary Tompa greeting her husband, John, as he returns from the No. 2 mines in upper Straight Hollow, about 1935. Among photos Dante residents collected for their display and book. Courtesy of the Dante History Project, Collection of Mary Tompa Harris.

and he guided my proposal. He's really good at doing that. And he said I needed to be more specific, exactly how was I going to display this thing? And I was thinking of some small, stand-up, wooden panels that I would move around. And the more I thought about it, the more I thought, "Well, you know, I'm not sure about that." I submitted a proposal that kind of sounded like that, but then it grew. By the time I was ready for it, it needed a lot more space.

I don't know how specific I was, but it was specific enough to get the funding. And I do think I said, "I will interview fifty people." And he wanted a nice variety of people. And I did interview, I think, forty-five. And the interviews were fairly lengthy—one to three hours each. I was working from the senior center, using that facility to go out and do my interviewing and copying the pictures there and everything.

And they were quilting. That was their daily activity. And so I realized that quilts would be a nice backdrop and got them involved in making the quilts to hang these panels on. Now as the exhibit got underway, even before we actually installed it the first time in Lebanon, my right-hand woman—Lucille Whitaker—said, "Well, this is real nice, honey, but when are we going to get a book?" And I kept telling her, "Lucille, we're not going to have a book; this is going to be an exhibit." And I knew she was really disappointed.

13. James Mabry's crew at Camp Branch mine, 1979, where Mabry was earlier credited with saving the life of Carson Mutter, trapped in a continuous miner after a roof fall. Mabry is pictured at far right, next to Mutter. Mabry is the father of James Mabry Jr., mentioned by Matthew Kincaid in chapter 11. Among photos Dante residents collected for their display and book. Courtesy of the Dante History Project, Collection of Clinchfield Coal Company.

The next thing she said is, "Well, I've raised $800." She had gone door-to-door telling everybody, "There's going to be a book, there's going to be a book. Give me money." And I began to be alarmed about this. So I thought, all right. So we went down to visit a local publishing company and hoped to interest them in the idea, because I had no idea of how to go about writing a book at all. And the publisher said, "No, I won't start a book project unless I'm sure I can sell fifteen hundred copies; that's my minimum. If you want to create the book and bring it to me to print, that's fine. We can do that, but I'm not going to publish a book on Dante. Not enough people are going to buy it."

And I had Lucille with me and Ethel with me from the seniors. Ohhh, they were brokenhearted. And on the way home, it was like "on the road to Damascas." This bolt hits me, and all of a sudden I find myself saying, "Ladies, there's going to be a book, and I guess I'm gonna write it." So that's where it started. We have sold right about two thousand. And we are in our second printing.[1]

14. The Dante branch of the Dickenson County Bank about 1930, later to become a beer garden, then a teen center, and now being renovated by Dante Lives On into a museum and coffee shop. Among photos Dante residents collected for their display and book. Courtesy of the Dante History Project, Collection of Eugene Addington.

Kathy Shearer, Nannie Phillips Gordon, and Frank Gordon: We are creating a new corporation, and it's going to be owned by the people in Dante. And they chose the name the other night—Dante Lives On. With or without the coal company.

I believe that eventually coal will come back.

You do?

Yes, I do.

Nope.

Yeah, I believe it will come back.

Now what makes you think so?

Well, I'm going to tell you. I'm an old lady. And there's been coal here all my life. And I can watch the coal go up and down the tracks on the train. I been in the mines. I been at the mines. And it's not worked out. It's not worked out. Eventually it will come back if time lasts. I'm gonna say it that way. But I also believe we're living down in our last days anyway. And I may never see it, but I believe it will be back.

Nope. The coal she sees going down the tracks they're hauling from Kentucky out of here because they done finished up out of here. They've gone to

Kentucky now, hauling it out. And coal will not come back to Dante. There will never be another coal boom in town like it was in the '50s.

James Thomas: There was supposed to be some flood money coming in here in February, and we haven't seen any of the money. We're having problems with that. You go to Lebanon, and you see how it's built up, all your roads and everything, they built up. Even Sword Creek, when they had the flood, they took and fixed every driveway in the community. When the flood hit here, nothing was done. We ain't just talking about one holler. We're talking about all the community of Dante. Something need to be done.

We're going to try to do the right thing when we go to these committees and stuff, the board of supervisors. The community need to get involved. That's the biggest problem. One will say, "They ain't gonna do nothing anyway." You don't know what they gonna do unless you try. They formed this committee that we can go in there and get something done. All I want is everything done right. You get tired of people sticking their hand in your pocket, and I can't stick my own and see what I can find in my own pocket.

Kathy Shearer: I knew that the people here from the coal company had vacated the office building, and I was aware it was empty. And about two months ago, I got a call from Bill Steel, who is the asset manager for Alpha Natural Resources, which bought out all of Pittston's coal holdings and properties.[2] That's almost a year ago. And he asked if People Incorporated, my agency, would be interested in becoming the owner of this building, the office building. And I was just astonished because the coal company's first response has always been, "If you don't need it, tear it down." They've never asked anybody to my knowledge if they wanted a building.

And I said at that time, "Bill, I'll bring my director up, and we'll certainly take a look at it. What about the old bank building?" Which has been my favorite building in the town, along with the depot. And he checked into it and got back to me. And he said, "Yeah, you can have the old bank building. That's fine. We are getting rid of everything." And at that point I was hoping our agency would take both buildings. My director decided eventually to take just the office building because it's in very good condition. It's pretty much a move-in situation; tenants could move right in. He decided not to take the bank building because it's going to take a lot of renovation.

We've had a call for a barber and a beauty shop. There's a florist who's considering coming here. So that was this obviously, I thought, great potential. People Incorporated has to own it for at least two years. The coal company will donate it to People Incorporated and will get a tax credit for doing that.

We have to hold onto it for two years. At the end of that time period, we will have to see what kind of situation we're in, but we'll be the owners at least that long.

So then we had the bank to consider. I didn't want to let that get away, and I didn't want them to tear it down. And I thought, "Well, this is the chance for the community to for the first time actually own something." So I called up people I knew who had been very interested in what goes on here—the woman who actually made the complaint about the school—and I told Catherine, "Get some of your friends together." Well, I asked her first, "Do you think this sounds like a good idea?" "Oh yes," she was very excited. I said, "Get a few of your friends together, maybe ten or twelve, and we'll have a small meeting at the fire hall, and we'll just talk about what could we do with it." And I got there, and there were twenty-three people. She had called all sorts of people, and people had talked with each other, and they were very excited.

Catherine Pratt: Back in the late fall of 2000, my sister and I were just out walking. And the old Dante Elementary School up there, it's just demolished. Kids have got in it and destroyed it. And the windows are all broke out, and that's such a sight in the community to be sitting there. And then Kathy Shearer has been real good friends, helped out in the Dante history and stuff, she contacted us, said they'd consider taking the old Clinchfield-Pittston building up there. And from then, we started working with her and approached them about getting the old bank/beer garden. Kathy came and met with a few of the citizens up there. Really, she's the one that got us hepped up and interested in doing some things. She said it was a shame to lose such a heritage that we have. We've had twenty to twenty-five. We had a real good turnout in October for a spaghetti dinner.

And it seems like the people are really interested in getting out and doing some things. There's no places to meet, other than the fire department, and that's owned by the county. We'd just like to try to get us a little area that the community could meet and people could get together, that the community could work together and have something of our own that we could pass on to our children. And put some things in it about the coal mining and the railroad, and let our children and our grandchildren get involved in it and see where we came from and hopefully that we can keep that and instill it in the lives of our children.

Kathy Shearer: At the spaghetti supper, we had a cakewalk. And I'd never been to a cakewalk before. I didn't know what that was—I couldn't imagine what it was. People donate cakes, and everybody donates a quarter in a box. And they stand all the way around this floor. And on the floor at the fire hall are painted numbers, and the band plays. And you walk around and walk around and walk around, and it's like "musical chairs." When the music stops, you jump on a number, a number is pulled, a ball with a number on it like the lottery is pulled out of a bag, the number is read out, and the person standing on that number wins a cake. So for twenty-five cents, you have a chance for a really nice cake. We had thirty cakes donated; this went on a long time. You put a quarter down each time.

We had probably a hundred people cakewalking. It was amazing, just amazing. A lot of kids really enjoyed it. People went home with two and three cakes. So there was that music all night. And then there was a little dancing, impromptu dancing. And then towards the end of the evening in a lull, and Pete Castle was in charge of the music so he was just hot to go on all night long. But there was a lull—he was taking a break or something. All of a sudden up at the front of the room, this woman stands up, and she's not facing the tables where people are eating, socializing. She's facing the wall basically. And she starts to sing gospel a cappella. And everybody quieted down. Who was that? That was Barbara Holbrooks. And she has this just wonderful voice. She is just obviously moved to sing, and it wasn't a religious gathering whatsoever. But this is what she wanted to do.

And other people—Bill Castle—joined in with her, and some other folks. And I said, "Gosh, this is beautiful. Why don't we have a gospel singing sometime?" And folks liked the idea. So it was arranged. The board of directors of Dante Lives On organized it, and they held it at the First Mount Calvary Baptist Church at the head of Sawmill Holler, which is a church in the black community, has been historically black, built by the black people. The woman from Sawmill who is on our board of directors, Emogene Kincaid, suggested the use of her church, recommended that and checked with her pastor. And he said that would be just fine.

And so it was held there. And I thought it was significant. I'll bet that 98 percent of the people who were there had never set foot in that church before. Because you looked out and you saw, what, probably a hundred white people. Or seventy-five white people and maybe five black people sitting in the back, who came in late. So just a handful of black people, all of whom had been in the church many times. This is their church. But I thought that was very significant. People enjoyed the gospel event, which was planned as a tribute to the Virginia Travelers, which is an old gospel group that grew out of Sawmill back after World War II. It's been going ever since with children and grandchildren of the original people, and folks have come and gone.

But I thought it was significant in that it was appropriately the day after Martin Luther King Jr.'s birthday. We had a nice coming together of the community, and people are very generous in their giving toward this project. We raised over $400 in a love offering from people who probably are spending quite a bit of money on medicine and food and heat. They don't have a whole lot to spare, but they're very generous. They want to see this Dante Lives On project succeed, and they're very supportive of it.

And I thought people really had a good time. You could tell when Jim Pratt said, "Don't just run off; stay and socialize." And people did. And most everybody there, as far as I could tell, made an effort to come up and thank James Thomas and the other black deacon who stood at the front of the church at the end there, to thank them and express their appreciation. I think it made them feel really good.

Pete Castle: We have an old building here that we're trying to preserve right now, which used to be the old bank building in the 1930s. It was a branch of the Dickenson County bank, and it, so to speak, went broke at that particular time. And as time passed on, because of all of the miners here who'd like to have a beer from time to time, they made it into an old, what they called a beer garden and a sandwich shop. You could even buy your dinner. It was in the '30s during the Depression.

Shirley Glass: I can remember the Dante beer garden that we are trying to turn into a museum. When I was a teenager, we had a teen center in there. And everybody would meet, and we would dance and have potato chips, just a place for us to meet.

Catherine Pratt: They wanted to put in a little coffee shop. People could come in and have some of the homemade goodies that people in this area have. We thought we would get some of the specialties—fried apple pies and the rum cakes and some of the things the elderly people have passed down through the years. Have those little specials during the day. Just give us a chance for people to come in, sit down and talk, get to know each other more, and visit, basically just to get together in fellowship. And that's things that we're just letting gradually slide by. We miss out on a lot by not being together with a community.

Years ago, we'd sit out on the front porch, and everybody hollered back and forth and visited, and if you had beans to string or fruit or something to work out, everybody just pitched in and worked together. Through the years,

I can see how some of that has slid away. A lot of the elderly ones have passed on, and a lot of the young ones has had to leave because of work. There's just no work or nothing here. So it's changed some in that way. There's no places to congregate at all. Churches is really about the only activities that we have there.

I try not to think about it, but it's close to $60,000 to get the building put back. We need a new roof, and there's just a lot of work inside that's going to have to be done on it, and some plumbing and electrical work. Hopefully, everybody that's got different traits in the community will come out and work and pitch in. I'm just new at it, and I'm wading through high water because I've never been involved in anything quite as deep as this.

We got a committee through the board of supervisors trying to get the old Dante School turned into a home for the elderly, either that or tear it down and make a park. We just want to clean up the area. There's a lot of houses where people has moved away that's fallen in. We'd like to get some of the lots and things like that cleaned up, just get our area back to where we can be proud of it. Not that we're not proud of our heritage and stuff, but we'd really like to revitalize it, get some things going.

Kathy Shearer: As a grassroots organization, we're very new here. I think it's been coming for a long time as people have gotten more and more dissatisfied. They are really tied to this community, they remember it fondly in its heyday, and they want it to live again. And, of course, it will never be what they remember, but it still could be something good. The book is a history, and that is to celebrate what was. And now if we think about that as part A, now we're at part B, which is what could be. And I was quite happy with the book, and this is wonderful, and now we have it all neatly put together, and no one will forget, and everybody will be very proud. And that was very satisfying and very satisfactory. But then when this opportunity came up, and I never saw any opportunity before because the company had such a tight grasp on everything, but when this building became available, I realized suddenly that here is maybe the last chance for these people to do something for their community that they hadn't been able to do before.

We had two meetings, and we went through a whole list of suggestions that they threw up there, and they decided that they would like to have a museum/cultural center with a coffee shop where people could come and sit down and eat. There's no place in Dante where you can do that. And they wanted to have a place for people to come and search for their ancestors through the genealogical hunt, meet other people in the community whom they might be related to, look at old pictures, all that kind of thing. And look at the mining equipment. We've got lots of people who have that kind of old stuff they would like to donate.

And we've got people who are ready to shovel that building out, ready to start working on it. So they are very excited. They have voted to go ahead and incorporate it. The first meeting they passed the hat and raised $139. That was actually the second meeting, where they voted to do it, passed Pete's hat. He said, "I've got $20 here." That was his idea. And so that was enough to cover the incorporation fee.

And tonight I'm meeting with the organization committee and some people from St. Paul. Suzie Harrison and Lou Ann Wallace are going to meet with us and talk to us about how they went through the nonprofit exemption process, getting that because we have to get that before they will give us the building. But Alpha has said that they will hold the building for us if we can do it in a timely manner.

There's transportation money—ISTEA [pronounced *ice tea*; Intermodal Surface Transportation Efficiency Act of 1991] money used to restore buildings. You can also go directly to the legislature and try to get a grant for an historic property. Bud Phillips is our delegate, and you know, he's a Phillips. And yes, his roots are right here in Dante. And he's always been very helpful. I think that we will get the money. Probably it's going to cost $10,000 or $12,000 to do the roof. It's a flat roof; it's got to be one seamless piece. It's got to be done professionally. A lot of the framing's going to have to be replaced first because it's been let go for so long, but we'll get it done.

That crack, we have pretty much determined, is a settlement crack. The back wall is a solid concrete, poured wall. It's the back of the vault. They made it that way so that nobody could drill in from the back. And the back wall is sitting on rock. The rest of the building is sitting on fill. And as the building settled, only part of it could settle. The back wall didn't go anywhere, so basically what you are seeing is something sort of split open. I talked to a guy who used to work in that building. He said it hasn't opened up in years; it's stable. And I've talked to another fellow who is a professional historic renovator, and he's told me how you go about fixing just that kind of problem.

Nannie Phillips Gordon: It means a lot to me for people to come and visit me. Some people that has lived here in Dante all these years, that I've known ever since I was a little girl, and if I see them out they speak; otherwise, no, they don't. As a for instance, the lady who lived next to my mother up in Bear Waller. We was friends for years. And after I found out she was sick about a month ago, I called up there to check on her. I've never heard one thing.

And that bothers me because I love my friends. My friends means more to me than money. And there's a lot of people don't have any. I don't know how they make it. If Kathy's in this area, if nothing else she'll come in and say hello. And that means a lot to me, because when people gets old, they're forgotten anyway. I can't say that.

Kathy Shearer: I'm from New Jersey. And I don't have any ties to New Jersey at this point. My parents left there when I graduated from high school. My dad retired. We had a very small family which was not very close, no reason to stay in New Jersey. So they moved to North Carolina, I went to college, I married a Virginian. He felt very tied to Virginia, and so we moved here. He's not from this part though; he's from Arlington. But we had worked in the mountains in VISTA in Georgia. When we decided to move to Virginia, we decided we'll just sort of move up the Appalachian chain, and ended up here.

And I guess one thing that has influenced me has been both of my grandmothers. One grandmother was very interested in family history, and she passed that on to me. She gave me some things, a wine decanter that her mother brought over on the ship with her from France. And I have that. And then the story and a copy of her passport. And I was able eventually in 1967 to go to France to the little village, and do that "going back home" sort of thing, go to the graveyard and all of that. So I've been interested in family history for a very long time. And then being in VISTA, I became very interested in Appalachian culture. I went to college in North Carolina, but I had no connection with the Appalachians whatsoever. So I began learning about Appalachia and Appalachians in 1969 when I went into VISTA.

My other grandmother influenced me right before she died, and this is very strange. I did not know this was the family secret. My other grandmother was Jewish and worked in the Triangle Shirtwaist Factory, the big one that burned in New York, and all the women jumped out of the window in 1913, 1914. She was working there, and that day she had stayed home to take care of someone in the family who was ill. I didn't know my grandmother was Jewish. I grew up in a Baptist church up north, and my mother had turned her back on all of that. She wanted to marry a non-Jew and get ahead in the world. She came out of a culture where Jews were spat on and could not join the country club and could not do this and could not do that.

I never learned my family's history until my grandmother was very close to death, and she revealed this secret to me, which she'd been sworn to never tell. And I realized that I had lost all of that. I would love to have talked to her about working at the Triangle Shirtwaist Factory. That is the foundation for the International Ladies Garment Workers Union. That's where it started. It's a fascinating, brutal part of labor history. But I missed that opportunity. I grew up in a Republican household, and I married a Democrat.

And he's always talked about labor history, labor struggles. And being in VISTA, you become much more aware of the other side of every issue and thinking about people who don't have a lot of money. And living here in this area, which has become such an anti-union area. A lot of people will tell you the reason industry won't come here is because of the union background. They don't want to be in an area where there is union. The employers say, "We'll move to southwest Virginia because of the strong work ethic." Which means "because they are willing to take really low wages." It doesn't mean they are working any harder than anywhere else.

But all that together, I felt like I had really lost that opportunity to know. She was my favorite of the two grandmothers. She was wonderful; she just adored me. But we could never share this history, and I thought this is really sad. And I was very angry about that. So that then was part of my mission, to not let those opportunities go by again, when I saw an opportunity, to think, "Well, I want to capture this."

I have been fortunate as an outsider in gaining almost immediate acceptance by the people of Dante. I went door to door with Frank Gordon. That was the key. I came into the community with a respected community member; I didn't just start knocking on the door. And I came bringing something. I brought them the possibility that the sewer would be installed and that they would then be able to continue living here and would be able to sell their homes—no one was able to finance a house through a bank here without the sewer. So that was going to be fixed up. But the key was really going door to door with Frank, for me. And then I also did it with Roger Blackstone in West Dante. So that was how I got in. And once people started seeing me here, they associated me with the sewer, which overall was a good thing. And so they have been very friendly, almost without exception.

I don't actually physically live here. I don't get totally involved in the life of the community. And for me that works better. I would like to see people at their best. I don't really want to know everything about everybody, and that's what you get when you're living here. I'm going to be much more successful at my work if I interact in meetings and events and things like that, and then I leave. That too is part of taking over, becoming part of the community, thinking that you have a voice too because "now I live here." When I go home to Emory, I'm in a totally separate place. And I'm fine with that, that's okay.

I do like the fact that this is different from Emory, and it certainly has a very tight feeling here, and this is what I still hear from people. I like that

that still exists somewhere. That's very important to me. I don't think it is that important for me to experience in my own personal life because I never had it. I grew up in an apartment building where we knew our neighbors, but we weren't all that close with them. And my family wasn't close. But it is important somehow for me to help maintain that for them. If they want it, I certainly think it's a worthy goal. And it's something that doesn't exist in many communities.

Again, I think it is a peculiar feature of company towns, where everybody worked for the same boss. And particularly a coal-mining town, where you had that element of danger, death always hanging over you. Some men have described coal mining as being very similar to being in war, because you and your buddies kept each other alive. And coal mining was somewhat like that. And so you have that very intense bond. Matthew said he "loved coal mining." I doubt that he really loved setting roof bolts, one per minute. But what he loved was being with a group of men, all of whom were white basically on his last crew, and whom he spent all this time with without any problems. They were buddies.

Community action varies from agency to agency. But I would say ours, like most, do programs where we go in and we offer a service. And you can take it or leave it. We don't knock on people's doors and say, "Hey, do you want this?" Now in the old days we probably did. We had to pull people in; now we have waiting lists. What I'm doing—grassroots organizing—is not your typical thing at my agency. I have to say this. My director has said to me, "This is not what we do." He's not happy about me doing this. In fact, at first he said, "You will not do this." And then he kind of backed off. I guaranteed him that I would do all my other work. I promised him. I am working four days a week at the agency. The fifth day I do my publishing, which is totally separate.

I want it to be grassroots. These people have had people from the outside telling them what to do their entire lives. And I said to them, "We're not coming in here as another parent. You guys are going to have to do this. I don't have the time and energy or the desire to come in here and do that. But if you want to, I will bring you resources, and I will help you through this process as much as I can. But you've got to make it happen. And once it's happened, you've got to keep it going."[3]

CONCLUSION

My instinct as a storyteller is to let this narrative stand without comment. I have nothing to say that will add to its eloquence. My editors have convinced me, however, that I should share my perspective on the narrative. After all, I am the one who decided the story deserved a wider audience than just myself and some students, and I am the one who selected what to leave in and take out. Having done that, what do I make of it all?

First of all, stereotypes, even generalizations about Appalachia, almost always fade into obscurity as the clarity of specific people and specific details march to the fore. I suspect this observation holds true of stereotypes and generalizations about any region, about any subject for that matter. With regard to Appalachia, however, stereotyping and overgeneralization have been particularly virulent in obfuscating reality, becoming a nation's excuse for exploiting people and then "saving" them. That doesn't mean there isn't an element of truth to a stereotype or generalization. There usually is. It is just that stereotypes and generalizations pretend to be more informative than they usually are. And the specifics almost always turn out to be more interesting.

Take Lou Ann Wallace, for example. Lou is an attractive woman whose blonde hair and southwestern Virginia drawl are consistent with a Daisy Mae stereotype. She was brought up to believe a woman's place was at home taking care of her man and her children. Yet her mother apparently never fully bought into the helpless, subservient role. And Lou bought into it even less. While she embraced marriage and family life, she also became a member of the St. Paul town council, challenged the status quo, and founded the St. Paul Tomorrow movement with a goal of sustainable, environmentally friendly, economic development.

And then there's Dink Shackleford. Dink's grandfather was killed in a duel over a card game. His father and uncles were all coal camp owners and operators. They raised Dink in Keokee, a place reputed in some quarters to be the roughest part of the state, even rougher than the Western Front of St. Paul. Dink now serves as executive director of the Virginia Mining Association, which represents mine owners all over southwestern Virginia. From stereotypes of coal company bosses, one might expect him to be an intimidating figure focused on getting coal out of the ground and little else. To be sure, he is focused on getting coal out of the ground. But he becomes most animated when talking about kayaking and riding his motorcycle, both rather remarkable hobbies for Dink since he is paraplegic.

When generalizing, one has a tendency to think in terms of extremes, often oppositions. In Appalachian coal country, that dichotomy often takes shape as company versus union. But as Debbie Penland points out, such thinking often overlooks salaried employees of the company such as her husband, mid-level managers who are not union members but also not top management or owners either. These people frequently live near, go to church with, and, as Tommy Penland did, marry into union families. When a strike occurs, many strikers expect these salaried employees to go on the picket line with them or at least stay away from work. But the company expects them to show up and even take the place of strikers. These people have no union protection if they stop working and are frequently vulnerable to union intimidation if they do not. Debbie's account illustrates a complexity in labor conflict appreciated neither by the general public nor apparently by many coalfield Appalachians themselves.

One of the main generalizations clarified by *Do, Die, or Get Along: A Tale of Two Appalachian Towns* is the term "coal towns." Coal camps or towns, such as Dante, were owned and operated by coal companies. The company owned the hotel, hospital, movie theater, store, schools, churches, and housing. In addition to employing all the town miners, the company also hired the doctors, police, teachers, store clerks, and even "ringers" for the company baseball team. As explained by Kathy Shearer, people living in such a place had few opportunities to gain civic or entrepreneurial talents. But there were also towns in the coalfields not owned by the companies, so-called bedroom communities, such as St. Paul, which frequently grew up at railheads near mines. Though dependent on the coal economy, these communities often incorporated as independent towns. The chapters of this book related to St. Paul show how a town council ran the local government, how politics became part of the texture of life, and how various entrepreneurs found ways to make money. The significance of these differences between the company-owned towns and the incorporated towns becomes evident as the coal economy played out, and coal companies began moving out and selling their properties. The narrative shows how Dante has declined to little more than a community of homes and churches, whereas St. Paul remains a viable economic, political entity with basic services intact. It is a pattern seen over and over in southwestern Virginia.

Do, Die, or Get Along focuses on people who are or have been involved in significant projects of benefit to the two communities. Their accounts of the early history of the area are included partially to provide background information, but mainly to give insight into how their sense of the past gives shape to what they do now. Some of their observations or experiences also comment on issues of interest to scholars of the region.

One of those relates to which Europeans displaced the Indians in various parts of Appalachia, and once there, whether or not they had any legal title to their land. The majority initially were Irish and German settlers following the great valley route from Pennsylvania. Presumably, the people most likely to do them harm in this enterprise were those they were displacing, such as Chief Benge described by Dink Shackleford. We learn from Frank Kilgore and LeRoy Hilton, however, that one of the first settlers in the St. Paul area was a Frenchman. An aristocrat fleeing France in fear of peasant uprisings, he purchased his land in 1790 from colonial speculator Richard Smith, the same speculator Kathy Shearer mentions as having the first recorded title to lands around what would eventually become Dante. In his new American home, the fear of Indians apparently displaced his fear of peasants, and one night he befriended a couple of wayfarers, who promptly murdered him in return for his kindness. While court records show that the Frenchman had clearly bought his land from Smith, the same kind of records are silent on the earliest Dante area settlers, suggesting that they were likely squatters.

Communities on the frontier tended to grow up at significant points along transportation routes; at sources of abundant natural resources such as wood, iron, and coal; at places where speculators thought they could make a fortune; and around settlements designated as court towns. St. Paul and Dante are excellent examples of a town developed along a transportation route and of a town developed near a natural resource. Lou Ann Wallace and her family live in an example of the third—a speculation community (slated to become "Minneapolis") that went bust before the first people moved in. The people driving Appalachian investment in the 1880s, 1890s, and early twentieth century often came from places outside the region. The principal financiers of St. Paul and Dante, however, were local and regional. According to LeRoy Hilton, there are hotel records of a Vanderbilt and Jay Gould visiting St. Paul, but apparently they found it less attractive than other opportunities. George L. Carter, through whose investments Dante emerged as a major coal town, was from nearby Carroll County, Virginia.

Much has been written about the Appalachian sense of place. For those narrators associated with St. Paul, the sense of place seems closely tied to family history in the region. Most of them trace their ancestry in the area back several generations, some to the Civil War. Frank Kilgore can trace parts of his ancestry back to the Revolutionary War. His father and grandfather both mined coal, his grandfather daily walking the twelve-mile round trip between his home on Honey Branch and the Dante mines, rather than moving to the coal town to live. Presumably, that decision related to his sense of place. Frank's family heritage has spurred him to collect all kinds of regional artifacts from postcards to furniture, turning his law office into a museum. LeRoy Hilton traces his lineage back to Revolutionary War ties to the Carter family of Appalachian music fame. LeRoy's home is testament to his sense of place, featuring an impressive collection of arrowheads he has found locally, furniture and other wood carvings he has made himself, a freezer full of trout, and a cardboard box full of photos and manuscripts about St. Paul.

The Dante citizens who talked with me expressed an equally strong, if different, sense of place. Old-timers Roy Phillips, Lucille Whitaker, and Nannie Phillips Gordon (Phillips were the first settlers in the Dante area) remember how dealing with mining accidents, labor disputes, omnipresent coal dust, alcohol abuse, and other hardships over the years defined their community, their sense of place. Somehow, with God's help they insist, they managed. Matthew Kincaid's memory of place is all that plus the smell of frying fish and the sounds of mothers shouting messages house to house from the bottom of their segregated holler to the baseball field at the top. Catherine Pratt remembers as a kid finding ways to play in the narrow hollers, swinging out on vines over the steep slopes and playing on the railroad tracks.

All this raises the question of the accuracy of people's memories. Appalachian scholars Henry Shapiro and Allen Batteau have written persuasively that much of what we think we know about Appalachia is really a fiction created by writers and other influential persons with an ax to grind or perhaps just a stereotypical image of their subject. But the memories of people who live in a place can also produce a fiction. Some parts of what happened to them get stuffed into forgetfulness, and other parts shoved to the fore and served up in language. Did the good times that people experienced in Dante really outweigh the pangs of living under the thumb of the company? Or is that just the way they remember it? It is a fascinating question but, as I have indicated, not the central concern for this narrative. Here the primary interest in memories is how they shape a narrator's values and actions, not how accurate or reliable they are.

A related problem occurs when a narrator's experience appears to confirm a stereotype that supposedly has been debunked. In chapter 19, Frank Kilgore states that he is frustrated by people using Calvinistic fatalism to justify inaction regarding their health. Frank is reacting to personal experience, not something he has read about or heard second hand. Yet compelling research by Appalachian scholars, especially Dwight Billings and Kathleen Blee, suggests that poverty centered in long-standing, local inequities is more foundational as a cause of intransigence, where it occurs, than is Calvinistic fatalism (or than is oppression by outside economic interests). Perhaps in his law profession, Frank runs across more fatalists than are truly representative of their numbers. Maybe Frank happened to encounter one or two particularly memorable fatalists just before I showed up with my recorder. This much is clear. When he spoke with me, Frank was frustrated by them, however representative they may be. And that is important to this narrative.

Surely a mix of fact and myth, *Do, Die, or Get Along* is above all a story. The central plot of that story involves, first, the ups and downs of two towns dependent largely on the vicissitudes of the coal economy. By all accounts it was a tough life, in the mines and out. LeRoy Hilton describes St. Paul's Western Front, a row of saloons and brothels along the railroad track that became legendary in its rowdiness. Tom Fletcher, son of the mayor who presided over the town during much of this time, explains how his father tried to maintain some semblance of control there while still letting the men "have some fun," freed for a time from the much stricter mores found across the tracks in the church-dominated part of St. Paul and from the tighter company control found in Dante.

Through good economic times and bad, confrontation seemed the dominant method of solving problems, even finding a bride. Matthew Kincaid talks about confronting inherent dangers of mining itself, especially securing the roof. Dean Vencil focuses more on how miners have had to stand up to lax standards set by the company. And from Nannie Phillips Gordon's and Lucille Whitaker's accounts, in the old days ripping coal out a seam seemed easier (and maybe safer) than getting a Dante woman away from her parents, even when one's intentions were entirely honorable. Frank Kilgore, too, talks about difficulties of playing the mating game when he was a youth. He speculates that confrontational problem-solving strategies of the past may have been inflamed by unrequited passions. However accurate that theory may be, Frank clearly has been no stranger to confrontation. When he was leading the fight in southwest Virginia for strip mine regulation during the 1960s and 1970s, he recalls wrestling one opponent and exchanging gunfire with others after being taunted and red-baited.

The "doing" or "dying" configuration of the story's plot shifts, however, as a culture of "getting along" slips into the action. The interest factor for readers becomes more subtle as raw conflict changes into rhythms of males/females, insiders/outsiders, blacks/whites, activists/authoritarians finding their place in common cause. In chapter 4, Frank Kilgore recalls listening to his grandfather talk about immigrant miners, how they were recruited to break strikes but later became some of the strongest union members and "part of the fabric of the community." At some point, hostility gave way to cohesion. In chapter 6, Democrat LeRoy Hilton tells how a Republican friend saved his job as postmaster. It is a humorous variation of a theme I heard repeatedly during the interviews. Democrats and Republicans in southwestern Virginia learned early on that they had to resolve differences if they were going to have any clout in Richmond.

This culture of "getting along" was nourished by connections to what was happening in the rest of the country. By the mid-1920s, there were hard-surfaced roads connecting St. Paul to all major localities in Wise County, as well as east to Abingdon and west into Kentucky. A good road to Dante was slower coming (in the 1930s with a New Deal work project), but people still got in and out. LeRoy Hilton comments on how Dante's company executives would take a Friday train from Dante to St. Paul, pick up their cars parked there, take a weekend trip, and then return to Dante by train on Sunday night. For ordinary people throughout the area, however, travel was apparently still a luxury. LeRoy recalls packing a car with friends for an all-day trip to Bristol, how special that was and how people talked about it for days.

In chapter 13, Bruce Robinette relates the problems he had in the 1960s even as an "insider" getting communities to buy into the idea of regional plan-ning. Ask people from St. Paul when an isolationist mentality gave way to seeking partnerships with outside agencies, and they will likely point to the river relocation project that Bruce started. Begun in the early 1970s and com-pleted in the early 1980s, it was pretty much an all-male venture still in the shadow of patriarchy. But chalk one up for the guys. Even if you are skeptical that a small town is worth $25 million, you have to be impressed by what they were able to do.

At the time, St. Paul was facing several problems. The Clinch River fre-quently flooded much of the town, the housing in the floodplain was sub-standard, there wasn't space for a water treatment plant, and there was no reasonable route for a four-lane highway that had already been funded. The first thing they decided was to bring in outside help. They made this deci-sion in typical male fashion—they had a fight. More accurately, they had an election, which Bruce remembers being as contentious as most fights. Then they made another macho decision—to solve all these problems at once by moving the river. To do that, they formed a team, made up of local, state, and federal agencies. They had to steer this team through conflicting budget cycles, a funding freeze, bureaucratic intransigence, and the new regulations that occur when a project drags on for more than a decade. In the end, they managed to hold their coalition together and prevail. It is an amazing story of cooperation, political savvy, persistence, and plain luck.

The river channelization project generated momentum toward coopera-tive, broad-based problem solving. Then came the Pittston strike of 1989–90. Again, it was "Whose side are you on?" There was little middle ground between the company side and the union side, little attention to working to-gether toward a stronger region. The conflict also tore at family cohesion, as Debbie Penland and Terry Vencil attest. Yet, no one was killed, and this strike did not reach the levels of violence that labor history in Appalachia might lead one to expect it would. I have no reason to doubt Jackie Stump's assertions of the United Mine Workers of America's commitment to civil dis-obedience, imperfect as the practice turned out to be. Frank Kilgore sup-ports that sentiment, adding the observation that many of the strikers were also community, youth, and church leaders who did not want to tarnish their images with headstrong acts. Finally, while strikes are divisive, labor unions in themselves remain, as they have always been, powerful forces for inclu-siveness and cohesion. Jackie Stump's last-minute, write-in victory over an incumbent congressman is clear testament to that.

The strike ended any lingering hope that coal would ever again be the foundation of the region's economy and way of life. Though Pittston was forced to make concessions to the union, it also began a process of divesting itself of its coal holdings in Virginia. Regional leaders began stepping up ef-forts to diversify the economy, hoping to capitalize on infrastructural impacts made largely through the Appalachian Regional Commission and other state and federal agencies (the St. Paul river relocation project being an exam-ple of such an infrastructural project). After the strike ended, Frank Kilgore turned his energies to a number of cooperative regional ventures, most no-tably Buchanan County's Appalachian School of Law and the Appalachian Pharmacy School. The idea of developing an Appalachian university focus-ing on leadership fields important to the area addresses several challenges simultaneously: providing a new economic development engine, increasing the intellectual resources (and reputation) of Appalachia, and addressing le-gal and health problems endemic to the region.

In the meantime, both environmental priorities and changing roles of women were playing into the stories of St. Paul and Dante, though envi-ronmentalism got off to a bumpy, confrontational start in both towns. It was, recall, the federal Environmental Protection Agency that almost derailed the river relocation project in St. Paul. And it was the Virginia Environmental Protection Agency that threatened to erase Dante from the map if it didn't put in a sewage system. Apparently, there were few serious efforts at sewage treatment anywhere in the area until the 1970s. Then in 1990, the Nature Conservancy opened an office in Abingdon. A national inventory of biodiver-sity had designated the Clinch River running through the Virginia coalfields as a treasure trove of rare and endangered species. Unlike many confronta-tional conservation organizations, the Nature Conservancy prefers working cooperatively with landowners, businesses, and local governments. Hence Bill Kittrell's association with Lou Ann Wallace and St. Paul Tomorrow. And hence an especially inclusive, cooperative species of environmentalism now introduced into the area. That partnership, explained in chapter 17, produced a vision for St. Paul useful to any rural community seeking economic sustainability in an environmentally friendly setting. And Lou Ann Wallace becomes one of many women who are turning "getting along," southwestern Virginia style, into innovative community leadership.

Another is St. Paul High School science teacher Terry Vencil. Chapter 18 describes an unorthodox pedagogy using a local wetlands as the basis for students' engagement in all sorts of learning. The project began in 1999 and has been passed from class to class—Team Estonoa—ever since. After the students convinced the Army Corps of Engineers to declare Estonoa a wetlands, they decided to make it an educational center. So they cleared a trail around Estonoa and installed floating docks. After that, they decided that a $136,500 learning center would be a good idea. To do all this, they sought help from the town council, the Job Corps, the Lions Club, the American Electric Power company, and anybody else who would listen. They wrote grants, they planned budgets, they made PowerPoint presentations. They also learned how wetlands ecology works, not just well enough to pass a class test but well enough to explain those dynamics to the many elementary, high school, college, and other groups that have come to visit. They have shared their experiences as far away as San Francisco and as far up as the White House. In all this, Terry was where many educational theorists believe a good teacher should be, at the side of the action encouraging, questioning, and making soup.

St. Paul High School is one of the smaller high schools in Virginia. Yet Terry Vencil is not a jewel standing alone. Chelsea Salyer and Jason Boone were both part of Team Estonoa when I conducted their interviews. Yet both discussed close relationships with several other teachers they admired, not just Terry. Principal Tom Fletcher attributes students' above-average Standard of Learning scores to small classes and dedicated teachers, both related to a long-standing county commitment to school funding. All this suggests there may be another ecology lesson here, this one a lesson in community ecology. Throughout Appalachia (indeed elsewhere as well), small schools are being consolidated to achieve economies of scale. But if learning is linked to the learner's own community (such as with Team Estonoa), what happens when the learner is uprooted and moved elsewhere? And if a student somehow at odds with parents cannot lean on a teacher he or she gets to know well enough to trust, where is that student going to lean? And what happens to the ecology of a community when the one place that rallies everyone's loyalties, perhaps the one place where everyone can gather, gets shut down and boarded up?

If St. Paul provides insight into maintaining and improving community, Dante provides insight into reviving community. It is difficult for me to imagine a more illuminating example of effective grassroots organizing. In chapter 20, Kathy Shearer remembers starting out like most organizers do—call a meeting, lay out the plan, sign people up. It's the way most outside agencies have traditionally operated in Appalachia. The difference here is that Kathy learned something from what obviously did not work. Tactics changed. Teams of people including locals called house to house in each holler. And they did more than explain: they listened and learned. Then Kathy brought to the town something only an outsider could bring. She brought excitement for what their individual experiences and memorabilia collectively represented, a sense of value that they had forgotten or dismissed.

The person-to-person approach won the day on the sewer question. More importantly, it stirred an awakening. People began digging out old photos and sharing their memories before a tape recorder. They produced an oral history display and set up a coal miners' memorial. They convinced Kathy that they needed to expand the display into a book. All that is what Kathy calls "Part A" of the story. A dying town had found meaning in its past and made a decision to live. But what kind of life can a town expect with little economy beyond that provided by entitlement checks? That's what Kathy calls "Part B" of the story. They decided that the coal company was no longer going to define for them what their expectations for life were going to be. So they formed a tax-exempt organization called Dante Lives On. Then the community did what it had apparently never done. It took legal ownership of something and gave it direction. And the new coal company, Alpha Natural Resources, did something Clinchfield and Pittston had never done. It helped the community make it happen by donating the old bank building to be renovated into a museum and coffee shop. Citizens of Dante are doing much of the labor themselves, plus applying for grants and developing creative ways to raise the $60,000 plus they need to complete the project. The white and black communities have found common cause, with one interracial gospel sing I attended raising several hundred dollars.

Unlike much fiction, the story of real people and real communities does not end in a neat denouement. No one knows if the stories of St. Paul and Dante will become blips on the downward spiral of American communities or an opening chapter in their renaissance. Lack of funding and a weak economic base often seem overwhelming. Like everywhere else, it seems, drugs weaken the social fabric. And there is another meaning of "get along," as in "move out of here." Lacking meaningful employment, many people in coalfield country still do just that, even with diminishing jobs elsewhere in the manufacturing or mining kinds of jobs they often seek.

Yet all the major projects that the narrators described are still moving forward at this time, two to four years after the interviews about them were conducted. As of March 2006, the pharmacy school described by Frank Kilgore is in its second semester, having raised $12 million in funds and real estate and having attracted a thousand applicants for the next year's class. The Conservation Forestry Program envisioned by the Nature Conservancy's Bill Kittrell now manages more than 20,000 acres of forestlands in the Clinch River watershed. St. Paul Tomorrow continues working with local government on downtown revitalization projects and for several years has organized what has now become an annual Clinch River Festival (www.clinchriverfestival.com), featuring bands, food, canoeing, and an environmental exposition sponsored by a number of environmental organizations. The Estonoa Wetlands Learning Center that Terry Vencil's students dreamed about and worked toward was completed in March and opened on April 22 (Earth Day), 2005. Through several significant grants and many small donors, Dante Lives On has now raised almost all the money needed for renovating the old bank building into a museum and sandwich shop. With the continued help of a lot of volunteer labor, they expect to be in the building greeting guests and selling goodies by the time you read these lines, load the car, and get over there.

The southern edge of what the Appalachian Regional Commission considers Appalachia was once home to one of America's most influential twentieth-century novelists. Often considered a fatalist himself, William Faulkner inspired a revaluation of his work after his Nobel Prize acceptance speech, wherein he declared that "man will not merely endure, he will prevail." Faulkner wrote a lot about community, his best-known works being set in a mythical county he made up. In Yoknapatawpha County, Mississippi, the individual characters collectively make up another character called "the town." Since "the town" represents the gossipy, prejudicial, herd instinct in people, Faulkner shows the people as individuals to be superior to the collective, even those individuals who pursue a very self-centered, materialistic notion of the American Dream. Faulkner's observation rings true to most of my experience with individuals in the context of their communities.

But I believe *Do, Die, or Get Along: A Tale of Two Appalachian Towns* reveals a different dynamic. The people who tell this story seem to find who they are as individuals primarily by working through and for their communities. They speak of their American Dream in terms of family and church, sustainability, education, enjoyment of place and heritage, and the social fun of community building. I am not sure what explains this different dynamic, beyond the story they tell here. Only a few of the twenty-six narrators are what I would describe as particularly civic minded. Rather, they seem like a normal cross section of a community drawn into and transformed by something bigger than they ever imagined experiencing. And, excited as new parents, they speak eagerly to us, bringing us into their story, telling it as if they would not believe it either if they had not seen it themselves. In doing so, they transfer their excitement, not just to fellow Appalachians, but to anyone who embraces the vital kinship between healthy local communities and a healthy nation and world. So after the last page, like any child drawn into a good story and left hanging, we put down the book, wishing we knew the ending, hoping things will turn out okay, and wondering whether our own lives will some day offer so much.

NOTES

Preface

1. Clifford Geertz, *The Interpretation of Cultures* (New York: Basic Books, 1973).

2. Alasdair MacIntyre, *After Virtue: A Study in Moral Theory* (Notre Dame, Ind.: University of Notre Dame Press, 1981).

3. Mary Field Belenky, Lynne A. Bond, and Jacqueline S. Weinstock, *A Tradition That Has No Name: Nurturing the Development of People, Families, and Communities* (New York: Basic Books, 1997).

4. See, for example, Jerome S. Bruner, *The Culture of Education* (Cambridge, Mass.: Harvard University Press, 1996).

Introduction

1. John Alexander Williams, *Appalachia: A History* (Chapel Hill: University of North Carolina Press, 2002).

2. Mary Beth Pudup, Dwight B. Billings, and Altina L. Waller, eds., *Appalachia in the Making: The Mountain South in the Nineteenth Century* (Chapel Hill: University of North Carolina Press, 1995).

3. Henry D. Shapiro, *Appalachia on Our Mind: The Southern Mountains and Mountaineers in the American Consciousness, 1870–1920* (Chapel Hill: University of North Carolina Press, 1978); Allen Batteau, *The Invention of Appalachia* (Tucson: University of Arizona Press, 1990).

4. In *Feud: Hatfields, McCoys, and Social Change in Appalachia, 1860–1900* (Chapel Hill: University of North Carolina Press, 1988), Altina Waller shows that violent conflicts between families often had less to do with clannishness than with competing economies and land disputes.

5. Harry Caudill, *Night Comes to the Cumberlands: A Biography of a Depressed Area* (Boston: Little, Brown, 1963), is widely credited (or blamed) for initiating this stereotype.

6. See, for example, John Gaventa, *Power and Powerlessness: Quiescence and Rebellion in an Appalachian Valley* (Urbana: University of Illinois Press, 1980); Stephen L. Fisher, ed., *Fighting Back in Appalachia: Traditions of Resistance and Change* (Philadelphia: Temple University Press, 1993); and Mary Ann Hinsdale, Helen M. Lewis, and Maxine Waller, *It Comes from the People: Community Development and Local Theology* (Philadelphia: Temple University Press, 1995).

7. For a thorough breakdown of the complex geology of Virginia and the Appalachians, one that is comprehensible to a nongeologist, see Lynn S. Fichter and Steve J. Baedke, *The Geological Evolution of Virginia and the Mid-Atlantic Region*,

13 September 2000, accessed 1 March 2005, http://csmres.jmu.edu/geollab/vageol/vahist/index.html.

8. See Crandall A. Shifflett, *Coal Towns: Life, Work, and Culture in Company Towns of Southern Appalachia, 1880–1969* (Knoxville: University of Tennessee Press, 1991).

9. Among recent studies of Appalachian ecology and diverse natural history, and of the growing threats thereto, are Scott Weidensaul, *Mountains of the Heart: A Natural History of the Appalachians* (Golden, Colo.: Fulcrum, 1994) and Steve Nash, *Blue Ridge 2020: An Owner's Manual* (Chapel Hill: University of North Carolina Press, 1999). For the Weidensaul quote, see page x.

10. Stephen J. Chaplin et al., "The Geography of Imperilment: Targeting Conservation toward Critical Biodiversity Areas," in *Precious Heritage: The Status of Biodiversity in the United States*, ed. Bruce A. Stein, Lynn S. Kutler, and Jonathan A. Adams (Oxford: Oxford University Press, 2000), 169–70.

11. Katharine C. Shearer, ed., *Memories from Dante: The Life of a Coal Town* (Abingdon: People Incorporated of Southwest Virginia, 2001).

12. Frank Kilgore and Katharine Shearer, *Far Southwest Virginia: A Postcard Journey* (Emory, Va.: Clinch Valley Press, 2004).

Chapter 1. Frontier Times

1. See, for example, N. Brent Kennedy and Joseph M. Scolnick Jr., eds., *From Anatolia to Appalachia: A Turkish-American Dialogue* (Macon, Ga.: Mercer University Press, 2004). Both Frank Kilgore and Dink Shackleford subscribe to local author Brent Kennedy's widely circulated theory of Melungeon origins. In fact, there are many fascinating theories as to the Melungeons' roots, none of them definitive.

2. Mountaineer patriots won one of the pivotal battles of the Revolutionary War at King's Mountain, South Carolina, on 7 October 1780. The victory stymied the British southern campaign and gave General Nathanael Greene time to reorganize the colonists' army.

3. Republican Jerry Kilgore (a distant cousin of Frank Kilgore) lost his gubernatorial bid to Democrat Tim Kaine in November 2005.

4. Frank Kilgore expressed knowledge on so many wide-ranging subjects that I did accuracy checks. In most instances, I found his statements soundly corroborated. Where experts disagree or add informative detail, I have appended notes. Roddy Moore, director of the Blue Ridge Institute and Farm Museum at Ferrum College, doubts that many subsistence farmers made their own furniture. According to Moore, furniture making required specific skills and tools the ordinary farmer wouldn't have had. There were estate sales where people could acquire furniture, and young couples

often got furniture for wedding gifts. Moore's research of agricultural records of southwest Virginia indicates farmers raised and sold more livestock than might have been expected, so they did have some cash. Roddy Moore, telephone interview, May 2004. See Pudup, Billings, and Waller, *Appalachia in the Making*, for further evidence that subsistence farmers were not as isolated as was once thought.

5. For a broad view of European displacement of Native Americans throughout Appalachia and subsequent development of settlements and towns, see Williams, *Appalachia*.

Chapter 2. Incorporated Town—Early Years

1. Hilton remembers people talking about this transaction as an outright sale, but the description suggests a sale of mineral and timber rights.

2. For more about the history of Wise County, Virginia, see Luther F. Addington, *The Story of Wise County (Virginia)* (Johnson City, Tenn.: Overmountain Press, 1956).

Chapter 3. Company Town—Early Years

1. Shearer's observation about land in Russell County already being owned by absentee speculators and Revolutionary War veterans, even before the earliest white settlers arrived, corroborates the findings of Wilma A. Dunaway, "Speculators and Settler Capitalists: Unthinking the Mythology about Appalachian Landholding, 1790–1860," in *Appalachia in the Making* (50–75). Dunaway notes that "after Virginia opened her western lands for sale in 1792, the state sold 2,590,059 acres to just fourteen speculators" (53).

2. Ronald D. Eller, in *Miners, Millhands, and Mountaineers: Industrialization of the Appalachian South, 1880–1930* (Knoxville: University of Tennessee Press, 1982), shows how speculators such as George L. Carter acquired extensive tracts of mineral-rich, timber-rich land following the Civil War. Eller also explains the important role of railroads in bringing this speculation to fruition. A study conducted in the late 1970s, early 1980s, by the Appalachian Land Ownership Task Force, ranging over eighty counties in six states, shows the extent to which land ownership by industrial interests continues throughout the United States but particularly in Appalachia: *Who Owns Appalachia? Landownership and Its Impact* (Lexington: University of Kentucky Press, 1983). Moreover, while Carter and other speculators after the Civil War were often of local or regional origin, *Who Owns Appalachia?* shows predominant ownership in the twentieth century to be by national (and multinational) railway and energy corporations, as well as by the federal government (mostly national forests and national parks).

3. The 1999 film *October Sky*, directed by Joe Johnston (Universal Pictures), dramatizes the early life of Coalwood's most famous citizen, "rocket boy" and author Homer Hickam, among whose writings is an autobiographical trilogy about the town.

4. During this interview, Shearer spoke with *Memories from Dante* nearby and occasionally checked out dates and other facts as she spoke.

Chapter 4. Immigrant Labor

1. Shearer's and Kilgore's impressions of large influxes of immigrant and African American labor in the decades surrounding the beginning of the twentieth century are illuminated by Joe William Trotter Jr.'s research related to the adjacent southern West Virginia coalfields: "Immigrants from southern, central, and eastern Europe grew from only fourteen hundred in 1880 to eighteen thousand (6 percent of the total) in 1910. The black population's growth was even greater, moving from forty-eight hundred in 1880 to over forty thousand in 1910 [from 6 to 14 percent of the total]." See "The Formation of Black Community in Southern West Virginia Coalfields," in *Appalachians and Race: The Mountain South from Slavery to Segregation*, ed. John C. Inscoe (Lexington: University of Kentucky Press, 2001), 284. Taking into account the considerable overall population increase, the combined African American and immigrant percentage increased from less than 8 percent to more than 17 percent of the total.

Chapter 5. Wild Times in St. Paul

1. Maybelle Carter was one of the original three of the famous Carter family country singers of Scott County in southwestern Virginia. Her daughter June Carter was married to Johnny Cash, a relationship referenced in chapter 11 by Dean Vencil.

2. The problem of community drug abuse has been thoroughly aired in Harlan County, Kentucky, thanks to a three-year community-designed project coordinated by the Appalachian Program of Southeast Kentucky Community and Technical College and funded primarily by the Rockefeller Foundation but also by the U.S. Department of Education, the Appalachian Regional Commission, and the Appalachian College Association. According to Roy Silver and Robert Gipe, two of the organizers, the project has involved interviews with over four hundred community people, a play and other artistic responses made public in the fall of 2005, and a structure for creating a community response to drug abuse and its causes in Harlan County. Community-centered research, empowerment, and problem solving of this kind, with outside agencies providing assistance and encouragement, fosters precisely the kind of regional development long called for by many people who live in and study Appalachia.

Chapter 6. Civility in St. Paul

1. Hilton's comments suggest a larger Republican presence than one might expect at this time in Virginia history. However, mountain Republicans have had a strong influence in Appalachian politics since the Civil War, a phenomenon Gordon B. McKinney explains in *Southern Mountain Republicans, 1865–1900* (Chapel Hill: University of North Carolina Press, 1978).

Chapter 9. Unionization

1. LeRoy Hilton and Frank Kilgore echo Kathy Shearer's positive assessment of the Episcopalian deaconesses and their impact on the region. For a critical look at missionary activity in the Appalachian coalfields, see David E. Whisnant, *All That Is Native and Fine: The Politics of Culture in an American Region* (Chapel Hill: University of North Carolina Press, 1983). In order to really help the Appalachian people, according to part of Whisnant's argument, the missionaries should have focused on underlying economic and social injustices of capitalist exploitation rather than on preserving musical and crafts traditions whose authenticity is questionable anyway. Although it is true that the Episcopalian deaconesses mentioned by Shearer did not challenge directly the capitalist bosses and church hierarchy that hired them, they did teach reading and writing and instill a love of learning in many lives they touched, Frank Kilgore being one of the beneficiaries of that legacy.

2. Nannie Phillips Gordon's statement about her father's religion reflects the kind of misperceptions about Primitive Baptist Universalists common in areas where this small but distinctively Appalachian Baptist sect can be found. Actually, the so-called No Hellers believe that hell is a real but earthly experience. Far from believing in no God, they actually believe Christ's atonement is so universal that it applies to everyone. Thus there is no hell in the afterlife. See Howard Dorgan, *In the Hands of a Happy God: The "No Hellers" of Central Appalachia* (Knoxville: University of Tennessee Press, 1997). Nothing is more distinctive about Appalachian culture than its religion. For an insightful overview, see Bill J. Leonard, ed., *Christianity in Appalachia: Profiles in Regional Pluralism* (Knoxville: University of Tennessee Press, 1999).

Chapter 11. Mining Safety

1. David M. Johnson, professor of chemistry and environmental science at Ferrum College, offers this critique of Kilgore's analogy: "Methane production from compost is entirely from biologically mediated reactions (certain types of anaerobic bacteria produce methane). With coal methane (and oil), the process is mostly chemical-physical—huge pressure and high temperature causing the transformation of plant material to fossil fuels. The similarity is that both processes require that oxygen not

be present or the plant carbon would all go to carbon dioxide rather than various forms of reduced carbon (that can then be burned in air, 21% oxygen, to release energy). The end-products are similar but the biological process is associated with ecosystem functioning and the short-term recycling of carbon, while the chemical-physical process is geologic, with long-term recycling of carbon." David M. Johnson to Peter Crow, e-mail, 3 May 2004.

2. Bennett M. Judkins observes a correlation between major mining disasters and mining safety regulations, with the Federal Coal Mine Health and Safety Act of 1969 being passed on the heels of the 1968 Farmington, West Virginia, explosion that killed seventy-eight miners. The search for survivors, which continued for over a week, was covered during the Thanksgiving holiday by national television. "In 1910, after explosions during the three previous years had killed a total of 1,013 men, the U.S. Bureau of Mines was established. A year after a 1940 explosion killed ninety-two men in West Virginia, Congress passed legislation that allowed Federal Bureau of Mines inspectors to actually enter and inspect the mines. The Federal Coal Mine Health and Safety Act of 1952 was passed a year after 119 coal miners were killed in an explosion at a mine in Illinois." See *We Offer Ourselves as Evidence: Toward Workers' Control of Occupational Health* (New York: Greenwood Press, 1986), 66.

Chapter 12. The Strip Mine Act of 1977

1. Mountaintop removal generates intense opposition in West Virginia, where the practice is much more widespread than in southwestern Virginia. See, for example, Appalachian Voices, www.appvoices.org, and the Ohio Valley Environmental Coalition, www.ohvec.org. Also, many Virginians, such as James A. Burger and Carl E. Zipper of Virginia Tech's Department of Forestry, see room for improvement in the state's strip mine reclamation practices: "How to Restore Forest on Surface-Mined Land," *Powell River Project: Reclamation Guidelines for Surface Mined Land in Southwest Virginia*, Virginia Cooperative Extension Publication 460–123, (Blacksburg: Virginia Polytechnic Institute and State University, rev. 2002), available at http://www.ext.vt .edu/pubs/mines/460-123/460-123.html, accessed 4 February 2006. The impact of coal mining on water quality, even with best practice reclamation, is widely debated among environmental hydrologists.

Chapter 13. Regional Planning and River Politics

1. Jamie Singleton, meteorologist with WSLS TV in Roanoke, Virginia, agrees with Kilgore's basic assessment, adding these details: "The steep mountains with creeks in the valleys act as lift for clouds and heavy rains. In the daytime, the air in the valleys and along the mountainsides heats and rises, following the slope of the mountains.

We call this orographic lift. In the summer, especially, when there aren't any major cold fronts nearby, just warm and humid weather, we'll see storms pop up pretty much right over the mountain ranges." Jamie Singleton to Peter Crow, e-mail, 18 May 2004.

2. Bruce Robinette credits the breakthrough to a different source: "We got a fellow, and his name is Michael Moscow—I'll never forget that name for obvious reasons. And he was with OMB, Office of Management and Budget. Don't ever know how I got a hold of him, but he had worked in a political campaign for someone in Virginia and had spent some time and was in college with a friend from Lynchburg. 'Yeah, I'll look into that for you.' He actually revived it. He asked me to write him a descriptive letter, which was about three pages single-spaced. I did him the entire résumé on the project, where we were. And it was revived, and we got it to going. We ended up getting up to where we could go to construction. And HUD did get very enthusiastic when their Richmond people got in it. They sold the Philadelphia and Washington people on the idea that we've got a mess down there."

3. Robinette is probably referring to the Clean Water Act of 1972, though it was indeed in 1975 that the courts included nonnavigable rivers such as the Clinch in its provisions.

4. For a critical view of federal agencies involved in Appalachian development, see David E. Whisnant's *Modernizing the Mountaineer: People, Power, and Planning in Appalachia*, rev. ed. (Knoxville: University of Tennessee Press, 1994). Whisnant sees a direct link between the Tennessee Valley Authority (TVA), Area Redevelopment Administration (ARA), Office of Economic Opportunity (OEO), and Appalachian Regional Commission (ARC) and the economics and politics of early coal and land barons. With regard to TVA, Whisnant aims his criticism primarily at agricultural policies that favor large farms and at energy policies that initiated large-scale strip mining to feed coal-fired electric facilities. The St. Paul river relocation project, for the most part, seems to fit the model of community improvement originated by community request that was part of TVA's original mission, which Whisnant applauds.

5. This entire story relates to the issue of how local government in Appalachia steers resource use for public and private benefit. For an insightful study of that issue, see Dwight B. Billings and Kathleen M. Blee, *The Road to Poverty: The Making of Wealth and Hardship in Appalachia* (Cambridge: Cambridge University Press, 2000). As an interviewer, I did not set out to undertake investigative journalism but rather to encourage people to tell their authentic story, wherever that might lead. What they revealed on their own, however, leads me to several conclusions relative to Billings and Blee's observations about heavy-handed leadership styles, corruption, and cronyism in Clay County, Kentucky. In the St. Paul river relocation project, a patriarchal pattern of governance was much in evidence wherein plans and decisions were made by a comparatively affluent leadership without significant input from poorer constituents, who in the end were most affected. However, while there was some talk of profiteering by

one town official, none of the principal negotiators and none of the people interviewed or mentioned in the narrative was implicated. Finally, though the final location of the highway helped some private enterprises at the expense of others, there seems to be general agreement that benefits of the river relocation project to the community as a whole far outweighed the public liabilities (or gains made by private individuals).

Chapter 14. Company Town with No Company

1. According to David Fields, vice president and chief financial officer of the Pittston Coal Company, the company moved to Lebanon because it had outgrown the facility in Dante. At the time of our conversation in the fall of 2004, the Pittston Coal Company was a subsidiary of the Brink's Company (see note 1 in chapter 20).

Chapter 15. The Pittston Strike of 1989–90

1. Reference to a popular union rallying song attributed to Florence Reece, written during the early 1930s "bloody Harlan" strike.

2. In 1950, UMWA president John L. Lewis and the Bituminous Coal Operators of America (BCOA) worked out an agreement by which the coal operators would pay into a union-managed health and welfare benefit program in return for the union's agreement to increased mechanization in the mines and thus decreased numbers of miners. In 1984, when Paul Douglas became chairman of Pittston, the company reportedly was losing $79 million a year, almost half from the coal division. Among cost-saving measures Pittston instituted was withdrawal from BCOA and the health and welfare benefit program Lewis had negotiated. The company argued that the coal industry had declined dramatically since 1950 and that surviving companies could not afford to pay the skyrocketing costs of benefits to retirees whose companies had folded. The UMWA argued that Pittston was reneging on a bedrock labor-management agreement at the expense of loyal workers who were now sick and elderly and thus highly vulnerable. The inability of labor and management to resolve this impasse led to the eleven-month Pittston strike of 1989–90, directly involving thousands of people in three Virginia counties and one each in Kentucky and West Virginia. The strike ended only after intervention by Secretary of Labor Elizabeth Dole. The ensuing mediation mandated significant concessions to the union, but Pittston subsequently pulled out of the coal-mining business altogether (see note 1 in chapter 20). For a lively, award-winning account of events and participants, see Dwayne Yancy, *Thunder in the Coalfields: The UMW's Strike against Pittston*, a series of articles organized into a supplement of the *Roanoke Times and World News*, 29 April 1990. For an extensive, worker-sympathetic examination of the legal ramifications of the massive civil resistance of the strike, see Richard A. Brisbin Jr., *A Strike Like No Other Strike:*

Law and Resistance during the Pittston Coal Strike of 1989–1990 (Baltimore: Johns Hopkins University Press, 2002).

3. "Jackie Stump is a decent man but he is giving you the UMWA spin." In 1989, Joe Farrell was president of the Pittston Coal Company and a vice president of Pittston's parent company. According to Farrell, now retired, he assumed the role of chief negotiator some months after the strike began "to meet the UMWA position that a change was necessary if progress was to be made." Citing continued decline into the twenty-first century of both Pittston coal operations and UMWA membership, Farrell says the company's goal was to "stanch financial losses by stimulating production and lowering the cost per ton" and thereby save thousands of jobs. "Our strategy was to convince the union leadership that the world was changing and it was time to take action before their membership suffered irreparable harm. The UMWA saw the strike as an attack on all they stood for and mounted an all out and very expensive effort. I was not surprised at the membership's ability to hold out given the resources the UMWA committed." Joe Farrell to Peter Crow, e-mail, 16 December 2004.

4. Five months into the strike, ninety-eight striking miners and a United Methodist minister illegally entered and occupied for several days Pittston's Moss 3 preparation plant in what was clearly the strike's most daring act of nonviolent civil disobedience.

Chapter 16. Changing Attitudes

1. Considerable insight into what happened before and especially after World War II to people who out-migrated from Appalachia is supplied by Phillip J. Obermiller, Thomas E. Wagner, and E. Bruce Tucker, eds., *Appalachian Odyssey: Historical Perspectives on the Great Migration* (Westport, Conn.: Praeger, 2000). The editors point out that in just twenty years after 1940, seven million people left Appalachia, with only three million moving in, much of this caused by jobs lost to mechanization of coal mining. Even as out-migration has slowed in more recent years, that is not necessarily a sign of economic recovery in the region, according to Richard Couto, "The Future of the Welfare State: The Case of Appalachia" in *Appalachia in an International Context: Cross-National Comparisons of Developing Regions*, ed. Phillip J. Obermiller and William W. Philliber (Westport, Conn.: Praeger, 1994). One of the reasons currently unemployed Appalachian coal miners or mill workers may not want to leave is the diminishing number of industrial-based jobs elsewhere.

Chapter 19. Changing Strategy for Regional Renewal

1. According to Virginia Tourism Corporation statistics for 2001, tourism ranked third as an employer throughout the state, behind business services and health ser-

vices. Tourism also ranked third in retail sales, behind automobile sales and food (grocery) sales, generating $12.9 billion in visitors' spending.

2. The strategy outlined here by Kilgore, if successful, will contravene an unfortunate pattern described by Richard A. Couto, *An American Challenge: A Report on Economic Trends and Social Issues in Appalachia* (Dubuque, Iowa: Kendall/Hunt, 1994). According to Couto, public capital such as education and healthcare normally follows in the wake of private capital such as jobs and cash in the local economy. When employment is declining, as it is in much of coalfield Appalachia, then underfunded public services tend to decline also (and at a time when they are needed most). In Buchanan County, however, the plan is to use investments in higher education and health resources (public capital) to increase employment (private capital) as well as benefits to the public welfare.

3. When the issue of poor health arises in reference to Appalachia, one immediately thinks of health and safety challenges miners have traditionally faced. For a study of workers' response to black lung, for example, see Judkins, *We Offer Ourselves as Evidence*. As Kilgore points out, however, much of Appalachia exhibits serious health problems that extend far beyond mining itself. Discussions of causes often focus on tobacco and alcohol use, unhealthy diets, and lack of exercise. Because of cultural factors, debilitations of poverty, and lack of adequate healthcare, making inroads into these problems has proven difficult. See Jennifer L. Gatz, Graham D. Rowles, and Suzanne L. Tyas, "Health Disparities in Rural Appalachia," in *Critical Issues in Rural Health*, ed. Nina Glasgow, Lois Wright Morton, and Nan E. Johnson (Ames, Iowa: Blackwell, 2004). Recently, the University of Pittsburgh received a $6.3 million, seven-year research grant to study the causes of oral health problems in Appalachia, said to be the worst in the United States.

4. Probably the most controversial study of intransigence in Appalachian people is Jack E. Weller, *Yesterday's People: Life in Contemporary Appalachia* (Lexington: University Press of Kentucky, 1965). Like Kilgore, Weller identifies religious fatalism as a leading reason Appalachian people don't take better care of their health. My own interviews suggest that the mountaineer profile was always more complex than Weller implies and that the profile has also changed considerably since 1965. Billings and Blee, in *The Road to Poverty*, explore a more seminal explanation than fatalism as to why many Appalachians seem loath to take action on their own behalf: poverty lodged in long-term local inequities. Whatever the causes, community leaders throughout the region, many of whom are themselves economically stressed, echo Kilgore's frustration with people resisting basic personal and community improvement. Anita Puckett's sociolinguistic study *Seldom Ask, Never Tell: Labor and Discourse in Appalachia* (Oxford: Oxford University Press, 2000) examines how social and family contexts can influence radically the often-negative responses of Appalachian people

(the more isolated of them) to the commands or requests of others. From that line of thinking, one could argue that the "fatalism" response to a stranger is a verbal equivalent of shutting a door in his or her face, not necessarily an expression of Calvinistic conviction.

Chapter 20. No-Company Town Fights On

1. See Katharine C. Shearer, ed., *Memories from Dante: The Life of a Coal Town* (Abingdon, Va.: People Incorporated of Southwest Virginia, 2001).

2. Keeping track of the corporate history of the coal companies involved in the history of Dante is no easy task. In 1906, George L. Carter combined his coal operations—most notably the Clinchfield Coal Company, Crane's Nest Coal and Coke, and Dawson Coal and Coke—into the Clinchfield Coal Corporation, the headquarters of which he moved from Bristol, Virginia, to Dante in 1912. In 1956, the Clinchfield Corporation was merged into the Pittston Company, operating henceforth under its former name, the Clinchfield Coal Company. In the same year, the Pittston Company purchased Brink's. Pittston's headquarters moved to Dante and remained there until the 1972 move to Lebanon, Virginia (discussed in chapter 14). According to documents made available by Pittston, in the 1980s the company expanded its diversification beyond the coal business and in the 1990s (just after the Pittston strike described in chapter 15) shifted its coal operations from union subsidiaries to nonunion production. Beginning in December of 2000, Pittston proceeded to divest itself of the coal business, a move largely completed by 2003 when the Pittston Company became the Brink's Company. Alpha Natural Resources, formed in 2002, bought Pittston's coal assets, including those of the Clinchfield Coal Company and including various buildings in Dante, among them the old bank building turned over to Dante Lives On. However, Alpha Natural Resources did not buy all of Pittston's liabilities. The Pittston Company, and under its umbrella the Clinchfield Coal Company, continue to exist as legal entities largely paying benefits. The majority of Alpha Natural Resources' management and production employees formerly worked for Pittston's coal subsidiaries.

3. Kathy's experience speaks to issues addressed in Allen Batteau, ed., *Appalachia and America: Autonomy and Regional Dependence* (Lexington: University Press of Kentucky, 1983), a collection of essays focused on how a bureaucratic, top-down management style among education, health, and social service professionals has replaced heavy-handed coal company ownership as the predominant form of alienation among Appalachian people, who have a strong family and community orientation. Kathy's success derives largely from her early realization that her interventional style needed to become much more community and family responsive. My observation while con-

ducting these interviews suggests that people in the region are increasingly joining into these professions and that at least some of the outside professionals are adjusting their manner of operation to local sensitivities. In addition, Appalachian allegiances to family and community, like those of people throughout the United States, have themselves changed over the last two decades and in widely varied ways.

INDEX

Clinchfield Railroad. *See* Carolina, Clinchfield and Ohio

Clinch Mountain, 118

Clinch Mountain Press, xxiii

Clinch River, xiv, 5, 9, 28; pollution of, 85; rare ecosystem, xxii, 145–46, 149–51, 157, 192, 195; tourist attraction, 167. *See also* McConnell, Charles; Robinette, Bruce

Clinch River Festival, 150

Clinch River trails, 5, 150

Clintwood, VA, 116, 135–36, 162, 172

Coalfield Economic Development Authority, 167

Coalfield Expressway, 167

coal formation, xiv, 1

Coal Miners Memorial, Dante, 172

Coalwood, WV, 22, 200n3

Coeburn, VA, 42, 65, 102, 104, 109, 164

Coldiron, Paul, 104

Coleman, George, 37

company store, 21–22, 43, 47, 50, 63–64, 115–17

Conservation Forestry Program, 153

Consolidated Coal (formerly Island Creek), 126

continuous miner, 68, 77, 90, 175

cook stove, 55

Cooley, Ethel, 175

Cooper, B. V., 94

Cornett, Tyler, 107

Couch, Kareen, 65, 172

Couch, Rab and Dule, 113–14

courtship, 31, 144. *See also* Gordon, Nannie Phillips; Kincaid, Emogene; Kincaid, Matthew; Vencil, Dean; Vencil, Terry; Whitaker, Lucille

Couto, Richard, 205n1 (chap. 16), 206n2

Covy (French), 70

Cox, Mr., 58

CSX Corporation, 14, 115

Cumberland Plateau, 170

Dante, William Joseph, 19, 21

Dante history project, xxiii, xxiv, 172–75

Dante Lives On, xxi, xxii, xxiii, xxiv, 176–82, 195

Davis, William A., 118

Dawson Coal and Coke, 19

deaconesses, Episcopalian, 59–60, 80, 201n1 (chap. 9)

Democrats, 35, 107, 190–91

Department of Environmental Quality (DEQ), 147, 161

Dickenson County, VA, 4, 8, 13, 135, 162, 180

Dickenson-McNeer Wholesale, 64

Dillon rule, 100

Dingus, John, 14

distillery, government, 28

drug awareness, 167–68

drugs, illegal, 31–33, 144, 194, 200n2. *See also* healthcare problems

drugstore: Dante, 51, 117; St. Paul, 38

Duffield, VA, 100, 127

Dunaway, Wilma A., 199n1 (chap. 3)

economic development, 186, 192; Coalfield Economic Development Authority, 167; Economic Development Administration (EDA), 101. *See also* Kilgore, Frank; Kittrell, Bill; McConnell, Charles; Robinette, Bruce; Wallace, Lou Ann

education, xvi, 195, 206n2, 207n3; of Episcopalian deaconesses, 80; generational difference in attitude toward, 97, 124, 130, 151, 163; George L. Carter and, 22–23; of miners, 63; and need for male role models,

education (*continued*)
162–63; post-secondary, 167–68; small
classes and, 158. *See also* Estonoa
Wetlands project; St. Paul High
School
electricity, xxiii, 89, 91–92, 96; solar
alternative, 155
Eller, Ronald D., 199n2 (chap. 3)
Emory, VA, 184
endangered species, xv, xxii, 112, 149–51,
192
English, John, 5
environmentalism, xv, xvi–xviii, 83–86,
94–96, 151–53, 195; Virginia's record
on, 93. *See also* Nature Conservancy,
The
Environmental Protection Agency
(EPA), 101, 109–12, 146–47, 161, 169
Episcopal Church (St. Paul), 36
erosion, soil, 10–11, 37, 95–96, 153–55
Estonoa Wetlands project, 157–65, 193,
195

Farrell, Joe, 127, 205n3
fatalism, Calvinistic, 168, 189, 206n4
Federal Emergency Management
Agency (FEMA), 98
Ferrum College, 162
Fichter, Lynn S., xiv, 197n7
Fields, David, 204n1 (chap. 14)
fighting: company law and, 58; over girls,
143–44; interracial, 51; strike related,
139; over strip mining, 86–89; on
Western Front, 31, 65, 143
First Mount Calvary Baptist Church,
xxiv, 49, 179–80
Fish and Wildlife Service, 109–10
Fisher, Stephen L., xiii, 197n6
fishing, 149. *See also* Hilton, LeRoy
Fletcher, Holland, xxi, 64–65, 102–4

Fletcher, Tom, xvii, xxi, 102, 190, 193;
coaching during integration, 52–53;
on his father as mayor, 93, 103–4; St.
Paul described by, 37–38, 114; on St.
Paul High School, 158–59
float dust, 78
flooding, xxii, 9, 52, 98–114
Food Lion, 92, 136
Ford, Gerald, 86
Forest Stewardship Council, 154
Free Will Baptist Church (Dante), 59
French drain, 95–96
furniture: from company store, 50, 117;
and Fornier (Bush Industries), 136;
from local, sustainably harvested
wood, 155–56; of subsistence farmers,
8–9

gambling, 28, 34, 84
Geertz, Clifford, ix
geology, Appalachian, xiv, 1, 197n7
getting along, culture of, xvi, 2, 143–45,
190–91, 193
Gipe, Robert, 200n2
Glass, Shirley, xviii, xxi, 117–18, 172, 180
Global Learning through Observation to
Benefit the Environment (GLOBE),
160, 162
Glover family, 4, 114
Gordon, Bill, 43, 48
Gordon, Frank, xxi, 169–71, 176, 184
Gordon, Nannie Phillips, xviii, xxi, 189,
190, 201n2; on courting and marriage,
48; describes father as "no-heller,"
60; on future of mining, 176; on
Kathy Shearer, 182–83; on life during
the Depression, 41–44; and Phillips
family, 12–13; on UMWA in Dante,
55–56
Gould, Jay, 15, 188

timber industry, xiii, 10–11, 17, 145; lack of regulation of, in Virginia, 153, 154–55; sustainable management practices of, 153–54, 155–56. *See also* sawmills

Tom Dean and Company, 31

tourism, 167, 205n1 (chap. 19)

town council, St. Paul, 63, 144, 151–52, 160, 186–87, 193

trains, 7, 30–31, 36, 64–65, 121–22, 191; Santa train, xxi, 121. *See also* railroads

Trammel, VA, 21, 40, 119, 148

Trammel Mountain, 56

Triangle Shirtwaist Factory, 183–84

Trinity Pentecostal Church (Buchanan Co.), 126

Trotter, Joe William, Jr., 200n1 (chap. 4)

Trumka, Donald, 126, 140

TuBeuf, Francois Pierre de, 4–5

Tucker, Bruce E., 205n1 (chap. 16)

tunnel, railroad, 21, 24–25

Tunnel Holler, 118

Turkey Foot (Dante), VA, xiv, 11, 18, 21

Turner, W. A., 37

twin cities, 14

Tyas, Suzanne L., 206n3

Udall, Morris K., 86

Union Baptist Church (Dante), 60

Union Church (Dante), 59–60

United Mine Workers of America (UMWA), xxiii, 62, 71, 85, 204n2, 205n3. *See also* Lewis, John L.; Pittston Strike of 1989–90

U.S. Department of Agriculture (USDA), 161

U.S. Forest Service, 86, 152

Vanderbilts, 15, 188

Vencil, Dean, xvii, xxiv, 190; and Dr. Davis, 118; on father's generation of miners, 71; friend of, killed, 70–71; marriage to Terry, 67–68; on mine examiner job, 68–70; and Pittston Strike of 1989–90, 136; and role at Estonoa Learning Center, 162–63

Vencil, Terry Kern, xvii, xxiv; and Dr. Davis, 118; interviewing Dean, 68–71; and marriage to Dean, 67–68; St. Paul ancestors of, 26–27; on strikes' effect on families, 137–38, 192; on strike music, 141; on Team Estonoa, 157–65, 193, 195; and tour of St. Paul, 38–39

ventilation, mine, 56, 68–69, 72

violence, xvii, 89, 130, 143, 192. *See also* fighting

Virginia, Commonwealth of, 17, 83, 91, 129, 167, 183; legislature of, 3–4, 12, 93, 100, 142, 154–55

Virginia, University of, 67, 104, 109; at Wise (Clinch Valley College), xviii, 2, 87, 164

Virginia and Tennessee Coal and Iron, 17

Virginia Citizens for Better Reclamation, xviii, 85–89

Virginia Department of Mines, Minerals, and Energy, 94

Virginia Department of Transportation (VDOT), 102, 104–9

Virginia Foundation for the Humanities, 173–74

Virginia Iron, Coal, and Coke, 20

Virginia Mining Association, xxiii

Virginia Pocahontas, 126

Virginia State Troopers, 133, 135–36

Virginia Tech, 94, 163